Enterprise Messaging Using JMS and IBM® WebSphere®

ON DEMAND COMPUTING BOOKS

On Demand Computing
Fellenstein

Grid Computing
Joseph and Fellenstein

Autonomic Computing
Murch

Business Intelligence for the Enterprise
Biere

DB2 BOOKS

DB2 Universal Database v8.1 Certification Exam 700 Study Guide
Sanders

DB2 Universal Database v8.1 Certification Exams 701 and 706 Study Guide
Sanders

DB2 for Solaris: The Official Guide
Bauch and Wilding

DB2 Universal Database v8 for Linux, UNIX, and Windows Database Administration Certification Guide, Fifth Edition
Baklarz and Wong

Advanced DBA Certification Guide and Reference for DB2 Universal Database v8 for Linux, UNIX, and Windows
Snow and Phan

DB2 Universal Database v8 Application Development Certification Guide, Second Edition
Martineau, Sanyal, Gashyna, and Kyprianou

DB2 Version 8: The Official Guide
Zikopoulos, Baklarz, deRoos, and Melnyk

Teach Yourself DB2 Universal Database in 21 Days
Visser and Wong

DB2 UDB for OS/390 v7.1 Application Certification Guide
Lawson

DB2 SQL Procedural Language for Linux, UNIX, and Windows
Yip, Bradstock, Curtis, Gao, Janmohamed, Liu, and McArthur

DB2 Universal Database v8 Handbook for Windows, UNIX, and Linux
Gunning

Integrated Solutions with DB2
Cutlip and Medicke

DB2 Universal Database for OS/390 Version 7.1 Certification Guide
Lawson and Yevich

DB2 Universal Database v7.1 for UNIX, Linux, Windows and OS/2—Database Administration Certification Guide, Fourth Edition
Baklarz and Wong

DB2 Universal Database v7.1 Application Development Certification Guide
Sanyal, Martineau, Gashyna, and Kyprianou

DB2 UDB for OS/390: An Introduction to DB2 OS/390
Sloan and Hernandez

MORE BOOKS FROM IBM PRESS

Enterprise Messaging Using JMS and IBM WebSphere
Yusuf

Enterprise Java Programming with IBM WebSphere, Second Edition
Brown, Craig, Hester, Stinehour, Pitt, Weitzel, Amsden, Jakab, and Berg

Enterprise Messaging Using JMS and IBM® WebSphere®

WebSphere

Kareem Yusuf, Ph.D.

PRENTICE HALL
Professional Technical Reference
Upper Saddle River, New Jersey 07458
www.phptr.com

Editorial/production supervision: *Mary Sudul*
Page layout: *FASTpages*
Cover design director: *Jerry Votta*
Cover design: *IBM Corporation*
Manufacturing manager: *Alexis Heydt-Long*
Publisher: *John Neidhart*
Editorial assistant: *Linda Ramagnano*
Marketing manager: *Robin O'Brien*
IBM Consulting Editor: *Tara B. Woodman*

Published by Pearson Education, Inc.
Publishing as Prentice Hall Professional Technical Reference
Upper Saddle River, NJ 07458

Prentice Hall PTR offers excellent discounts on this book when ordered in quantity for bulk purchases or special sales.þ For more information, please contact: U.S. Corporate and Government Sales, 1-800-382-3419, corpsales@pearsontechgroup.com. For sales outside of the U.S., please contact: International Sales, 1-317-581-3793, international@pearsontechgroup.com.

Printed in the United States of America

Second Printing

ISBN   0-13-146863-4

Pearson Education LTD.
Pearson Education Australia PTY, Limited
Pearson Education Singapore, Pte. Ltd.
Pearson Education North Asia Ltd.
Pearson Education Canada, Ltd.
Pearson Educación de Mexico, S.A. de C.V.
Pearson Education — Japan
Pearson Education Malaysia, Pte. Ltd.

For Patti, My heart, My Life, My love, My Wife

CONTENTS

Preface xi

Acknowledgments xv

Part 1   Enterprise Messaging and JMS

Chapter 1 Enterprise Messaging   3

Defining Messaging   3

Messaging Architecture   5

    Message Distribution Paradigms   6

    Interaction Patterns   7

    Connectivity Options   12

Summary   13

Chapter 2 Java Message Service   15

Key Concepts   15

Messaging Domains   19

    What's New in JMS 1.1   23

JMS Messages   25

Application Server Facilities   26

    Concurrent Processing of Incoming Messages   27

    Distributed or Global Transactions   27

Summary   28

Chapter 3 JMS Messages   29

Message Definition   29

    XML   30

    Tagged/Delimited   38

    Record-Oriented   40

JMS Message Structure   41

    Message Header   42

    Properties   44

    Message Selectors   47

Message Body   48

Using the JMS Message Interface   50

Summary   56

Chapter 4   Using the JMS API   57

The JMS Client: Implementation Considerations   57

Point-to-Point Interface   61

Connecting to a Provider   61

Sending Messages   65

Receiving Messages   66

Additional Facilities   70

Publish-Subscribe Interface   72

Connecting to a Provider   73

Publishing Messages   74

Creating Subscribers   75

Additional Facilities   78

Handling JMS Exceptions   79

Handling Local Transactions   81

Unified Interface   84

Summary   86

Part 2   Using JMS with IBM WebSphere

Chapter 5   IBM JMS Providers   89

The WebSphere Software Platform   89

WebSphere MQ   92

System Components   92

JMS Support   95

WebSphere MQ Everyplace   100

JMS Support   100

WebSphere Business Integration Message Broker   101

System Components   102

JMS Support   104

WebSphere Application Server   108

JMS Support   109

Summary   112

Chapter 6 IBM JMS—Administered Objects   115

Administered Objects Revisited   115

WebSphere JMS Provider (Embedded JMS Server)   116

    WebSphere QueueConnectionFactory   117

    WebSphere TopicConnectionFactory   118

    WebSphere Queue   120

    WebSphere Topic   121

WebSphere MQ JMS Provider   122

    MQQueueConnectionFactory   123

    MQTopicConnectionFactory   127

    MQXAQueueConnectionFactory and MQXATopicConnectionFactory   134

    JMSWrapXAQueueConnectionFactory and JMSWrapXATopicConnectionFactory   135

    WebSphere Application Server Runtime Properties   135

    MQQueue   136

    MQTopic   138

Creating Administered Objects   141

    WebSphere Application Server Administration Console   141

    JMSAdmin   143

Summary   146

Chapter 7 JMS Implementation Scenarios   147

Development Environment   148

Scenario 1: Exchanging Messages Using EJBs   149

    Create the Sender Session Bean   150

    Create the Message-Driven Bean   169

    Test the Scenario Implementation   177

Scenario 2: Implementing Publish-Subscribe   184

    Create the Publisher Session Bean   186

    Create the Subscriber Message-Driven Beans   192

    Test the Scenario Implementation   198

Scenario 3: Communicating with Non-JMS Clients   202

    Using the WebSphere MQ JMS Provider   206

    Testing the Scenario Implementation   211

Scenario 4: Securing JMS Communications   213

    SSL Concepts   215

    Configuring WebSphere MQ SSL   219

    Testing the Scenario Implementation   238

Summary   239

Chapter 8 Enterprise Deployment   241

JMS Provider Location   241

Clustering Topologies   244

      High-Availability Clusters   245

      Workload Management Clusters   248

      Message Broker Collectives and Clones   250

JNDI Namespace Provider   251

Summary   252

Appendix A JMS Specification Excerpts   253

Message Selector Syntax   253

JMS Standard Exceptions   256

Appendix B Implementing XA Global Transactions   259

Development Environment   259

Using XA Global Transactions   259

      Create the Entity Bean   260

      Create the Session Bean   278

      Modify the MDB   282

      Test the Scenario Implementation   284

Appendix C Implementing Publish-Subscribe II   289

Development Environment   289

Using Message Broker   290

      Broker Configuration   290

      Update Application Configuration   309

      Test the Scenario Implementation   313

Appendix D Resources   315

Index   319

PREFACE

When I first started working for IBM in 1998 as a software engineer, Java was still in its infancy and the development of messaging applications in Java was virtually nonexistent. I recall the first major customer I worked with, who was trying to use Java servlets to send messages via MQSeries (as it was then known) to a mainframe application (CICS). Comments like "Customers have started doing this?" were shared by teammates as we stepped up to address the issues at hand. Now Java has grown, server-side Java has exploded, and the use of messaging as a means of integrating applications and processes is as strong as, if not stronger than, ever. Alongside this growth has evolved the importance and benefit of open standards. In the Java world, J2EE adoption has become a given, and JMS as a standards-based API for messaging has become one of the most popular APIs in current use.

I still work with IBM customers, and they are my inspiration for writing this book. Over the years, I have handled numerous queries associated with how to use standards-based APIs such as JMS with IBM WebSphere software. These queries have run the gamut, ranging from architectural to implementation considerations. It is these answers, my thoughts and experience, that I share here.

Purpose of This Book

The overall goal of this book is to serve as an authoritative guide to using JMS and IBM software to implement messaging solutions within the enterprise. It covers the role and use of messaging, explores JMS in great depth, and provides guidance on how to design, develop, and implement JMS-based solutions. It does this using a combination of discussions, code examples, and hands-on tutorials. My personal objective is to provide you, in a simple, clear, and concise manner, with a rich resource that serves not only as a learning aid, but also as a ready reference on the subject of enterprise messaging using JMS.

This book does not aim to be a product manual, and in all cases I discuss underlying product technology to a level of detail appropriate to understanding the subject under discussion. Consequently, this book is not (nor does it aim to be) an exhaustive reference on a given product set. Should you desire to explore certain technologies discussed in this book to a depth greater than what is offered here, you'll find a detailed resource list in Appendix D to guide and support further reading.

Who Should Read This Book

The primary audience for this book are developers and technical architects who are developing messaging infrastructure and are interested in using JMS, particularly with IBM WebSphere. While the book focuses on the JMS implementations offered by IBM WebSphere, it is still useful to those not using IBM software, as it includes extensive generic material that is not dependent on a specific vendor's implementation. The book is also useful for technical managers and students who need to gain a better understanding of JMS and enterprise messaging systems.

The book assumes some familiarity with programming languages in general and with Java in particular. While you do not need to be a seasoned programmer to appreciate and benefit from the book, you do need to be comfortable with Java concepts and to a lesser extent J2EE to follow the code examples and tutorials. The resources in Appendix D can provide you with more background in specific subject areas.

What's in This Book

This book is split into two main parts: "Enterprise Messaging and JMS" and "Using JMS with IBM WebSphere." Part 1 (Chapters 1 to 4) discusses enterprise messaging and JMS from a generic perspective, focusing on patterns and utilization of the standards-based API. Part 2 (Chapters 5 to 8) introduces IBM JMS implementations and explores their use and configuration in support of JMS solutions. A set of appendices complete the book, providing reference information and extensions to tutorials.

Part 1: Enterprise Messaging and JMS

Chapter 1, "Enterprise Messaging," defines messaging and explores how it is used within the enterprise. It examines enterprise messaging architecture, reviews associated paradigms, and discusses patterns governing how applications interact using messaging. It then explains how an application can utilize messaging infrastructure, which sets the stage for our examination of JMS as such an option for Java applications

Chapter 2, "Java Message Service," provides a technical overview of JMS, introducing key concepts and terminology. It reviews important aspects of the specification, such as messaging domains, JMS messages, and Application Server Facilities (ASF), and highlights what's new in the latest version of the specification. It thus forms the platform from which we delve deeper into JMS in following chapters.

Chapter 3, "JMS Messages," undertakes a detailed examination of the JMS message, which is the entity communicating applications exchange. It examines the concepts and considerations associated with creating a message, discussing how message content is defined and how physical formats are used to structure message content. It then reviews in detail the structure of the JMS message and considers the suitability of various message types for enterprise messaging applications. Finally, using code examples, it shows how the JMS message is manipulated by the application.

Chapter 4, "Using the JMS API," extends our discussion to the actual use of the JMS API. It starts by considering our implementation choices regarding the software component used to implement the messaging application: standalone application, Enterprise Java Bean, and so on. It provides a detailed review of the JMS API. Extensive use of code examples is employed to illustrate usage and implementation approaches, and by the end of this chapter you should be fairly comfortable with writing JMS applications.

Part 2: Using JMS with IBM WebSphere

Chapter 5, "IBM JMS Providers," switches our focus from the generic use of JMS to its use with specific implementations. To this end, Chapter 5 details and reviews IBM JMS implementations (called JMS providers) that provide the operating environment and messaging infrastructure for communicating JMS applications. It addresses the IBM software used to implement a JMS messaging solution and reviews a number of popular offerings in terms of their support for JMS, including WebSphere MQ and WebSphere Application Server.

The glue that binds a JMS application to a JMS provider is the administered object, and Chapter 6, "IBM JMS–Administered Objects," details the administered objects defined for two IBM JMS providers: the WebSphere JMS Provider embedded within the WebSphere Application Server and the WebSphere MQ JMS Provider, which comprises WebSphere MQ and WebSphere Business Integration Message Broker. We examine the properties exposed by these administered objects and how they influence the behavior of the JMS application. We also review IBM supplied tools for creating these objects.

Chapter 7, "JMS Implementation Scenarios," provides a number of hands-on tutorials that guide you through implementing some common JMS usage scenarios. It ties together the knowledge gained in the previous chapters and illustrates useful implementation approaches to real-world problems. The scenarios cover exchanging messages using Enterprise Java Beans, communicating with non-JMS applications, and securing JMS communications. By the end of this chapter you would have built a number of functional prototypes, rounding out the basic skills you acquired by end of Chapter 4.

The successful conclusion of any application development project is the operational deployment of the application. Chapter 8, "Enterprise Deployment," reviews a number of important considerations associated with deploying JMS applications in the enterprise. These include resource location and physical topologies for availability and workload management.

Appendices

Appendix A, "JMS Specification Excerpts," reproduces specific sections of the JMS specification that are relevant to discussions in the book. They are reproduced strictly as a convenience.

Appendix B, "Implementing XA Global Transactions," extends one of the JMS implementation scenarios discussed in Chapter 7 to include message handling and database updates within a single global transaction

Appendix C, "Implementing Publish-Subscribe II," extends one of the JMS implementation scenarios discussed in Chapter 7 to include configuration of a different JMS provider.

Appendix D, "Resources," provides a detailed, annotated list of useful publications and reference sites that provide further insight into specific subject areas.

How to Use this Book

I generally recommend that this book be read in a linear fashion, as each chapter lays the foundation for the one that follows. That being said, there are no hard-order dependencies between chapters, and I have generally written in a style that accommodates readers who might want to read specific chapters. The one exception is the hands-on tutorials detailed in Appendix B and Appendix C, which are dependent upon completion of associated tutorials in Chapter 7. For clarity, I recommend that they only be attempted after you have familiarized yourself with the scenarios in Chapter 7.

If you are already familiar with messaging and JMS and are more interested in how to use IBM JMS implementations, you may choose to skim through Part 1 and focus on Part 2. However, note that both Chapter 3 and Chapter 4 in Part 1 contain discussions on design and usage considerations that might prove valuable even to a JMS expert.

Software and Versions

This book covers two versions of the JMS specification: JMS 1.0.2b and JMS 1.1. Where appropriate, I distinguish between them; otherwise, I simply use the term JMS to refer to both versions.

While this book does offer code examples illustrating the use of the unified messaging domain introduced by JMS 1.1, it is important to note that at the time of this writing the JMS providers used in the hands-on tutorials support JMS 1.0.2b only. Thus, the functional prototypes developed are based on this version of the specification.

ACKNOWLEDGMENTS

First my thanks to Professor Nigel Smith who taught me everything I know about technical writing, and without whose foundational teachings I would never have been able to write this book.

To Peter Niblett my sincere gratitude for introducing me to the world of messaging and JMS, those whiteboard sessions in your office served me well.

To James Kingdon and members of the WebSphere MQ JMS development team, my thanks for your patience and tolerance over the years of my unending stream of questions: Andrew Leonard, Stewart Addison, Rachel Norris you have my thanks.

My technical reviewers did an outstanding job of keeping me honest and providing valuable insights as development of the book progressed: Alex Koutsoumbos thank you for your friendship and support; Ian Parkinson thank you for always being so ready to help, it is much appreciated.

My thanks also go to Maria Menendez and Patrick Verdugo who served as a test audience, and willingly subjected themselves to the ramblings that constituted my early drafts.

Special thanks to my management; Chuck Bergmann and John Ramieri, and my IBM retail publishing manager, Tara Woodman, for their support throughout the process.

This book could not have been published without the wonderful efforts of my publishing team; John Neidhart, Mary Sudul, Carol Lallier and others, thank you for making this work a reality.

For putting up with the many late nights and working weekends, for her love and undying support, I have nothing but the deepest love for my wife, Patricia.

To my family, my mother, brother and sisters, as always words are never quite enough, but once again thank you for all your love, support and faith. Mum, as you have always said, a mother's prayers never go unanswered, I thank you dearly for them.

To my friends and team mates, thank you for your support, but most especially thank you for the laughter.

To the good Lord goes all praise, without whom none of this would have been possible.

And to William James, whoever you are, it happened like you said it would, thank you.

Enterprise Messaging and JMS

n the first part of this book (Chapters 1 to 4), we focus on enterprise messaging and JMS from a generic perspective. We are concerned here with clearly defining concepts, establishing usage patterns, and developing a detailed understanding of how to use JMS to develop messaging solutions.

Enterprise Messaging

We begin with a definition of messaging and explore how it is used within the enterprise. We examine enterprise messaging architecture and review the major paradigms that govern the distribution of messages around the enterprise. Consideration is given to how applications interact via messaging in terms of associated patterns, key implementation issues, and the options available for an application to utilize messaging infrastructure. This sets the stage for our examination of a particular option for Java applications, Java Message Service (JMS), in the rest of the book.

Defining Messaging

As a concept, messaging has existed since the dawn of man, in its most basic form referring to the exchange of messages between two individuals, whether verbally or in written form. In the world of computing the term messaging was coined to describe the exchange of data between interacting software components ranging from objects to full-blown applications. Though messages communicated between software components can be generated by humans for consumption by humans—for example, email—we are not concerned in this book with email but rather with the automated exchange of messages between software applications that enable the fulfillment of desired functions. For example, an order is generated by a Web-based or a customer relationship management (CRM) application (such as SIEBEL) and sent as a message to an enterprise resource planning (ERP) application (such as SAP) for order fulfillment. The message contains precisely formatted data that describes the order or, in more generic terms, relevant business data. The use of messaging as a communication style for software components is characterized by two primary attributes. The first is the data (message) that is to be exchanged, and the second is the basic mode of interaction: synchronous or asynchronous.

Synchronous messaging defines a tightly coupled interaction that requires both applications to be available simultaneously (analogous to having a phone conversation with an individual). The interacting applications are required not only to understand the nature of the data (message) that the other will accept, but also how to directly establish a communication link with each other.

In contrast, asynchronous messaging defines a loosely coupled style of interaction that introduces an intermediary, whom we will call the messaging provider. Rather than communicating directly, applications hand off messages to the messaging provider, specifying some level of addressing information. The messaging provider then delivers the message to the target application (analogous to using an answering or postal service). As with the postal service, the messaging provider offers the application varying levels of quality of service guarantees (for a price, usually in terms of performance overhead), assuring that messages are delivered, that message sequence is maintained, that no duplicates are delivered, and so on.

With asynchronous messaging, the sending and receiving applications do not necessarily need to know of each other's existence or the nature of the messages that each application understands. Instead, each application is concerned with defining the format of the messages with which it will communicate and establishing access to the services of the messaging provider. The messaging provider in turn focuses on providing value-added services to dynamically route and potentially transform the message so that it is received and understood by the recipient.

There is no question that synchronous messaging has its place in the enterprise: business requirements might dictate that the given interaction is only meaningful if both applications are available simultaneously and communicate directly. Synchronous messaging might also be adopted when the latency or performance overhead introduced by communicating via an intermediary (messaging provider) is deemed inappropriate for the functional requirements. For instance, the required response time for a human-driven query from a Web-based application to a payroll system might necessitate a direct (synchronous) connection between the applications. However, one of the problems that the tightly coupled nature of synchronous messaging poses is that changes to either of the interacting applications, such as an upgrade or change in the choice of application, necessitates changes to the other application (typically in terms of the messages it must now support or the communication protocol it must be aware of).

In an enterprise, numerous applications are required to interact with each other in support of the business and, in addition, these applications change as business requirements evolve. Consequently, loosely coupling applications using a messaging provider is key to building an enterprisewide messaging infrastructure with which disparate applications distributed across the enterprise can exchange and leverage data.

It is with asynchronous messaging that we are concerned in this book and to which the term messaging hereafter refers. In the next section we discuss (asynchronous) messaging architecture and ascertain how the application avails itself of the services of the messaging provider.

Messaging Architecture

Figure 1–1 portrays a typical enterprise messaging architecture. The architecture depicts loosely coupled business applications, which connect to the messaging provider layer and exchange messages in fulfillment of some business function. The interface between the communicating applications is defined by the messages they exchange. Each message represents data that may have meaning independent of the applications that process it; for example, the message might represent an employee's personnel record. Messages are typically self-contained, containing sufficient information so that they can be processed independently. However, some applications may choose to group messages into a logical group, defining the order in which the set of messages should be processed.

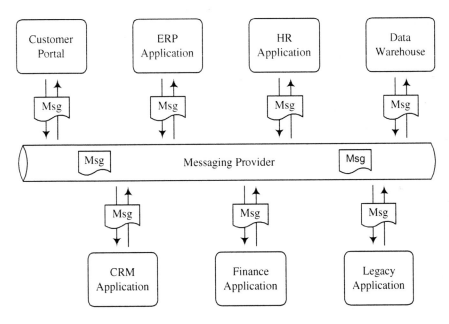

Figure 1-1 Enterprise Messaging Architecture

In considering the interaction between applications, the enterprise messaging architecture highlights three main areas of interest:

- The distribution paradigms associated with the exchange and delivery of messages.
- The interaction patterns between the application and the messaging provider.
- How the application achieves connectivity to the messaging provider.

Message Distribution Paradigms

The messaging provider is responsible for delivering messages to target applications. As mentioned previously, the provider can offer varying levels of service in support of this function. For instance, the messaging provider may offer a store-and-forward mechanism (generally called a queue), which enables the provider to store and later forward a message if the target application or network access to the target application is unavailable. The messaging provider may also offer a means of prioritizing messages or expiring messages that have not been retrieved. The manner in which the messages are distributed by the messaging provider to the target destination is governed by two primary paradigms: point-to-point and publish-subscribe.

Point-to-Point

Point-to-point messaging is characterized by the sending application explicitly identifying the target destination for the message. The messaging provider delivers the message to the destination, where it is retrieved by the receiving application (Figure 1–2). The pattern defines a one-to-one relationship between the message sender and message receiver, and implies that if the sender wishes to send the message to more than one receiver, it has to send the message separately to each target application.

Point-to-point messaging is typically adopted when an application communicates with a single application or a small number of known applications. In most point-to-point scenarios, the applications have a single target for a given message—for instance, sending updated personnel data to an HR application.

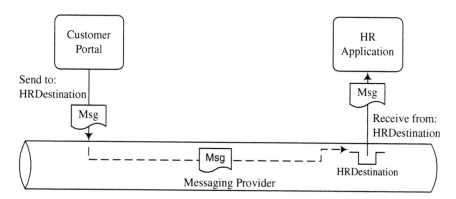

Figure 1-2 Point-to-Point

Publish-Subscribe

Publish-subscribe isolates the sending application from the receiver, using the concept of topics. A topic defines a category or subject with which messages can be associated, and applications register their interest in a given topic by subscribing to that topic with the messaging provider.

Applications that are interested in receiving messages associated with given topics are called subscribers, and applications that send messages associated with given topics are called publishers. Before sending a message, the publisher associates the message with a topic, then "publishes" the message to the provider. The provider matches the message's topic with the subscription list and delivers the message to all subscribers that subscribe to the topic (Figure 1–3). For any given publication, the pattern defines a one-to-n relationship, where n could be zero or more interested subscribers.

Publish-subscribe is typically used when data needs to be distributed to a potentially varying number of receivers (subscribers), which can change dynamically. Its use is most closely associated with event-driven scenarios, such as the distribution of sport scores, sensor readings or stock prices.

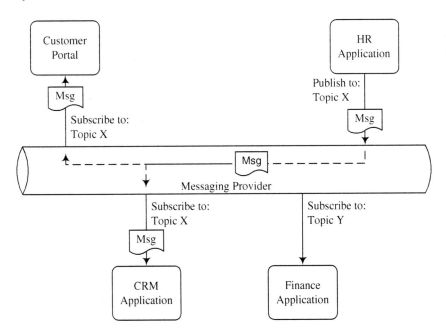

Figure 1-3 Publish-Subscribe

Interaction Patterns

The interaction between the application and the messaging provider generally entails the sending or receiving of messages. On examination, the application can be viewed as implementing one of three base patterns:

- Message producer
- Message consumer
- Request-reply

Message Producer

The message producer pattern, sometimes called the "fire and forget" pattern, involves the application simply sending a message (Figure 1–4). The application's interaction with the messaging provider ends once the message has been accepted by the provider. Common usage scenarios include sending a data record such as account information, registration details, a bill, or a stock quote. The message sent maybe delivered using point-to-point or publish-subscribe, based on the business need.

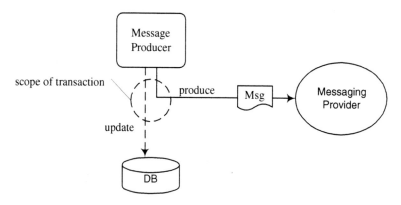

Figure 1-4 Message Producer

Before sending the message, the application needs to ascertain what qualities of service are required of the messaging provider. A major consideration in designing the application is deciding whether the message should be marked as persistent or nonpersistent. A persistent message is stored by the messaging provider in a persistent store (depending on the messaging provider implementation, a flat file or a database might be used). This offers an increased level of robustness, as in the event of process failures, the messaging provider can recover the message from storage and process it. Such robustness, however, comes with the price of increased read/write activity, which affects message throughput performance. In contrast, nonpersistent messages do not get logged in a persistent store, avoiding the associated overhead. However as a nonpersistent message is held only in memory, it would be lost if the messaging provider process failed.

The decision to use persistent or nonpersistent messages is generally governed by business requirements. In the case of publishing stock quotes, data is being updated within a relatively small time window. Consequently, the loss of a message could have very little impact, as the relevance of the data would soon be superseded by the next publication. In such scenarios, the messages would typically be nonpersistent. However, in the case of sending registration details, the user expects to submit this data once and once only, and as such persistent messaging could be chosen to ensure that the information gets delivered regardless of whatever outage might occur.

The sending of the message does not necessarily occur in isolation. As shown in Figure 1–4, the sending application might wish to coordinate the sending of the message with an update to a status table in a database. Thus, transaction scope is an important consideration in implementing the message producer pattern. Note, too, that even though the pattern ends once the message has been sent, the application may very well return some response to its user confirming completion of the task.

Message Consumer

In the message consumer pattern, application logic is initiated by the arrival of a message (Figure 1–5). This initiation could occur in either a pull or push mode. In the pull mode the application checks (polls) the messaging provider at suitable time intervals for a message. In the push mode, the messaging provider invokes the application when a message arrives, passing it the message. The message consumer pattern is commonly used by business applications that service requests, such as an inquiry application. The pattern can also be found in applications that listen for events, such as an application that subscribes to weather data.

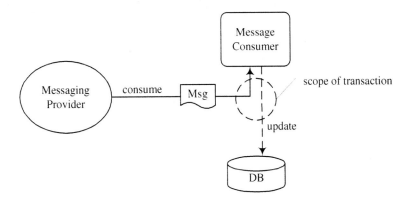

Figure 1-5 Message Consumer

On receipt of the message, the application invariably needs to process it, extracting and acting upon the data contained in the message. Given that errors may occur when processing the message, it is common to find that the message is retrieved from the messaging provider within the scope of a transaction. This gives the application the ability to roll back the message to the messaging provider in the event of processing errors. The application can then attempt to retry processing the message. A key consideration when implementing the message consumer pattern is how to handle processing errors, such as corrupt or incorrect data caused by the nature of the message itself. Simply rolling back such a message would result in an infinite retry loop, as processing would repeatedly fail. As we see in Chapters 3 and 7, support by the messaging provider for concepts such as back-out or retry counts allows this issue, often called "poison messages," to be addressed.

Request-Reply

The request-reply pattern combines the message producer and message consumer patterns to implement a conversation between the sending and receiving applications. As would be expected, the conversation involves the exchange of a set of related messages. As shown in Figure 1–6, the pattern involves the requester sending a message and waiting for a reply. A typical usage example is an inquiry—for instance, checking an account balance. The pattern might also be adopted when sending an order, the reply being the status of the order request: accepted or rejected.

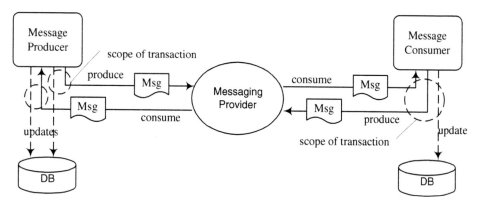

Figure 1-6 Request-Reply (Same Consumer for Replies)

In effecting request-reply, the requester specifies in the message a destination to which the reply should be sent. Once the receiving application processes the request, it sends the reply to the identified destination. The requester may be sending a number of requests to a variety of applications and may thus need to correlate the replies it receives with the requests it sent. Correlation also becomes an important consideration in situations where we are running multiple copies of the requesting application or running different applications that share the same reply-to destination. Correlation is achieved using the concept of message identifiers, which allow a message to be tagged with an identifier that marks it as being associated with the request (called a correlation identifier). We see how message identifiers are used to correlate requests and replies in Chapter 3.

In most request-reply scenarios the overriding factor is time, that is, the time taken for a reply to arrive. For this reason, inquiry requests such as account balance are typically handled as nonpersistent messages. This is because recoverability of the message is noncritical. If a reply has not been received within a given amount of time, an exception path is taken by the application, potentially resubmitting the request. However, if the use case involves sending a registration request (as in the message producer example) and waiting for a confirmation reply, it is likely that the request will be a persistent message, with failure to receive a reply within the given timeframe triggering a "check back later" mechanism.

Often, use cases involving action-initiation and waiting for a confirmation (the send order or registration details examples) are good candidates for the variation shown in Figure 1–7.

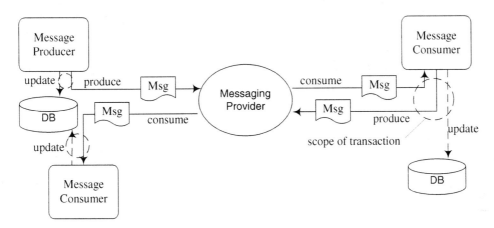

Figure 1-7 Request-Reply (Different Consumer for Replies)

Instead of having the application send a request message and then wait for its reply, the application sends the message (message producer), then passes a correlation identifier to another application, which, acting as a message consumer, processes replies. The replies could be logged to a status table that can be checked later by the user. This variation is particularly useful when the processing time is such that having the requester block and wait for the reply might be unattractive or when the business need does not demand that the originator of the request need to be informed at that instance of the results of the reply. For example, I purchase a book online, the Web site gives me an order identifier, and I can check back later or get sent an email regarding the actual status of my order (credit card accepted, proposed delivery date, and so on).

In either case, thought must be given to what to do with late replies, as it must be remembered that in light of the potential store-and-forward capabilities of the messaging provider, failure to arrive within the stipulated timeframe does not imply that the message will not arrive at all. The ability to specify the expiration (time to live, or TTL) of the message proves useful in this case. The expiry of the reply message is set so that if it is not retrieved within a given timeframe, the messaging provider discards it.

For those unfamiliar with messaging applications, defining the transaction scope associated with the sending of requests and receiving of replies can be an area of concern. As shown in Figures 1–6 and 1–7, the message is sent and received in different transactions. It is not possible to send a request and receive its reply in the same transaction, because until the transaction ends, the request does not get sent and thus no reply can be received. It is instructive to note, however, that the application servicing the request can retrieve and process the request, then send the reply within the same transaction, allowing the request to be reprocessed if errors occur.

Although request-reply scenarios are often implemented using point-to-point message distribution, as the conversation typically involves a known number of participants, publish-subscribe does allow some sophisticated conversation patterns to be implemented. For instance, an application publishing a request to multiple recipients could form the basis for a quote-gathering system. Conversely, a single request could be used to trigger the publication of relevant data.

Message producer, message consumer, and request-reply are base patterns that form the building blocks for enterprise messaging between applications. If you trace the path of a message through the enterprise and trace the messages it might cause to be generated, you can expect to see composite delivery and interaction patterns established on the base patterns we have discussed here. We will revisit these patterns as we progress through the book.

Connectivity Options

In exploring messaging architecture, we have examined patterns governing how messages get delivered and how the application interacts with the messaging provider. The final piece in the jigsaw puzzle, and indeed the primary focus of this book, is concerned with how the application actually connects to and avails itself of the services of the messaging provider.

A messaging provider invariably provides an application programming interface (API) with which applications can access its services. However, modifying an existing application's code to enable the application to connect to a given messaging provider is not always an option, as may be the case with shrink-wrapped, off-the-shelf applications. In such instances a bridging application, commonly called an adapter, is required. The adapter implements both the API or protocol required to communicate with the application and the API for the messaging provider. The adapter serves as the interaction link between the application and the messaging provider, which both interact with the adapter. With the ever-growing implementation of off-the-shelf ERP, CRM, and other business-critical applications within the enterprise, the need for messaging providers that facilitate the integration of these applications continues to grow. Consequently, the market for adapters is particularly vibrant.

The emergence of open standards as a major force in enterprise application development, especially the advent of the Java 2 Enterprise Edition (J2EE) platform, has seen a growing number of business applications implemented in Java. These applications similarly require access to messaging providers so that they can interact with other applications within the enterprise.

The main problem facing developers trying to enable applications (be they adapters or the business application itself) to connect to a messaging provider was that they needed to understand the specific messaging provider's API. This implied a steep learning curve for the developer and the greater potential for bad programming practices and bugs due to misunderstandings, since a messaging vendor's proprietary API typically provides a wealth of options that can prove fatal in the hands of an inexperienced developer. In addition, there was the question of skills portability, as expertise with one messaging provider's API did not imply that the learning curve for a different messaging provider was flattened. This of course had implications for productivity and for the cost to an enterprise of adopting a given messaging provider and acquiring skilled resources.

What was needed was an industry-standard API that insulated the developer from the specifics of any given messaging provider. Such an API would have to be learned only once and could be used in developing applications with little regard for the actual messaging provider they would be accessing. More importantly, the API could incorporate, by design, programming best practices with regard to accessing messaging providers. It was such an API that Sun Microsystems, IBM, and other major messaging provider vendors set forth to create for Java. The resulting API is the Java Message Service (JMS) API, defined in its specification *(http://java.sun.com/products/jms/docs.html)* as an API for accessing enterprise messaging systems from Java programs.

This book is focused on the use of JMS, particularly with the messaging providers delivered as part of IBM WebSphere. We are concerned not only with how to program to the API but also with how to configure the underlying messaging providers in support of the application. By using real-world scenarios and addressing common technical challenges, the rest of this book provides deeper insight into the world of enterprise messaging and the use of JMS with IBM WebSphere.

Summary

In this chapter we defined *messaging*—the automated exchange of messages between software applications that enables the fulfillment of desired function. We also established our specific focus on the asynchronous style of messaging, which involves the use of a messaging provider that receives and delivers messages on behalf of communicating applications.

We examined the two primary paradigms that govern message distribution—point-to-point and publish-subscribe—then discussed basic interaction patterns between the application and the messaging provider. For each interaction pattern—message producer, message consumer and request-reply—we detailed the pattern and reviewed key considerations associated with implementation.

Finally, we discussed how applications avail themselves of the services of a messaging provider, primarily via messaging provider APIs. We established the value proposition for an industry-standard API and introduced JMS as such a standard for Java applications. In the next chapter we examine JMS in further detail.

CHAPTER 2

Java Message Service

In Chapter 1 we established the value of an industry-standard API for accessing the services of messaging providers and introduced the Java Message Service (JMS) API as such a standard for Java applications. We now undertake an introductory tour of JMS, exploring key concepts and associated terminology, and gaining insights into how it is structured and implemented.

It is useful to note that at the time of this writing there are two active versions of the JMS specification: 1.0.2b and 1.1. JMS 1.0.2b are part of the current J2EE 1.3 specification, while JMS 1.1 will be included in the forthcoming J2EE 1.4 specification. In this book JMS refers to both versions, but if a feature described is specific to one version, the version is identified explicitly.

Key Concepts

JMS defines an API for accessing the services of a messaging provider. It defines an industry-standard interface for Java programs to create, send, receive, and read messages using messaging providers that support the JMS API. JMS is closely associated with the Java 2 Enterprise Edition (J2EE) platform *(http://java.sun.com/j2ee/)*, which defines industry standards in support of a component-based approach to the design, development, assembly, and deployment of enterprise applications. The J2EE platform consists of a set of services, APIs, and protocols that support the development of a multitiered architecture (Figure 2–1). It defines components such as Servlets and Enterprise Java Beans (EJB), which are hosted in J2EE containers. The J2EE containers implement a standardized runtime environment, and are packaged as part of a J2EE Server, which provides a number of services, such as life cycle management, security, deployment, transaction support, and thread pooling.

The inclusion of JMS as part of the J2EE platform extended the J2EE platform to support enterprise messaging. The J2EE platform is currently at version 1.3, and this includes JMS

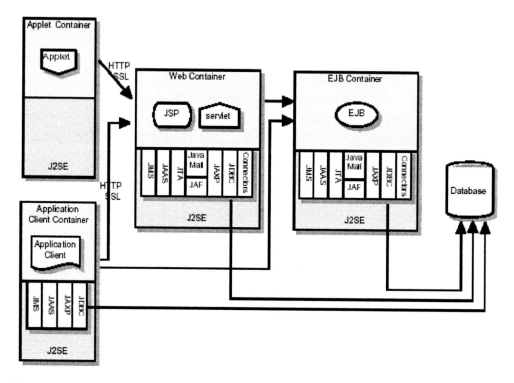

Figure 2-1 The Java 2 Enterprise Edition (J2EE) Platform

1.0.2b. In April 2002, JMS 1.1 was finalized, and it will be part of J2EE 1.4, which is currently in draft form. The inclusion of JMS in J2EE does not imply that JMS can only be used with J2EE-based applications. The services of the messaging provider are accessible to any Java application. However, it is fair to say that a majority of JMS applications will be J2EE-based, as most enterprise applications (written in Java) are developed on this platform.

A common misconception is that JMS defines more than an API, and in some shape, size, or form, is a software product in its own right. Let's be very clear: JMS defines an API and only an API. It is rendered as a set of Java interface classes that messaging provider vendors implement so that applications written to the JMS API can communicate with the messaging provider the vendor supplies.

JMS focuses on the behaviors that an application can expect in response to an API call. For instance, if the application sends a persistent message, it can expect the messaging provider to place the message in a persistent message store as part of processing. However, JMS does not define how the messaging provider implements the message store or what wire protocol it uses when transmitting messages. Similarly, the messaging provider's load-balancing and fault-tolerance characteristics and other such implementation details are not defined. This sometimes overlooked fact brings to light a number of interesting points:

- *Different JMS implementations do not necessarily interoperate:* It is sometimes thought that because two vendors provide messaging providers that implement JMS, these messaging providers can interoperate at a messaging level, that is, exchange messages. This is not true. Different implementation philosophies, protocols adopted and design choices made mean that both messaging providers are fundamentally different from each other. However, from the application's perspective, they can be accessed in the same way via JMS. Consequently, a JMS application can act as a bridge between two messaging providers.

- *JMS implementations are not necessarily created equal*: As previously mentioned, the inherent designs of messaging providers from various software vendors are different. They offer different network administration models, service implementations, configuration options, tools, and so on. Thus, even though they support the same behavior from the JMS application's perspective, they do so with differing levels of efficiency, robustness, and performance. This is not unique to JMS, but is indeed true of the entire J2EE platform. J2EE defines a standard. Implementation and the approach to implementation are left to the implementer.

- *Deployment of JMS solutions is vendor-specific*: The writing of JMS code in an application is vendor-neutral, as it is based on the standard API set. However, in order to achieve a working system, some administrative tasks require knowledge of the underlying messaging provider. The tools provided for administering a JMS environment are messaging provider–specific and detail attributes peculiar to the specific implementation.

JMS defines a number of key entities that form the JMS environment, as shown in Figure 2–2.

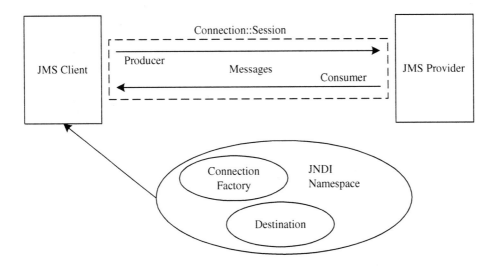

Figure 2-2 JMS Environment

The *JMS provider* is the messaging provider that implements support for JMS, providing the basis for the exchange of messages between applications. As has already been discussed, the JMS (messaging) provider will support the behaviors defined by JMS, although its functionality may extend beyond those defined. It is the entity with which the *JMS client* interacts. The JMS client is quite simply the component utilizing the JMS API, and it establishes a *connection*, then a *session* with the JMS provider in which its interaction with the provider is encapsulated. The session has additional importance in that it defines the scope of a transaction so that all interaction that occurs based on the session can occur within the same transaction. The JMS client interacts with the JMS provider acting as a *producer* (sender or publisher) and/or *consumer* (receiver or subscriber) of *messages*. The JMS client establishes its connection with the provider based on configuration information contained in a `ConnectionFactory` object and identifies the location where a message is to be sent to or retrieved from based on the attributes of a `Destination` object. These definition objects are retrieved from a *JNDI namespace* and are called *administered objects*.

Administered objects contain provider-specific information that allows the JMS client to access the services of the JMS provider. For instance, the `ConnectionFactory` contains the necessary parameters for establishing a connection, such as the server's hostname. These parameters differ between JMS providers, but the client is insulated from these differences because it never has to create or handle the provider's implementation of `ConnectionFactory`. Instead, the `ConnectionFactory` is created external to the application (using a provider-specific administration tool) and stored by a naming and directory service from which it is retrieved using Java Naming and Directory Interface (JNDI).

JNDI is a Java industry-standard API for accessing naming and directory services. It provides an API that allows objects to be stored in or retrieved from any naming and directory service that provides a JNDI implementation, called a JNDI namespace. The JMS specification establishes the convention that JMS administered objects should be defined and stored by an administrator in a JNDI namespace from where they can be retrieved by the JMS client. The choice of naming and directory service varies based on user preference, company policy, or application hosting environment; common choices found in practice are LDAP servers, J2EE servers, and simple file directories.

All provider-specific administered objects extend a Java interface class defined by JMS. The JMS client, on retrieval of the administered object from the JNDI namespace, casts the administered object to its parent interface. This protects the JMS client's portability because it does not need to contain any provider-specific code, as illustrated in the following example:

```
import javax.naming.*; //JNDI package
import javax.jms.*; //JMS package
......

//get Context to JNDI namespace
Context ctx = new InitialContext();
```

```
//retrieve connection factory using Context
ConnectionFactory factory =
(ConnectionFactory)ctx.lookup("MyConnectionFactory");
// factory retrieved
```

In the code snippet, the application uses JNDI to retrieve a provider-specific `Connec-tionFactory` called `"MyConnectionFactory"`, which is cast to the parent class. We examine this process in further detail in Chapter 4.

The practice of retrieving administered objects from JNDI namespaces offers some clear advantages:

- Based on the `ConnectionFactory` retrieved, the client can connect to different JMS providers with no change in the client code.
- The behavior of the client with a given JMS provider can be changed by simply changing the attributes of the administered object rather than changing client code. For instance, if the JMS client is required to send messages to a new destination, this can be affected by changing the attributes of the `destination` object. The new settings go into effect the next time the destination object is retrieved.
- Administered objects can be centrally managed and configured, ensuring consistency with the underlying messaging infrastructure.

The concept of administered objects is key to configuring a JMS application, and we examine in detail the attributes of the administered objects defined by IBM JMS providers in Chapter 6.

The JMS specification recognizes the point-to-point and publish-subscribe paradigms discussed in Chapter 1. JMS supports the semantics of both paradigms by defining messaging domains.

Messaging Domains

JMS defines two messaging domains, point-to-point and publish-subscribe, in support of the two common patterns of message distribution. A set of interfaces are defined for each domain, inheriting their attributes and behavior from a base set of interfaces (Table 2–1).

An application typically chooses which set of interfaces (point-to-point or publish-subscribe) it wishes to work with based on the messaging domain (distribution paradigm) it will be using. As we shall see shortly, JMS 1.1 now allows the application to use the common (parent) interfaces so that the application can send or receive messages in either domain using the same API set.

JMS defines a basic programming model, as shown in Figure 2–3.

Table 2–1 Messaging Domain Interfaces

Common (Parent)	Point-to-Point	Publish-Subscribe
ConnectionFactory*	QueueConnectionFactory*	TopicConnectionFactory*
Connection	QueueConnection	TopicConnection
Destination*	Queue*	Topic*
Session	QueueSession	TopicSession
MessageProducer	QueueSender	TopicPublisher
MessageConsumer	QueueReceiver QueueBrowser	TopicSubscriber

*Administered objects

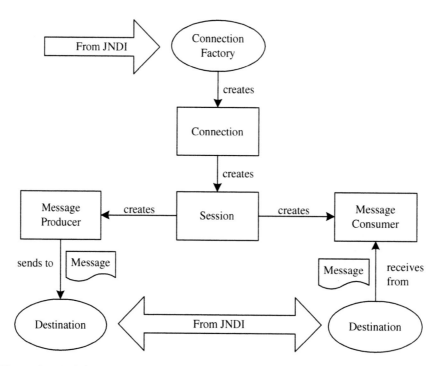

Figure 2-3 JMS Programming Model

The JMS client retrieves the `ConnectionFactory` from a JNDI namespace and uses it to create a `Connection`. The `Connection` creates a `Session`, and `MessageProducers` and/or `MessageConsumers` are created from the `Session`. The `Session` is also used to create `Messages`, which are then sent to or received from a `Destination` (retrieved from a JNDI namespace) using a `MessageProducer` and `MessageConsumer` respectively. Figure 2–4 illustrates the process in the point-to-point domain.

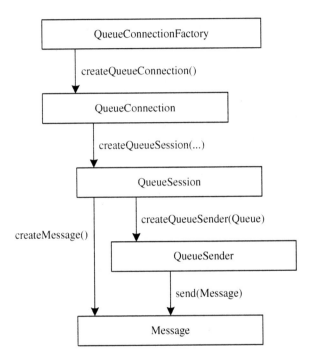

Figure 2-4 Application Flow: Point-to-Point Domain

Rendered in code, the sending flow looks like this:

```
import javax.naming.*; //JNDI package
import javax.jms.*; //JMS package
......


//get Context to JNDI namespace
Context ctx = new InitialContext();

//retrieve ConnectionFactory and Queue using Context
QueueConnectionFactory factory =
(QueueConnectionFactory)ctx.lookup("qServer");
Queue queue = (Queue)ctx.lookup("queueX");
```

```
// create connection
QueueConnection connection = factory.createQueueConnection();

//create session
QueueSession session = connection.createQueueSession(false,
Session.AUTO_ACKNOWLEDGE);

//create sender
QueueSender queueSender = session.createSender(queue);

//send the message
TextMessage outMessage = session.createTextMessage();
outMessage.setText("this is a test");
queueSender.send(outMessage);
```

Using the publish-subscribe domain, the basic application flow remains the same (Figure 2–5), except that here the publish-subscribe interfaces are used.

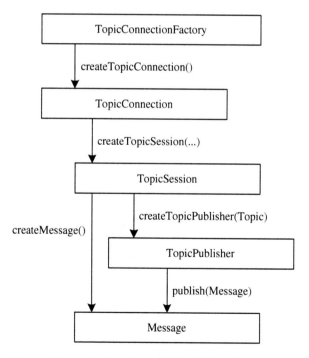

Figure 2-5 Application Flow: Publish-Subscribe

Observe how similar the code snippet to publish a message looks when compared with sending a message in the point-to-point messaging domain.

```
import javax.naming.*; //JNDI package
import javax.jms.*; //JMS package
......

//get Context to JNDI namespace
Context ctx = new InitialContext();

//retrieve ConnectionFactory and Topic using Context
TopicConnectionFactory factory =
(TopicConnectionFactory)ctx.lookup("tServer");
Topic topic = (Topic)ctx.lookup("topicX");

// create connection
TopicConnection connection = factory.createTopicConnection();

//create session
TopicSession session = connection.createTopicSession(false,
Session.AUTO_ACKNOWLEDGE);

//create publisher
TopicPublisher topicPublisher =
session.createPublisher(topic);

//publish message
TextMessage outMessage = session.createTextMessage();
outMessage.setText("this is a test");
topicPublisher.publish(outMessage);
```

JMS 1.0.2b provides no support for a client that wishes to access both messaging domains in a single session. For instance, the client might want to receive a message from a queue, process it, and publish the results to interested parties. While the application could be written to utilize both domains by creating a QueueSession and a TopicSession, there is no way to use a single session to access both a queue and a topic, and consequently the scenario described could not be executed as a single transaction. It is also difficult with JMS 1.0.2b to write a reusable client that can work with either messaging domain. As evidenced by the code snippets above, while the flow is similar, the actual interfaces and method calls do differ. In defense of JMS 1.0.2b, it must be said that the specification adopted two independent interfaces in support of software vendors whose JMS providers supported only one or the other distribution paradigms. Note that a JMS provider is not obligated to support both messaging domains unless the JMS provider is part of a J2EE 1.3 server.

What's New in JMS 1.1

JMS 1.1 has addressed the inherent difficulties of working with both messaging domains by unifying the domains. Thus, with JMS 1.1, in addition to using either the point-to-point or publish-subscribe interfaces, the client can now use the parent or common interfaces acting in a domain-neutral fashion. Our code fragment that sends a message, using the unified domain, now looks like this:

```
import javax.naming.*; //JNDI package
import javax.jms.*; //JMS package
......


//get context to JNDI namespace
Context ctx = new InitialContext();

//retrieve ConnectionFactory and Destination using Context
ConnectionFactory factory =
(ConnectionFactory)ctx.lookup("Server");
Destination destination =
(Destination)ctx.lookup("destinationX");

// create connection
Connection connection = factory.createConnection();

//Create session
Session session = connection.createSession(false,
Session.AUTO_ACKNOWLEDGE);

//create Producer
MessageProducer producer =
session.createProducer(destination);

//send message
TextMessage outMessage = session.createTextMessage();
outMessage.setText("this is a test");
producer.send(outMessage);
```

Using the common interfaces, the true nature of the send (i.e., a point-to-point send or a publish-subscribe publish) is determined by the nature of the Destination retrieved (i.e., Queue or Topic). Thus, the code snippet can be reused in either domain based on the definition of destinationX in the JNDI namespace.

The common interfaces offer the application developer an even simpler programming interface, as the developer can now write code that can be used in either point-to-point or publish-subscribe scenarios. It also facilitates mixed domain programming, enabling messages to be moved between queues and topics within the same transaction. In support of this feature, new methods have been defined for the common interfaces, enabling, for instance, the creation of a Connection from a ConnectionFactory. Previously, only QueueConnectionFactory and TopicConnectionFactory could create a QueueConnection or TopicConnection. In addition, JMS 1.1 details some clarifications on the behavior of the interfaces in terms of returned values and error conditions, which are of particular relevance to the software vendor implementing a JMS provider.

We have by no means exhausted the variations in the way the JMS interfaces are used or indeed introduced every single interface. We also have not yet discussed all the associated method calls and supporting infrastructure code, such as exception handling. However, the above illustrations provide basic insight into the workings of JMS. The attraction for the developer should now be obvious: JMS provides a simple API with clear lines of responsibility: a `ConnectionFactory` is required to create a `Connection`, a `Connection` is required to create a `Session`, and so on. The JMS API is fairly straightforward to use. In Chapter 4, we examine the API in greater detail and build a number of JMS client applications.

JMS Messages

JMS defines a set of interfaces for messages that address the basic forms of data that we might wish to send or receive. The JMS message is typed based on the data it contains. The defined message types are:

- `BytesMessage`: Stores data as a sequence of bytes, supports the most basic representation of data and thus can contain varied payloads.
- `TextMessage`: Stores data as a `String`, a common representation for enterprise data.
- `StreamMessage`: Stores data as a sequence of typed fields, for example, `JohnDoe33`, defined as sequence of two strings (John, Doe), and an integer (33).
- `MapMessage`: Stores data as a set of key-value pairs; the key is defined as a string and the value is typed (e.g., `Age:33`, where Age is the key and 33 the integer value).
- `ObjectMessage`: Stores a serialized Java object.

The JMS message (be it a `BytesMessage`, `TextMessage`, or other message type) is composed of three basic parts:

- **Header**: The header contains attributes (fields) that enable the message to be identified and routed. The attributes are prefixed with `JMS`. Examples include `JMSMessageID`, which uniquely identifies the message; `JMSDestination`, which contains the destination to which the message is being sent; and `JMSDeliveryMode`, which defines a message as being persistent or nonpersistent.
- **Properties**: JMS defines properties as a built-in facility for supporting property values, which are categorized by JMS as
    - **Application-specific:** These are properties specified and used by the JMS client. They are commonly used to set application-specific filters, allowing certain messages to be retrieved based on the value of the property.
    - **Standard**: These are defined by JMS and are in effect optional header fields. The properties are prefixed with `JMSX`. Examples include `JMSX-`

GroupID, the identity of the logical group the message is part of, and JMSXGroupSeq, the sequence number of the message within the group.
- **Provider-specific**: This property value provides a placeholder for provider-specific attributes that may be required when the JMS client is sending a message to a non-JMS client (i.e., an application that is using the provider's proprietary API). If such properties are defined, they are prefixed JMS_<vendor_name>.
- **Body**: The actual payload is carried in the body; as mentioned earlier, the nature of the payload determines the type of JMS message used.

The JMS message contains operations for accessing and setting header fields and properties. Depending upon the nature of the message body and consequently the message type, different methods are exposed for storing and retrieving the message contents. You may recall that in the code snippets in the section "Message Domains," we manipulated a TextMessage object, as shown:

```
TextMessage outMessage = session.createTextMessage();
outMessage.setText("this is a test");
```

In the code snippet we use the TextMessage, as the message data is defined as the string "this is a test". Note that the TextMessage object provides a setText method that allows the contents of the message body to be set. As would be expected, a corresponding getText method exists to retrieve the contents of the message.

JMS 1.1 introduced a couple of new methods in existing interfaces in response to the user community. Regarding JMS messages, one method of note is BytesMessage.get-BodyLength(), which returns the size of the BytesMessage body. This enables the byte array into which the contents of the body will be copied to be easily initialized. Prior to JMS 1.1, this required testing and resizing logic to be implemented.

In Chapter 3, we examine the operations defined for JMS messages in greater detail; more importantly, we examine the use of different message types in enterprise messaging applications and provide technical guidance on when a message type might be used.

Application Server Facilities

A J2EE server hosts J2EE components, such as servlets and EJBs. These components may implement JMS clients or wish to avail themselves indirectly of the services of a JMS provider, as is the case with message-driven beans (MDB). Application Server Facilities (ASF) are defined by JMS to enable J2EE servers to efficiently implement certain JMS-related processing functions in support of the components they host. It defines a set of server APIs (interfaces) that are implemented by the JMS provider and J2EE server vendors.

Application Server Facilities, as the name suggests, are targeted at the J2EE server and not the JMS client. ASF is an optional part of JMS and may not be supported by a given JMS provider. Thus, the JMS specification strongly advises against the direct use of ASF in a JMS client.

Rather, the client should exploit the facilities of the J2EE server and JMS provider, which may have been implemented with the help of ASF.

To round out our overview of JMS, we briefly examine two specific areas that ASF addresses: concurrent message handling and distributed transaction coordination.

Concurrent Processing of Incoming Messages

Message-driven beans, introduced in EJB 2.0 (part of J2EE 1.3) as a new type of message-oriented EJB, are designed to be invoked by the hosting J2EE server when a JMS message arrives. Prior to EJB 2.0, we had only the task-oriented session bean and data-oriented entity bean. MDBs provide a mechanism for implementing the message consumer pattern (see Chapter 1) in a J2EE server. The J2EE server is responsible for connecting to the JMS provider and monitoring the JMS destinations of interest (defined using deployment descriptors) for the arrival of messages. Once a message arrives, the J2EE server retrieves the message and passes it to the associated MDB.

ASF defines a special facility that is used by the J2EE server to create `MessageConsumers` that can concurrently process multiple incoming messages in support of its MDBs. This facility is implemented by a number of specialized interfaces: `ServerSessionPool`, `ServerSession`, and `ConnectionConsumer`. The responsibility for implementing these interfaces is shared between the JMS provider and J2EE server. Given that the JMS client is not the natural target of these facilities, we do not explore the use of these interfaces in any more detail. However, in Chapter 7 we examine the configuration of an MDB as part of a usage scenario.

Distributed or Global Transactions

As discussed in Chapter 1, it is common for an application to want to send or receive a JMS message and update another resource such as a database within the same transaction. J2EE servers perform the role of external transaction managers, managing updates to different resources in a single distributed transaction. The J2EE server's transaction management capability is defined by the Java Transaction Service (JTS) specification. JTS requires that resource managers involved in the transaction (in our case, the JMS provider) implement support for the Java Transaction API (JTA).

ASF defines an `XAConnectionFactory`, which is used by the JMS provider to expose its support for JTA. As might be expected, the `XAConnectionFactory` is used by the J2EE server to create an `XAConnection` and `XASession`. The `XASession` contains the resource handle (`XAResource`) used by the J2EE server to coordinate the transaction. The XA common interfaces are similarly rendered in the point-to-point and publish-subscribe interfaces. However, being administered objects, they are defined such that the JMS client never uses them directly, and thus their use has no impact on the programming flow previously discussed.

In Chapter 7 we see how a JMS client can be configured to take advantage of the transaction management capabilities of IBM's WebSphere Application Server.

Summary

JMS, which is part of the J2EE platform, defines an industry-standard API for accessing the services of a messaging provider. It provides a set of interfaces that applications use based on the messaging domain in which they are working: point-to-point or publish-subscribe. JMS 1.1, however; has now given the application access to the common interfaces, allowing applications to be written in a domain-neutral fashion, facilitating mixed domain programming.

Central to the JMS programming model are administered objects, which encapsulate provider-specific attributes. Administered objects are stored in a JNDI namespace (using provider-specific tools) from where they are retrieved by the application using JNDI. We saw how this feature allows the application to be written independent of the underlying messaging infrastructure, enhancing its portability.

We examined the JMS message, which is the "unit of exchange" between applications, detailing its structure and associated attributes. Finally, we briefly discussed Application Server Facilities (ASF), which, as part of the JMS specification, caters to the needs of the J2EE server in terms of the JMS-related processing services it needs to implement. Specifically, we reviewed concurrent message handling and transaction management.

In the following chapters, we delve deeper into JMS, beginning with a detailed examination of the JMS message. We explore its content, structure, and finally its usage.

JMS Messages

All too often when people think about messaging, their minds immediately focus on the mechanics of the process and the entity for which the process is being implemented—the message—is all too easily forgotten. The message is the unit of exchange and without first defining the message, we have nothing with which to communicate. Thus, before we explore the use of the JMS API, we examine in detail the JMS message. We review the process of message definition and learn what factors influence the nature of the message content. We detail the structure of JMS messages, discuss key attributes, and consider when a given message type should be used. We also answer questions regarding how the JMS client uses the JMS message interface. For instance: How do I select a specific message of interest or populate it with content?

Message Definition

Message definition is probably the most crucial and potentially the most challenging of all activities associated with enterprise messaging. It defines the process of determining message content (what makes up a message) and structure (how message content is organized), without which applications do not have the basis to communicate. The varied nature and number of applications that interact using the enterprise messaging infrastructure implies that the number and form of message definitions can vary widely. This typically suggests a requirement for transformation services that transform messages between different formats. Such services are often provided by messaging providers as part of the delivery service.

In approaching the problem of message definition proliferation, some encourage the use of a common message model or canonical form that all messages exchanged are based on. Of course, the main challenge is defining a suitable canonical form that addresses the needs of all the enterprise applications. Irrespective of the approach to message definition adopted, the problem still remains to define for any given message the message content and its physical format or layout. Together, the message content and physical format define the data block that will be contained within the body of the JMS message.

The message content problem is typically bounded by the actual functions of the applications that will be producing or consuming the message. For instance, for an application that is responsible for submitting an order, it's safe to assume that the message content representing the order will contain data consistent with how an order is defined in that enterprise. The content should address the needs of the application that will process the order as well as take into account the data the submitting application has available. Expected content could comprise an order identifier, customer details, and a list of ordered items.

Defining message content can thus be viewed as an exercise in understanding and interpreting the business context. In addition, the potential interactions between the communicating applications must be considered. For example, when the order is submitted, how is the status of the order communicated? We could adopt the approach that our order message contains a status field, which is populated by the order fulfillment application. In this case we use a single message type for submitting an order as well as for receiving or querying its status. Alternately, we could design an order status message that is returned when the order is submitted and also used when the status of the order is requested. Note that in both cases we would also have to define the dependencies among the data. For instance, in the case where I use the same message type for different purposes, what fields are mandatory or optional based on my usage?

Sometimes the message content is predefined by the application that ultimately produces or consumes the message. This is often the case when enabling existing off-the-shelf or custom applications to communicate via messaging. As an example, the message content of a message designed to move data to or from a database table could be expected to bear a close relationship with the columns and rows defined for the database table.

The physical format of a message refers to the actual representation of the message content. It specifies how the data is structured and laid out and defines the relationship between discrete items of data, usually called fields or elements. The physical format enables the sending or receiving application to make sense of the data contained within the message.

As an illustration of the problem, consider the data block:

    JOHN DOE 33

Is this a single data field? Or is it three fields, each separated by a space? What is the nature of the data? Is it a string? Is 33 an integer? The ways in which this data block could be interpreted are endless, and the physical format enables the data to be interpreted as intended.

To further our discussion of physical formats, we examine three physical formats commonly used to define messages: XML, tagged/delimited, and record-oriented.

XML

XML (Extensible Markup Language) is probably the most commonly used physical format in Java applications. It is a standards-based markup language (http://www.w3.org/XML/) that allows data to be described independent of the language the application is written in or the operating system on which the application runs. The inherent portability of XML data is a major factor in its popularity in the Java world, which is understandable given that Java itself is aimed at developing portable applications that can run on any operating system. XML is also widely used by non-Java applications and is definitely experiencing a boom in its usage. Indeed, it may not be inappropriate to suggest that XML could be considered the physical format of choice, or at the very least the first port of call, for representing data in today's business applications.

XML is a markup language: it uses tags to identify pieces of data. XML, like its sibling HTML, owes its existence to Standard Generalized Markup Language (SGML), which was defined in 1986 by the International Standards Organization in the standard ISO 8879. SGML had its roots in document representation and was designed to provide a basis for describing the various elements associated with a document, including text, formatting, linking, and embedding. It introduced the concept of providing start and end tags to identify a piece of textual data. Hence, a first name of John would be described <firstName>John</firstName>, with the addition of the forward slash (/) identifying the end tag. The use of start and end tags meant that data could be nested and described in a hierarchical form. For instance, the attributes of a given individual could be described as:

```
<person>
    <firstName>John</firstName>
    <lastName>Doe</lastName>
    <age>33</age>
</person>
```

In essence, SGML provided a way to identify, name, and describe the relationship between pieces of data so they could be managed and manipulated. That said, the SGML standard was by no means simple, as it provided a generalized framework and was consequently extensive in scope and detail. A key characteristic of SGML is that it is a metalanguage, which means that it defines how any given markup language can be specified. HTML was first introduced in 1990 as a markup language for describing data that is rendered in browsers as Web pages. HTML defined a strict set of tags and associated syntax to be used and provided the impetus for the explosion of the Internet, as any browser that could process HTML could display the resulting data. XML, introduced in 1996, was aimed at providing a simpler and lightweight generalized markup language for use on the Web. It differed from HTML in one key aspect: it did not define a tag set. This meant that XML was highly extensible and flexible, as tags could be defined to suit any given purpose. In addition, as long as the XML document was well formed (e.g., matching start and end tags), the data could be processed by any application that could handle XML. Of course with such flexibility there was the question of whether the tags would be understood by the processing application, and a number of specifications, which we will examine later, such as DTD and Schemas, evolved to enable the meaning of an XML document to be shared among applications.

XML describes data in a textual form that is typically human readable, it is used in a variety of applications ranging from presentation of information and storage of configuration options, to communication of data—a use we are obviously interested in. Being a meta-language in its own right, XML has formed the basis of other language specifications that define an explicit tag set and associated syntax for their use. Examples include SOAP, a standards-based format for describing messages sent using Web services, and WSDL, a format for describing Web services.

Anatomy of an XML Document

Figure 3–1 shows an XML document (a block of data rendered in XML) with key attributes of the document highlighted.

An XML document typically commences with an optional XML declaration that in the least identifies the version of XML in the document and additionally the character encoding. If the XML declaration is omitted, the version is assumed to be 1.0, and heuristics are applied by the processing application to guess the encoding. The XML declaration is known as a processing instruction (PI) and is characterized by the syntax `<?PITarget   instructions?>`. `PITarget` represents a keyword meaningful to the processing XML parser or application. In our example we specify a target `"XML"`, which refers to the XML standard set of PIs that a

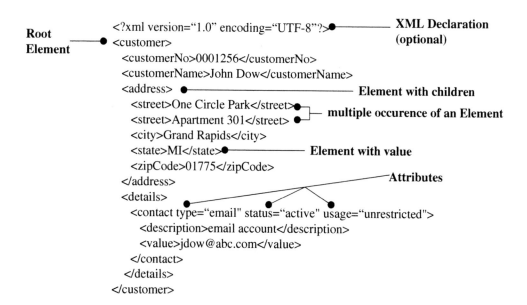

Figure 3-1 Anatomy of an XML Document

parser should recognize; the specific instructions identify version and character encoding. Application-specific PIs may be defined and included in the document.

The XML data is bound by a root tag `<customer>` ... `</customer>`. The root tag encapsulates all other tags associated with the data block and marks the start and end of the XML data. As would be expected with most hierarchical structures, there can be only one root tag. An element is generally defined by a start tag, end tag, and some value. The element itself may contain nested elements and may indeed be empty; that is, they may have no value or nested element assigned. In the case of an empty element, a special shorthand may be used specifying a start tag ending in a forward slash, for example, `<value/>`. Elements may optionally contain attributes, which are name-value pairs that provide an alternative way of structuring data. For example, element `contact` has associated with it three attributes: `type`, `status`, and `usage`.

The question that always arises is: When do I represent data as an element or as an attribute, given that either approach can be easily adopted? For instance,

```
<contact type="email" status="active" usage="unrestricted">
... .
</contact>
```

can just as easily be represented by

```
<contact>
<type>email</type>
<status>active</status>
<usage>unrestricted</usage>

...

</contact>
```

The simple answer is that it depends. It basically comes down to what constitutes a logical arrangement, what makes contextual sense, personal preference, and style.

In reviewing the XML example (Figure 3–1), you may have noted some simple syntactical rules. Element names must begin with a letter or underscore and may not contain embedded spaces. All start tags must have a corresponding end tag, and the order of nesting must be maintained. An XML document that conforms to these rules is said to be well formed; however, that a document is well formed does not mean that it is correct or valid from the perspective of the application that is processing it. As an example, assume I wish to send an XML-based message to a shipping application. The shipping application requires that a postal code (ZIP Code) be specified and the sending application sends the following:

```
<address>
        <street>One Circle Park</street>
        <street>Apartment 301</street>
        <city>Grand Rapids</city>
        <state>MI</state>
        <zipCode/>
    </address>
```

The XML document in itself is well formed, obeying all the syntactical rules; however, from the perspective of the shipping application, the XML document is not valid because it does not contain a required value: `zipCode` is empty. When viewed from the perspective of validity, you may have already begun to ask other questions, such as how the shipping application knows that the element `zipCode` is contained in the element `address`, or how the sending application can be notified that in preparing the XML document, `zipCode` is a mandatory element that must be populated. In other words, is there a blueprint or metadata that describes the structures and relationships in the XML document? This need is addressed by DTDs and XML Schema.

DTDs and Schemas

DTDs (Document Type Definitions) and XML Schemas define what an XML document should look like. They define the ordering of elements, mandatory and optional elements, allowable values, and a host of other characteristics that make it possible for an application to successfully interpret an XML document. While they are not required to successfully parse or construct an XML document, they define a reusable template for the XML document that can be shared among applications, and they provide a definition against which the document can be validated.

Initially, a DTD was the only means of describing an XML document, but as usage evolved, a number of restrictions became apparent:

- DTDs are not expressed in XML; they are simple text documents and are consequently not as easy as XML to process or manipulate.
- DTDs do not allow the value of an element to be typed as anything other than a `String`. While it was accepted that an XML document represented all data in textual form and was in itself one large `String`, users wanted the capability to say that the value of a given element was not actually a `String`, but an integer, for example, and should be treated as such by the processing application.
- DTDs do not provide a mechanism to define the scope of a tag to protect against name collision. For example, does the element `type` mean the same thing when defined as part of the element `account` and the element `phoneNumber`? Are the allowed values in both cases the same? And how do we address the ambiguity?

XML Schemas were introduced to address these and other limitations, and are the preferred option over DTDs. XML Schemas are written in XML. They allow elements to be typed and are closely associated with the concept of XML namespaces, which provide a solution to name collision. The concepts associated with XML Schemas, particularly XML namespaces, are nontrivial, and a detailed review is outside the scope of this book. However, a number of excellent references are suggested in the resource list in Appendix D. For our purposes, it suffices to say that armed with a DTD or Schema, our application can validate that the message content is appropriately formatted and populated before sending or on receipt. It is useful to note that from a performance viewpoint, the overhead associated with validating an XML document can be significant. It is thus not unusual for validation to be done as part of development and testing, and disabled when the applications move into production, as thorough testing should have confirmed the correctness of the exchanged XML.

Processing XML Documents

Generally, an XML-aware application is concerned with constructing XML documents from various data structures and/or parsing XML documents into data structures that can be accessed and manipulated. From the JMS client's perspective, the XML document will be inserted into or retrieved from the message body of a JMS message. Given the textual nature of the XML document, it is fair to assume that it would be contained in a JMS `TextMessage` or `BytesMessage`.

A number of APIs have been developed in Java that enable an application to process an XML document. In all cases the use of the API is associated with a supporting XML parser that implements support for the API. The XML parser is responsible for actually parsing the XML document and optionally validating it against a Schema or DTD. A good example of an XML parser is the open source Apache Xerces2 Java Parser (*http://xml.apache.org/xerces2-j/index.html*), which supports the full range of APIs. It is particularly popular among developers and is repackaged by a number of vendors, including IBM. Currently, Java developers have a choice of four APIs to use for XML processing: SAX, DOM, JAXP, and JDOM.

SAX   SAX (Simple API for XML; *http://www.saxproject.org/*) focuses on the parsing of XML documents only. It does not provide for the building of an XML document from scratch or the modification of an existing document. It offers an event-driven interface that enables the application to register content handlers that are called with parsing events as they occur. The parsing events are triggered as the document is parsed by the parser, and the content handler implements methods (callbacks) that are called based upon the nature of the event. Examples include `startDocument()`, `endDocument()`, `startElement()`, `endElement()`, and `characters()`. In all cases the callback methods are passed arguments, which are processed by the application. The `characters()` method receives the actual data associated with a given element.

Under SAX, the parser handles the document sequentially, triggering events as it progresses. Once an event has been triggered, it cannot be retrieved, and SAX does not store processed values. This offers a performance advantage, as large documents can be easily handled without constraining available memory. The downside is that SAX provides no means of accessing data randomly or at a specified location. It also provides no in-memory model of the document that can be accessed by the application.

DOM   The DOM (Document Object Model) API is aimed at providing an in-memory model of the XML document defined as a tree. A document object is provided by the API, which contains the parse tree and methods that enable the tree to be traversed. The API also allows a document object and thus a tree to be built from scratch, providing methods to create elements, attributes, and other XML constructs. Unfortunately, the API does not provide a means to easily render a built tree in XML, and custom string-generation methods are required if DOM is to be used this way. Such utilities may be provided by the parser vendor; for example, Xerces provides an XMLSerializer class for this purpose.

The greatest concern when using DOM is the resource constraints that can occur when parsing large documents, as in all cases the entire document must be read into memory before it can be accessed. It is instructive to note that DOM actually uses SAX to parse the document as it builds the tree.

DOM was not designed specifically for Java, but is rather a general specification (see *http://www.w3.org/DOM/*) that can be implemented in any programming language. This has resulted in what some developer's have described as an API that is foreign to Java programmers. While this is of course a matter of opinion, the API does offer certain idiosyncrasies such as treating everything, even data, as a node on the tree (one would expect data to be associated with a node and not be a node itself), which can make the API feel unwieldy.

JAXP JAXP (Java API for XML Parsing) was introduced by Sun to attempt to provide some standardized abstraction to the use of SAX and DOM with different parsers. One of the drawbacks of SAX and DOM is that they both require that the XML parser is explicitly specified, which of course means that code would need to be modified if a different parser is used. While one could work around this limitation using property files, JAXP (http://java.sun.com/xml/jaxp/) provides a standard pluggability layer that allows applications to be written independent of the XML parser used. It allows the XML parser to be specified using Java system properties, and provides factory classes that enable a SAX or DOM parser to be invoked. It does not change the SAX or DOM APIs, but simply adds some convenience constructs that abstract the vendor specific parser.

JDOM The JDOM API is an open source effort (*http://www.jdom.org/*) that addresses the limitations of SAX and DOM. Despite the name similarity, JDOM is not based on DOM, though it adopts a document object model. It was designed and optimized specifically for Java and harnesses the power of the Java language to provide a simple API with credible performance characteristics. It is not dependent on an XML parser implementing support for JDOM, as it uses SAX (or DOM) to invoke the parser; thus it can be used with existing parsers. As it is based on a document object model, it allows the parse tree to be constructed from scratch, and unlike DOM, it provides utility classes that can render the tree in a number of forms, including XML.

While not intended to be a full-fledged tutorial on using JDOM, to round out our discussion on XML, the code snippet below illustrates the use of JDOM to construct and insert a simple XML document into a JMS message. It also shows how to parse an XML document retrieved from a JMS message.

```
//JDOM imports
import org.jdom.*; //XML Processing API
import org.jdom.input.SAXBuilder; //Parser
```

```
import org.jdom.output.XMLOutputter;//XML generator

/*Sender*/
//build XML document from data
String firstName = "JOHN";
String lastName = "DOE";
int age = 33;

//create document object
Document doc = new Document(new Element("person"));
//retrieve root element and build tree
Element root = doc.getRootElement();
root.addContent(new Element("firstName").setText(firstName));
root.addContent(new Element("lastName").setText(lastName));
root.addContent(new
Element("age").setText(Integer.toString(age)));
//output tree as XML stream ready for transmission
XMLOutputter fmt = new XMLOutputter();
//XMLOutputter output method works with java.io.OutputStream
//though an outputString method is provided, its use is not
recommended by jdom
ByteArrayOutputStream out = new ByteArrayOutputStream();
fmt.output(doc, out);

//create TextMessage
TextMessage tOutMsg = session.createTextMessage();
tOutMsg.setText(new String(out.toByteArray()));

/*Receiver*/
//Unpack TextMessage
String message = tInMsg.getText();

//parse message content to generate document
ByteArrayInputStream in = new
ByteArrayInputStream(message.getBytes());
//create parser using default (Xerces) and no validation
SAXBuilder parser = new SAXBuilder(false);
Document doc = parser.build(in);
Element root = doc.getRootElement();
String firstName = root.getChildText("firstName");
String lastName = root.getChildText("lastName");
int age = Integer.parseInt(root.getChildText("age"));
```

Note that for the construction and parsing of the message, JDOM favors
java.io.InputStream, and I used the ByteArrayInputStream and ByteArray-
OutputStream. My reason for not simply using a BytesMessage (which would be a natural fit) is specifically related to the fact that with the BytesMessage, the receiver does not

know the size of the incoming message, which hampers its ability to extract the contents (a problem fixed in JMS 1.1). This is discussed in detail in the section "Using the JMS Message Interface," later in this chapter.

Tagged/Delimited

A tagged/delimited physical format uses tags, delimiters, or both to define the structure of a block of data, which is usually rendered as text. If we revisit our sample message data, JOHN DOE 33, we could define this as three fields delimited by a space. Alternately, JOHN;DOE;33 would be three fields delimited by a semicolon. Tagged/delimited physical formats have been in use for years and are found in many industrial-strength applications. For instance, the SWIFT message format, which is used to move money electronically between banks, is tagged/delimited. Automated commerce transactions between businesses often rely upon the exchange of messages that conform to the Electronic Data Interchange (EDI) format, which is also traditionally a tagged/delimited format. Indeed, in the strictest sense XML can be thought of as a formalized tagged/delimited format.

Using a tagged/delimited format simply comes down to deciding if your fields need to be tagged and how the fields are delimited. A number of approaches can be adopted to define the structure of the data:

Variable-Length Delimited

With a variable-length delimited approach, the data fields are separated from each other by a delimiter. The delimiter is a constant that marks the end of a field. Punctuation constructs such as commas (,), full stops (.), semicolons (;), and colons (:) are commonly used. This approach proves particularly useful when the length of a data field varies from message to message (hence the term variable-length). For example, the length of a person's name varies widely. Defining a fixed length for the data field that will contain a name requires you to define an allowable maximum. This runs the risk of someday proving inadequate or alternately proves inefficient because the full length is never used and thus a great portion of the message is essentially redundant space.

It is not uncommon to have data that contains a combination of fixed-length and variable-length fields. You can choose to simply delimit all fields using a delimiter, or you can choose to delimit fixed fields based on their length and variable fields with a delimiter. For example, in

```
1050JOHN;DOE;33
```

1050 is a value with a fixed length of four characters. The other fields are variable and delimited with a semicolon.

Tagged Delimited

As the name suggests, tagged delimited uses a tag to identify data fields. The tag generally precedes the data field and is itself separated from the data field either by a known tag length or by a specified tag data separator, which is essentially a delimiter that specifies the end of the tag. The data field is separated from the next tag by a specified delimiter. For example, in

        DATA:0001;DATA:0002;DATA:0003

DATA is the tag for each field, a colon is the tag data separator, and a semicolon delimits the data field from the next tag. A variation on this is tagged fixed length, in which the data fields are delimited by their known length.

It is certainly possible for techniques to be combined when defining data formats, and varied and complicated variations can occur. For example, if a field is delimited by its length, the data structure may be designed such that the length of the field is carried as part of the message, as shown:

        X:4;0001Y:6;000123

where X is a tag separated from the following data field by a colon. The data field containing the value 4 is delimited by a semicolon from a fixed data field whose length is the value contained in the preceding field: 4. The data structure then repeats the same pattern with a tag, Y, and a data field whose length is 6.

Processing Tagged/Delimited Formats   The tagged/delimited physical format offers considerable flexibility in defining the way data is structured. Consider the sample SWIFT message shown:

```
{1:F01IBMADEF0AXXX0000000000}{2:I100IBMADEF0AXXXN}{3:{108:abc}
}{4:
:20:X
:32A:940930USD1,
:50:X
:52A:CHASUS33
:53A:CHASUS33
:54A:CHASUS33
:56A:CHASUS33
:57A:CHASUS33
:59:X
:70:X
:71A:OUR
:72:/A/
-}
```

The message is defined by blocks of data grouped together. Each block is identified by a tag (1, 2, ...) which is separated from its data fields by a colon. Blocks are delimited by curly braces ({ }). Notice that in the block tagged with a 4 (known as the SWIFT message body; the others are headers), each data field is further tagged with a colon as separator, and the data is delimited with a carriage-return linefeed.

Clearly, the parsing or construction of such a message format is nontrivial; however, it illustrates an important point: if you decide to define a tagged/delimited format, you must typically design code to successfully parse and construct messages in that format. As an example, the following code snippet illustrates how our sample variable-length delimited message JOHN;DOE;33 might be parsed:

```
//parse received message
String message = tInMsg.getText();
//initialize variables
String firstName = "";
String lastName = "";
int age = 0;

//use java.util.StringTokenizer to parse string
StringTokenizer st = new StringTokenizer(message, ";");
while (st.hasMoreTokens()) {
    firstName = st.nextToken();
    lastName = st.nextToken();
    age = Integer.parseInt(st.nextToken());
}
```

It is useful to note that in the case of well-known, complicated formats such as SWIFT and EDI, vendor-supplied tools are generally available to assist in the processing of such data.

Why, you may ask, would I want to create a tagged/delimited format when I can use XML with all its associated tools? Performance considerations and optimizing message size are influencing factors. XML by design is a verbose format, and as previously discussed, processing XML documents can attract significant overhead. In contrast, representing the data using a tagged/delimited format such as variable-length delimited results in much less data that needs to be transmitted and, with careful choices, a structure that is not that hard to parse or construct. However, this is usually at the expense of readability and maintainability. Thus, in choosing a physical format, thought should be given to the use of the message and the impact the choice of physical format will have on development effort, performance, maintainability, ease of change, and ease of data sharing (remember that the physical format definition will need to be shared with at least one other application).

Record-Oriented

The record-oriented physical format is a fixed length–based format; that is, data is described based on the length of associated typed fields. For example, JOHNDOE33 is described as two strings of length 4 and 3 and an integer. Record-oriented formats were first introduced by mainframe-based applications as a means of formatting data that was to be exchanged between programs. Such applications were often written in COBOL, and COBOL copybooks defined the structure of data in terms of the number of bytes representing each field. For applications written in C, the *struct* provided a useful construct for representing record-oriented data. In Java, record-oriented formats are often rendered in byte arrays, and the JMS Bytes-Message object provides useful methods for rendering record-oriented physical formats, as we see later in this chapter.

While a record-oriented format can form the most concise description of a data block, this is done at the expense of readability and ease of sharing. For example, it is not as straightforward to share the definition of a record-oriented format between two applications that are written in different languages as it is to share an XML Schema. As discussed earlier, if fields may vary in length, then a maximum allowable length must be defined, with the attendant risks. Consideration also must be given to padding characters (often null or whitespace), which must be inserted when the actual data is less than the maximum length. The question of justification—Is data inserted from the beginning or end of the field so that blank space is either after or before the data?—also needs to be considered.

As with XML and tagged/delimited formats, record-oriented formats can be used to render quite complex data structures, and I would not want to convey the impression that they are obsolete, as they are widely used by today's enterprise applications. However, it is fair to say that new Java applications being developed today will most likely use XML rather than a record-oriented format for reasons discussed earlier. In the instance where the JMS application is sending or receiving a message from a non-JMS application that uses a record-oriented format, we may find ourselves handling record-oriented formats directly. However, recall that a messaging provider may offer value-added transformation services, which transform messages into physical formats appropriate for the recipient. If such services are available and are used, then the physical formats adopted by different applications do not need to be constrained. A given application simply speaks in a format that best suits its purposes.

JMS Message Structure

As discussed in Chapter 2, "Java Message Service," the JMS message is composed of a header, properties, and body, and it is typed based on the message data contained within the message body. The JMS message class hierarchy is organized such that the Message interface, which is the root interface for all the JMS message types, defines the header fields, property facility, and associated accessor methods. The Message interface is extended by the body-specific message interfaces—BytesMessage, TextMessage, StreamMessage, MapMessage, and ObjectMessage—which define the accessor methods associated with their specific body type.

It should be noted that in the interest of conciseness and clarity, when discussing attribute types I use the common interface classes (see Table 2–1), such as Destination. Depending on the messaging domain being used, the corresponding domain-specific interface, such as Queue or Topic, could be substituted.

Message Header

The message header is comprised of the following fields, which are present in every JMS message. Setter and getter methods are provided for all fields, but as detailed, setting a value often has no effect if the message is being sent and the field is populated by the provider on completion of the send.

JMSDestination: JMSDestination holds a Destination object that represents the destination to which the message is being sent—for example, Queue or Topic. Its value is set by the provider after completion of the send and matches the destination associated with the MessageProducer. A getter method is defined to allow the receiving application to access the value of JMSDestination. However, although a setter method is provided, the value of JMSDestination is ignored during a send.

JMSDeliveryMode: JMSDeliveryMode is used to define the persistence of a message. A nonpersistent message is not logged to a persistent message store by the provider, implying that the message cannot be recovered in the event of a provider process failure. Persistent messages, on the other hand, are logged and are thus recoverable by the provider when it restarts. JMSDeliveryMode holds an integer value defined by the interface DeliveryMode. DeliveryMode contains two static integer values: NONPERSISTENT and PERSISTENT. The value of JMSDeliveryMode is set by the provider after completion of the send. It is based on the value specified by the sending method, which can be either Delivery-Mode.NONPERSISTENT or DeliveryMode.PERSISTENT. The provider defaults to persistent delivery if no value is specified. As with JMSDestination, any value set by the setter method is ignored on send. A getter method provides access to the populated value.

JMSExpiration: JMSExpiration stores the expiration time of the message. This is calculated as the current time plus a specified timeToLive. The value of time-ToLive is specified on the sending method in milliseconds, and the provider populates JMSExpiration (type Long) with the computed value in milliseconds on completion of the send. If a value for timeToLive is not specified or is specified as zero, JMSExpiration is set to zero, signifying that the message does not expire. Any value set for JMSExpiration is ignored on the send. Once a message has expired, the JMS client is unable to retrieve the message. Typically, the message is discarded by the provider at this point. JMSExpiration provides a convenient way to clean up messages that have a well-defined relevance period, such as a reply to a request that has arrived late.

JMSPriority: JMS defines transmission priority levels 0 to 9, with 0 as the lowest priority and 9 as the highest. It additionally specifies that priorities 0 to 4 should be considered gradations of normal delivery and priorities 5 to 9 as gradations of expedited delivery. The provider populates JMSPriority (type int) on completion of the send based on the value specified by the sending method.

JMSTimeStamp: The JMSTimeStamp field is populated by the provider during the send; the value set is in the format of a normal Java millisecond time value.

JMSMessageID: JMSMessageID uniquely identifies a message. It is defined as a String and ignored if set when the message is sent. It is populated with a provider-assigned value on completion of the send. The provider-assigned identifier is prefixed with ID:.

JMSCorrelationID: The JMSCorrelationID field is typically used to link two messages together. For example, in order to link a given reply to a request, the JMS client could specify that the JMSCorrelationID of the incoming reply should match the JMSMessageID of the sent request. This requires the servicing client to set the JMSCorrelationID of the reply to the JMSMessageID of the request before sending the reply. Consequently, if used, this field is set by the JMS client, as shown:

```
//set correlationID
replyMsg.setJMSCorrelationID(requestMsg.getJMSMessageID());
```

JMS additionally allows for the case where the JMS client needs to use a specific value for linking messages; in this case an alternative string value can be set, but it should not be prefixed with ID:. If the JMS client is servicing a request from a non-JMS client and needs to assign a specific value for use with such clients, JMS defines a byte array optional type for JMSCorrelationID. However, providers are not required to implement support for this optional type.

JMSReplyTo: JMSReplyTo is set by the client and takes as value a Destination object that specifies where replies to this message are to be sent. This implies that this field is set only if a reply is required. By default it is set to null. JMSReplyTo can be set as shown:

```
//set reply to destination
Queue replyQ = (Queue)ctx.lookup(jmsReplyQ);
requestMsg.setJMSReplyTo(replyQ);
```

JMSType: JMSType contains a message type identifier that is set by the client. Its purpose is to enable clients of providers who provide a message definition repository to associate with the contained message body a reference to its physical format definition in the provider's message repository.

JMSRedelivered: The JMSRedelivered field takes a Boolean value set by the provider to signify that the message has been previously delivered to the client. It is only relevant when consuming a message and serves to alert the client (if checked) that it has previously attempted processing of this message. Recall from our discussion of message consumers and "poison" messages in Chapter 1, "Enterprise Messaging," that JMSRedelivered can help address the issue of infinite repeated processing, which could occur if the message is being processed within a transaction and being redelivered because processing failed.

Overriding Message Header Fields

JMS allows providers to provide a means for JMS administrators to override the client's settings for JMSDeliveryMode, JMSExpiration, and JMSPriority. This could be to enforce company policy or adopted best practice, or to change the behavior of the client without having to change code. JMS does not define specifically how this facility should be implemented, but IBM JMS providers utilize the administered objects, specifically the Destination object, to provide this feature. As discussed in Chapter 2, administered objects are stored outside the application in a JNDI namespace and contain vendor-specific settings. The Destination objects defined for IBM JMS providers allow values for JMSDeliveryMode, JMSExpiration, and JMSPriority to be set. By default they are set to "application specifies," but if set to an explicit value, they override any settings specified by the client on the sending method. We review the IBM JMS–administered objects in detail in Chapter 6, "IBM JMS–Administered Objects."

Properties

Properties are used to add optional fields to the header. A property can be specified by the application, be one of the standard properties defined by JMS, or be provider-specific. When sending a message, properties can be set using associated setter methods. In the received message, properties are read-only, and any attempt to set the properties on a received message results in a MessageNotWriteableException. If it is desired to modify the properties of a received message—for instance, the application is performing a brokering function and needs to modify the attributes of the message before forwarding it to the next destination—then the clearProperties() method is called on the message object.

Application-Specific Properties

Consider an audit application that tracks all orders being sent but wants to log an entry only if the order value is over a certain amount. An approach to solving this problem is to have the application process every order message passed to it and check the contents of the message to ascertain if the order value is above the threshold. A more efficient approach is to have the client application tell the provider that of all the messages sent to it, only those with an order value greater than some specified amount should be delivered. Application-specific properties enable this approach by offering a basis for a provider to filter messages based on application-specific criteria.

Continuing with our example, the sending application defines and assigns a value to an application-specific property, which we call `orderValue`. The message is then sent. The audit application defines a message selector (more on this in the next section) that details the selection criteria based on the application-specific property `orderValue`. The provider subsequently passes the sent message to the audit application only if the selection criteria are satisfied.

Why go through all this? Why not simply specify the selection criteria based on the "total cost" field in the message? The answer is quite simply that message selectors cannot operate on the message body. If message selectors did operate on the message body, then providers would have to have a means to successfully parse each message (a nontrivial task; see "Message Definition"), and we would be faced with the same performance bottleneck that having the application check each message would attract. In addition, this approach assumes that the data we want to filter on is contained in the message, which is not necessarily the case.

Handling the filter property as an optional header field is obviously much more efficient, as the provider understands the structure of the header, and given the typically small size of the header relative to the body, the property can be accessed much more quickly. Application-specific properties are typed and can be `boolean`, `byte`, `short`, `int`, `long`, `float`, `double`, and `String`. The properties are set by the sending application on the outbound message. For example,

```
//set property on outgoing message
outMessage.setIntProperty("orderValue", 3000);
```

Setter methods exist for each type, and they accept as arguments the property name and the associated value. A `setObjectProperty()` method is provided if the objectified version of the primitive types is to be used. As would be expected, corresponding getter methods are defined. Application-specific properties are used not only for selection criteria, but for a wealth of reasons, such as a means of specifying processing flags that can't be carried in the message. However, it is for use in message selection that they are most often considered. A list of application-specific properties defined for a message can be retrieved by calling `getProp-ertyNames()` on the message, which returns an `Enumeration` object.

Standard Properties

Standard properties are additional header fields defined by JMS, which further define the message. Apart from two noted exceptions, JMSXGroupID and JMSXGroupSeq, support for all other standard properties is optional. To determine which are supported by a given JMS provider, you can obviously read provider-specific documentation or use ConnectionMeta-Data.getJMSXPropertyNames() as shown:

```
// retrieve factory
ConnectionFactory factory = /*JNDI LOOKUP*/
// create connection
Connection connection = factory.createConnection();
//retrieve information describing the connection
ConnectionMetaData connInfo = connection.getMetaData();
//getJMSXPropertyNames
Enumeration propNames = connInfo.getJMSXPropertyNames();
```

ConnectionMetaData is a useful JMS interface that provides information that describes a JMS provider's implementation. It offers access to details such as JMS version, provider name, and other information. The IBM JMS providers support the following standard properties.

JMSXUserID: JMSXUserID contains the identity of the user sending the message. It is set by the provider on send and usually resolves to the user ID under which the client application is running. It is defined as a String.

JMSXAppID: JMSXAppID is the identifier associated with the application sending the message. It is similarly set by the provider on send. It is defined as a String.

JMSXDeliveryCount: JMSXDeliveryCount defines the number of times that a message has been delivered. It complements JMSRedelivered, which simply signifies that a message has been previously delivered, by providing a count of the number of times delivery as been attempted. It is set by the provider when the message is received.

JMSXGroupID and JMSXGroupSeq: JMSXGroupID and JMSXGroupSeq together uniquely define a message as belonging to a particular group of messages and being at a certain position (sequence) in the group. They are set by the client before sending and are defined using the set<type>Property methods as shown (they are defined as a String and int respectively):

```
//set group properties on outgoing message
outMessage.setStringProperty("JMSXGroupID", "10000001");
outMessage.setIntProperty("JMSXGroupSeq", 1);
```

Provider-Specific Properties

As the name suggests, JMS offers a means for providers to include specific fields in the header. The stated purpose is to support communication with non-JMS clients that might require certain properties set. Thus, they should never be used when knowingly communicating between two JMS clients. As would be expected, IBM JMS providers do specify a number of provider-specific properties, given that the messaging provider can be accessed using a variety of APIs and languages (see Chapter 5, "IBM JMS Providers"). Provider-specific properties are prefixed by JMS_<vendor_name>, in our case JMS_IBM; however, the properties are not detailed here because they do not add much to our JMS-specific discussion at this time. In Chapter 7, "JMS Implementation Scenarios," where we examine a usage scenario that involves knowingly communicating with a non-JMS client, we explore the use of provider-specific properties in a more appropriate context.

Message Selectors

A JMS message selector is used by a JMS client to specify which messages it is interested in. It is based on values contained in the message header, which includes standard header fields as well as optional fields that have been added via application-, standard-, or provider-specific properties. As noted earlier, a message selector cannot refer to message body values. A message selector is a Boolean expression that, when it evaluates to true, results in the matched message being passed to the client. It is defined as a String, and its syntax is based on a subset of the SQL92 conditional syntax.

Creating a selector involves generating a String that conforms to the defined syntax. For instance, continuing with our previous example of the audit application that wants to receive messages only if the orderValue (specified as an application-specific property) is greater than a certain threshold, the message selector would be of the form

```
//Set selector
String selector = "orderValue > 2500";
```

Another common use of message selectors is to match a reply message to the original request based on the JMSCorrelationID, as shown (note that the syntax requires quotes around Strings):

```
//Set selector
String messageID = requestMsg.getJMSMessageID();
String selector = "JMSCorrelationID ='" + messageID + "'";
```

The syntax for message selectors enables pattern matching whereby the selector can match a variety of messages. For example, to match all messages that have a postal code that begins with SO—such as SO53 2NW and SO51 2JN—the selector would be of the form

```
//Set selector
String selector = "postalcode LIKE 'SO%'";
```

Given that a message selector is a Boolean expression, expressions can be combined using constructs such as AND or OR:

```
//Set selector
String selector = "stock = 'IBM' OR stock = 'Microsoft' AND
price = 100";
```

Once a message selector is defined, it is associated with the MessageConsumer that will check the specified destination for messages (we examine this in more detail in Chapter 4, "Using the JMS API"):

```
//get reply
QueueReceiver receiver = session.createQueueReceiver(replyQ,
selector);
TextMessage replyMsg = receiver.receive();
```

JMS enables fairly sophisticated patterns to be defined for message selectors, and the rules regarding selector syntax defined by JMS are extensive. They are reproduced in Appendix A for your convenience. In all cases it is important to remember that message selectors can be specified only on header values and not the message body. It is thus not uncommon to find application-specific properties being defined that duplicate certain fields in the message body so that the message can be selected based on what is essentially message content.

Message Body

As discussed in Chapter 2, JMS supports five types of message bodies, with each body type represented by a different message interface: BytesMessage, TextMessage, StreamMessage, MapMessage, and ObjectMessage. The choice of message type used is to a great extent, but not exclusively, governed by the nature of the data being sent. To recap,

- BytesMessage stores data as a sequence of bytes, supports the most basic representation of data, and thus can contain varied payloads.
- TextMessage stores data as a String, a common representation of enterprise data.
- StreamMessage stores data as a sequence of typed fields, for example, JohnDoe33, defined as a sequence of two strings (John, Doe), and an integer (33).
- MapMessage stores data as a set of key-value pairs. The key is defined as a string, and the value is typed—for example, Age:33, where Age is the key and 33 the integer value.
- ObjectMessage stores a serialized Java object.

BytesMessage and TextMessage are probably the most common type of message used. Both handle data in a form that facilitates the easy exchange of data across the enterprise between JMS applications as well as non-JMS applications. The common physical formats adopted—XML, tagged/delimited, and record-oriented—readily lend themselves to byte or string representations and thus can be easily transported using BytesMessage or TextMessage. In particular, a record-oriented format rendered in a byte array is often the format of choice for exchanging data with legacy applications.

`ObjectMessage` is specialized in its use, as it stores a serialized Java object. Clearly, the recipient must be able to deserialize the received Java object, and thus the use of this message type is generally associated with JMS-to-JMS communication. The representation of data as a Java object can be efficient from the JMS client's point of view, as no explicit parsing or construction of the message body is required. The exchange of the object's class definition between JMS clients is also a trivial exercise, as this is part of everyday Java programming practice. However, when you consider messaging within an enterprise, rarely are all the interacting applications written in Java. More importantly, even if the ultimate destination is a JMS client, the message may pass through other infrastructure applications, such as message trackers that are not Java-based. Even when the target application is Java-based, another consideration, particularly with off-the-shelf packages, is whether the application supports the use of class definitions as the basis for defining data that will be exchanged. In truth, you are more likely to find support for XML than for Java objects. Consequently, the use of the `ObjectMessage` places more restrictions on who can ultimately process the contained data (object) and may not provide as flexible a solution in comparison to one built on the exchange of a non-language-based format such as XML.

`StreamMessage` and `MapMessage` are rather unique in that while JMS defines the interface, it does not actually specify the associated physical construct—string, serialized object, or byte array—in which the typed sequence or key-value pairs are contained. The stated reason for this is that JMS provides these message types in support of JMS providers whose native implementation supports some form of self-defining format, the idea being that the provider renders the `StreamMessage` or `MapMessage` in its native format, facilitating the exchange of data with native clients—that is, non-JMS clients that use the provider's native (proprietary) API. Given that the IBM JMS providers do not have a native self-defining format (data is generally treated as being opaque), the value of `StreamMessage` and `MapMessage` for this purpose is questionable.

With the IBM JMS providers, the contents of `StreamMessage` and `MapMessage` are rendered in XML, a standards-based self-describing format.

A `StreamMessage` is rendered in the following format:

```
<stream>
<elt dt='datatype '>value</elt>
<elt dt='datatype '>value</elt>
. . . . .
</stream>
```

Every field is sent using the same tag name, `elt`, where `elt` contains an XML attribute, `dt`, that specifies the data type of the field in the sequence and has as value the actual contents of the field. The default type is `String`, so `dt='string '` is omitted for string elements.

A `MapMessage` takes the form:

```
<map>
<elementName1 dt='datatype '>value</elementName1>
<elementName2 dt='datatype '>value</elementName2>
. . . . .
</map>
```

In this case, `elementName1 . . . . .` N maps to the key in the key-value pair.

Given that `StreamMessage` and `MapMessage` are rendered as XML by the IBM JMS providers, they do enable the exchange of data in a flexible form. In the case where the user does not want to develop XML data formats, they provide one out of the box that can be readily used. From the perspective of the JMS client, they do insulate the client from the fact that the data is XML, providing a simple interface to manipulate data, and unlike for `ObjectMessage`, the data can be handled by non-JMS and non-Java clients. However, because the implementation of `StreamMessage` and `MapMessage` is provider-specific, they should be used carefully. If it is desired to exchange data in XML, then defining an XML structure and using a `BytesMessage` or `TextMessage` provides a more generic, flexible, and portable approach.

As with properties, the body of a received message is read-only and cannot be directly modified by the receiving application. If the application wishes to populate the body of a received message with data, then it calls the `clearBody()` method on the message.

Using the JMS Message Interface

A message is created using the `Session` interface (see Chapter 2), and the `Session` interface defines create methods for all the message types, including the root `Message` interface (Table 3–1).

Table 3–1 Accessor Methods for Session Interface

```
createBytesMessage()
createMapMessage()
createMessage()
createObjectMessage()
createObjectMessage(java.io.seriablizable object) //create with content
createStreamMessage()
createTextMessage()
createTextMessage(String value) // create with content
```

As shown, `createObjectMessage` and `createTextMessage` are overloaded so that they can be instantiated with data at the time of creation. Creation of a message takes the form

```
//create message
BytesMessage bMsg = session.createBytesMessage();
```

If a message is being received, then the `MessageConsumer` creates the message and returns it to an object variable:

```
//receive message
TextMessage replyMsg = (TextMessage)receiver.receive();
```

This assumes that the type of message being received is known. In our example, if the message retrieved was actually a `BytesMessage`, then an exception would be thrown. Another approach is to use the root interface to receive the object variable, and then test the object and cast to the allowed type:

```
//receive message
Message msg = receiver.receive();
if(msg instanceof TextMessage){
      TextMessage tMsg = (TextMessage)msg;
      ......
}
```

The root `Message` interface defines the accessor methods for the header fields and properties; the typed `Message` interfaces extend this to include accessor methods for manipulating the data they contain in their message body. We examine the methods and sample usage for each of the typed interfaces in turn.

BytesMessage

Table 3–2 details the accessor methods associated with `BytesMessage`.

Table 3–2 Accessor Methods for BytesMessage Interface

`readBoolean()`	`writeBoolean(boolean value)`
`readByte()`	`writeByte(byte value)`
`readBytes(byte[] value)`	`writeBytes(byte[] value)`
`readBytes(byte[] value, int length)`	`writeBytes(byte[] value, int length)`
`readChar()`	`writeChar(char value)`
`readDouble()`	`writeDouble(double value)`
`readFloat()`	`writeFloat(float value)`
`readInt()`	`writeInt(int value)`
`readLong()`	`writeLong(long value)`
`readUnsignedByte()`	`writeObject(Object value) //works only for object primitive types`
`readUnsignedShort()`	`writeShort(short value)`
`readUTF()`	`writeUTF(String value)`

Use of these methods follow a simple rule: If you build the message body by using write methods in a certain order, then you unpack the message body by using the corresponding read methods in the same order. Let's use our familiar John Doe example laid out in a record-oriented format to illustrate:

```
/*Sender*/
//create and send BytesMessage
String firstName = "JOHN";
String lastName = "DOE";
int age = 33;

BytesMessage bOutMsg = session.createBytesMessage();
bOutMsg.writeBytes(firstName.getBytes());
bOutMsg.writeBytes(lastName.getBytes());
bOutMsg.writeInt(age);
sender.send(bOutMsg);

/*Receiver*/
//receive and unpack BytesMessage
BytesMessage bInMsg = (BytesMessage)receiver.receive();
byte[] data = new byte[4];
bInMsg.readBytes(data, 4);
String firstName = new String(data);
bInMsg.readBytes(data, 3);
String lastName = new String(data, 0, 3);
int age = bInMsg.readInt();
```

If we want to retrieve the entire contents of `BytesMessage` using `readBytes(byte [] value)`, we must determine the length of the message body so that we can appropriately initialize the byte array that will contain the read data. Unfortunately, JMS 1.0.2b does not provide any means for determining the length of the message body, and if the length of the incoming message is not known, we may be forced to adopt processing of the form

```
//receive and unpack BytesMessage
BytesMessage bInMsg = (BytesMessage)receiver.receive();
int msgLength = 0;
int BUF_SIZE = 50000; //some efficient maximum
byte[] data = new byte[BUF_SIZE];
while(true){
    int len = bInMsg.readBytes(data);
    if(len > 0){
    msgLength += len;
    }else{
    break;
    }
}
// now we know the message length
// so reset and read in one go.
byte[] message = new byte[msgLength];
//if msgLength <= BUF_SIZE, then we already
```

```
//have the contents
if (msgLength <= BUF_SIZE) {
        System.arraycopy(data, 0, message, 0, msgLength);
} else {
        bInMsg.reset();//reset cursor to beginning
        bInMsg.readBytes(message);
}
```

Notice that we introduce the utility method reset(), which repositions the stream of bytes to the beginning and allows us to read in the entire byte array. JMS 1.1 addresses this issue by specifying a getBodyLength() method in the BytesMessage interface, which allows us to greatly simplify the process of dynamically sizing our byte array as follows:

```
//receive and unpack BytesMessage
BytesMessage bInMsg = (BytesMessage)receiver.receive();
int msgLength = bInMsg.getBodyLength();
byte[] message = new byte[msgLength];
bInMsg.readBytes(message);
```

TextMessage

As shown in Table 3–3, TextMessage offers an interface that is quite simple to use.

Table 3–3 Accessor Methods for TextMessage Interface

getText()	setText(String value)

It provides a setText and a getText method, which enable the message body to be populated or content extracted:

```
/*Sender*/
//create and send TextMessage
String firstName = "JOHN";
String lastName = "DOE";
String age = "33";

TextMessage tOutMsg = session.createTextMessage();
String message = firstName + ";" + lastName + ";" + age;
tOutMsg.setText(message);
sender.send(tOutMsg);

/*Receiver*/
//receive and unpack TextMessage
TextMessage tInMsg = (TextMessage)receiver.receive();
String message = tInMsg.getText();
```

StreamMessage

`StreamMessage` represents a sequence of primitive types, as shown in Table 3–4.

Table 3–4 Accessor Methods for StreamMessage Interface

`readBoolean()`	`writeBoolean(boolean value)`
`readByte()`	`writeByte(byte value)`
`readBytes(byte[] value)`	`writeBytes(byte[] value)`
`readChar()`	`writeBytes(byte[] value, int offset, int length)`
`readDouble()`	`writeChar(char value)`
`readFloat()`	`writeDouble(double value)`
`readInt()`	`writeFloat(float value)`
`readLong()`	`writeInt(int value)`
`readObject()`	`writeLong(long value)`
`readShort()`	`writeObject(Object value)`
`readString()`	`//works only for object primitive types`
	`writeShort(short value)`
	`writeString(String value)`

It provides methods that allow the various primitives to be written or read:

```
/*Sender*/
//create and send StreamMessage
String firstName = "JOHN";
String lastName = "DOE";
int age = 33;

StreamMessage sOutMsg = session.createStreamMessage();
sOutMsg.writeString(firstName);
sOutMsg.writeString(lastName);
sOutMsg.writeInt(age);
sender.send(sOutMsg);

/*Receiver*/
//receive and unpack StreamMessage
StreamMessage sInMsg = (StreamMessage)receiver.receive();
String firstName = sInMsg.readString();
String lastName = sInMsg.readString();
int age = sInMsg.readInt();
```

As with `BytesMessage`, `StreamMessage` also provides a reset method with which the stream can be repositioned to its beginning.

MapMessage

The `MapMessage` interface (Table 3–5) introduces a name variable that represents the key associated with the typed field. Because data is accessed based on the name (key), it does allow random access to data fields.

Table 3–5 Accessor Methods for MapMessage Interface

getBoolean(String name)	setBoolean(String name, boolean value)
getByte(String name)	setByte(String name, byte value)
getBytes(String name)	setBytes(String name, byte[] value)
getChar(String name)	setBytes(String name, byte[] value, int offset, int length)
getDouble(String name)	
getFloat(String name)	setChar(String name, char value)
getInt(String name)	setDouble(String name, double value)
getLong(String name)	setFloat(String name, float value)
getObject(String name)	setInt(String name, int value)
getShort(String name)	setLong(String name, long value)
getString(String name)	setObject(String name, Object value)
	setShort(String name, short value)
	setString(String name, String value)

To facilitate key management, the `MapMessage` interface offers two utility methods: `itemExists` and `getMapNames`. `itemExists(String Name)` takes as argument a key name and checks for its existence, returning a Boolean. `getMapNames()` returns an Enumeration object containing all the key names defined in the message. The use of MapMessage follows the now familiar pattern:

```
/*Sender*/
//create and send MapMessage
String firstName = "JOHN";
String lastName = "DOE";
int age = 33;

MapMessage mOutMsg = session.createMapMessage();
mOutMsg.setString("first", firstName);
mOutMsg.setString("last", lastName);
mOutMsg.setInt("age", age);
sender.send(mOutMsg);

/*Receiver*/
//receive and unpack MapMessage
MapMessage mInMsg = (MapMessage)receiver.receive();
String firstName = mInMsg.getString("first");
String lastName = mInMsg.getString("last");
int age = mInMsg.getInt("age");
```

ObjectMessage

As with `TextMessage`, `ObjectMessage` (Table 3–6) offers a simple interface that supports the insertion or retrieval of objects from the message.

Table 3–6 Accessor Methods for ObjectMessage Interface

`getObject()`	`setObject(Object value)`

Objects passed must implement the `java.io.Serializable` interface:

```
/*Sender*/
//create and send ObjectMessage
String firstName = "JOHN";
String lastName = "DOE";
int age = 33;
Person pObj = new Person(firstName, lastName, age);

ObjectMessage objOutMsg = session.createObjectMessage();
objOutMsg.setObject(pObj);
sender.send(objOutMsg);

/*Receiver*/
//receive and unpack ObjectMessage
ObjectMessage objInMsg = (ObjectMessage)receiver.receive();
Person pObj = (Person)objInMsg.getObject();
```

Summary

We began our exploration of the JMS message by examining the concepts and considerations associated with defining messages. We discussed how message content is defined and reviewed three popular physical formats used to structure message content: XML, tagged/delimited, and record-oriented. Physical formats enable the application to make sense of the data, and for each format we reviewed its history and detailed how it could be used by the JMS client.

We then examined the structure of the JMS message and detailed the attributes that comprise the header, properties, and body. We considered how some of these attributes could be used to effect application processing and specifically devoted some time to examining the use of message selectors to control which messages are delivered to the JMS client. We also discussed which types of JMS messages are suited to various enterprise messaging scenarios, concluding that `TextMessage` and `BytesMessage` are the most flexible and versatile.

The chapter concluded with a detailed review of the accessor methods defined by each type of message interface, and using code snippets, we demonstrated how a JMS client creates, packs, or unpacks a `BytesMessage`, `TextMessage`, `StreamMessage`, `MapMessage`, and `ObjectMessage`.

In the following chapter we examine how our JMS message can be sent or received using the JMS API.

CHAPTER 4

Using the JMS API

Having established an understanding of our unit of exchange—the message—we are now ready to delve into the mechanics of messaging using the JMS API. In this chapter we begin with a discussion on implementation choices, examining our options regarding the software components with which we might implement a JMS client. We then undertake a detailed review of the JMS API, using code snippets to illustrate usage and implementation approaches. We do this by examining in turn each set of interfaces: point-to-point, publish-subscribe, and the unified or common interface. This will round out our knowledge of JMS and prepare us to consider a number of real-world scenarios based on a specific product family: IBM WebSphere.

The JMS Client: Implementation Considerations

The JMS client is the entity that utilizes the JMS API to interact with the JMS provider. It can be any Java artifact, and depending on the application environment, a number of choices exist as to how the JMS client is implemented. The JMS client could be a standalone Java application, serving as part of a desktop client, or acting as the connectivity module (adapter) for a business application. The JMS client could also be encapsulated in a J2EE component such as an applet, servlet or portlet, or Enterprise Java Bean (EJB). That the JMS client can be any Java artifact offers a great deal of flexibility in implementation. However, this comes at a price, as the decision-making process regarding your implementation choice becomes more involved.

The choice between a standalone Java application or J2EE component is one we need not address, as that decision is driven more by the nature of the application and its target runtime environment than by the JMS connectivity requirement. However, if the application is J2EE-based, then we still have the basic choices of applet, servlet, or EJB.

Servlets and EJBs are serverside components that run in containers in the J2EE server. They consequently have access to a host of services, such as security and transaction support (see Chapter 2, "Java Message Service"). Applets, on the other hand, are clientside (presentation layer) components that run in a browser and are most often used as user interface constructs. Current best practice recommends that J2EE applications adopt a lightweight presentation layer with business logic and connectivity to enterprise resources (such as messaging providers) residing in serverside components. This enables transaction and security services to be readily invoked if required and offers an important advantage in that it is much easier to scale and modify serverside components. Furthermore, it greatly simplifies the implementation of the presentation layer.

With this in mind, it is fair to say that applets are probably least suited to the role of JMS client. Besides the design considerations, there are practical implications to be considered as well. The applet needs access to the JMS libraries (standard and provider implementation), increasing its size and potentially impacting the time it takes it to download to the browser. In addition, the still existing inconsistencies in browser Java Virtual Machines (JVMs) and their support for running JMS must be addressed. Such inconsistencies can complicate the deployment of the solution and force you to have to specify browser versions or runtime plug-ins that will support your application. In solutions where applets are used (their current popularity is questionable), a better pattern is for the applet to call a servlet. The servlet then either calls an EJB, which implements the JMS client, or it implements the JMS client itself.

In deciding whether to implement the JMS client in a servlet/portlet or EJB, consider the following key questions:

- Does your programming model currently use EJBs?
- Is your application Web based?
- Based on your application design, where does business logic reside?
- Is the interaction with the JMS provider going to be transactional, potentially involving other resources?
- If it is transactional, do you want to use container managed or client-demarcated transactions?
- What is your considered approach to scaling your solution, particularly access to the JMS provider?
- Which interaction patterns will your JMS client implement?

J2EE best practice recommends that connectivity logic—that is, access to enterprise resources—reside in the business logic layer, which in J2EE is the EJB layer. This suggests that EJBs should be the first choice when implementing the JMS client. However, for Web-based applications, it is not uncommon to find the JMS client being implemented by a servlet or portlet, since they offer a simpler programming framework when compared to EJBs. If transactions are required, then the only choice open to the servlet developer is the use of client-demarcated transactions. This requires that the developer explicitly handle the transactions, making appropriate Java Transaction API (JTA) calls such as commit or rollback at the right time. In contrast, the EJB developer has the option of having transactions managed by the container, which simply involves specifying the scope of the transaction as part of the deployment properties and requires no explicit programming. This greatly simplifies building transactional components and is considered a best practice.

In comparison to servlets, EJBs offer considerable tuning options and efficiency savings in terms of how the EJB container manages its EJBs and, by extension, access to enterprise resources. The EJB container can be expected to provide pooling optimizations, load-balancing configurations, and other scalability and performance enhancements, which can have considerable benefits in terms of the scalability and reliability of the implemented solution. In addition, access to EJBs often tends to be more secure.

Recall from our discussion in Chapter 1, "Enterprise Messaging," that the interaction between the JMS client and the provider is composed of three base patterns: message producer, message consumer, and request-reply.

The message producer pattern involves simply sending a message; interaction with the provider ends once the message has been accepted by the provider. The session EJB readily lends itself to the role of message producer, being for the most part a stateless bean that can be reused by client applications such as servlets for sending messages. The same can be said for servlets, and here the choice is influenced by additional factors previously discussed, such as transaction requirements. For example, if the sending of the message is to occur as part of a global transaction, such as updating a database within the same transaction, then the container-managed transaction services offered by the EJB container further facilitate the implementation of this pattern.

The message consumer pattern is initiated by the arrival of a message. As discussed in Chapter 1, this initiation could occur in either a pull or push mode. In the pull mode, the application checks (polls) the messaging provider at suitable time intervals for a message. In the push mode, the messaging provider invokes the application when a message arrives, passing it the message. EJB 2.0 (included in J2EE 1.3) introduced support for implementing the message consumer pattern using EJBs by defining the message-driven bean (MDB). MDB support implements the message consumer pattern in push mode. The EJB container monitors the JMS destination using Application Server Facilities, or ASF (see Chapter 2) and invokes the MDB with a retrieved message as messages arrive.

In support of this facility, JMS defines a `MessageListener` interface, which the MDB implements. The `MessageListener` interface (discussed in the next section) was available before the advent of MDBs and can be used by servlets or other Java entities to implement the message consumer pattern. When the `MessageListener` interface is used by components other than MDBs, the JMS provider monitors the destination and invokes the component with the message on arrival. The use of MDBs, however, offers a number of distinct advantages. Using ASF, the EJB container can process multiple incoming messages from multiple destinations concurrently, providing a significant performance benefit. In contrast, the JMS provider can provide only serialized access to messages and destinations for other components using the `MessageListener` interface. In addition, the EJB container provides tuning, transaction, and message redelivery configuration options, which would have to be explicitly programmed into non-MDB entities.

It is useful to remember, however, that prior to J2EE 1.3 and EJB 2.0, none of this support existed, and the only option available to implement a push-mode message consumer was the `MessageListener` interface. The push-mode (some might say asynchronous) nature of the `MessageListener` interface does not readily lend itself to implementation using session EJBs, and thus prior to EJB 2.0, it was particularly difficult to implement the message consumer pattern using EJBs. A common workaround at the time was to have another component, typically a standalone application or servlet, monitor the JMS destination for a message and either retrieve and pass the message to the session bean or notify the session bean that a message was available for retrieval (used if retrieval needed to occur as part of a transaction managed by the EJB container).

The request-reply pattern combines the message producer and message consumer patterns to implement a conversation between the sending and receiving applications. There are two basic variations for this pattern (see Chapter 1). In the first, the requester (acting as a message producer) sends the request, then reverts to the role of message consumer and waits for its reply (pull mode). In the second variation, the requester sends the request, but a different component receives (consumes) the replies, usually operating in a push mode.

With the first variation, a critical factor is the length of time that the requester will wait for a reply to its request. JMS provides a receive method (more on this later in the chapter) that can have a wait time specified. The method returns with a message if it is available or with nothing after the specified wait time if no message has arrived. During the wait interval, the calling thread is blocked, and this is of particular importance if a session EJB is used to implement this pattern. Certain schools of thought totally abhor the concept of a blocked thread within the EJB container, particularly when it is considered that a large number of instances (blocked threads) of the session EJB can potentially exist. Consequently, when a session EJB is used in this manner, careful consideration must be given to the amount of time (specified in milliseconds) the session EJB will be allowed to wait and the impact that may have on the J2EE Server environment.

The second variation avoids this issue, as the requester session EJB doesn't wait for the reply and thus never blocks. The MDB readily lends itself to acting as the consumer of replies and, when paired with the requesting session EJB, provides a straightforward implementation for this variation.

We have detailed a number of considerations that should influence our choice of whether to use servlets or EJBs for JMS client implementations. All things considered, I recommend that JMS clients be implemented using EJBs. On the other hand, in cases where EJBs are not part of the adopted programming model and transactions (particularly global transactions involving other resources) are not required, servlets may prove attractive. However, as with all design decisions, the choice of what software component to use, is further constrained by factors directly associated with the nature of the project. Consequently, it is important to note that regardless of the entity adopted to implement the JMS client, the JMS API is used in the same way, and we examine its use in the following sections.

Point-to-Point Interface

As discussed in Chapter 1, point-to-point messaging is adopted when there is a one-to-one relationship between sender and receiver. In this message distribution pattern, the sender sends the message to a known destination, from where it is retrieved. Common usage scenarios include submitting an order or registration request to a processing application, effecting an account inquiry or update, and exchanging data between two systems that are being synchronized. JMS supports this message distribution pattern with a specific subset of the API that supports the semantics of point-to-point messaging. We examine the API by considering the three basic phases our JMS client will experience: connecting to a provider, producing a message, and consuming a message.

Connecting to a Provider

Connectivity to a provider is based on a `QueueConnectionFactory`, which contains the configuration details required to connect to the provider. As discussed in Chapter 2, the `QueueConnectionFactory`, a JMS-administered object, should be retrieved from a JNDI namespace. It is of course possible to create a provider-specific `QueueConnectionFactory` in code, but as this compromises the JMS client's portability and is not a recommended JMS practice, we will not explore that option further. Rather, we assume that a `QueueConnectionFactory` has been defined and stored in a given JNDI namespace, using a provider-specific administration tool (we explore how this is achieved in Chapter 6, "IBM JMS–Administered Objects"). Our first task is thus to establish a context to the JNDI namespace.

Creating an InitialContext

JNDI offers a rich API, but from the JMS client's perspective, we are interested in creating an `InitialContext` object with which we can look up named objects, specifically the `QueueConnectionFactory`. The `InitialContext` class acts as a starting point for accessing the naming system (namespace) and is created thus:

```
import javax.jms.*;   // JMS classes

import java.io.*;        // Standard Java imports
import java.util.*;
import javax.naming.*;   // JNDI imports
......

String jmsICF = "com.sun.jndi.fscontext.RefFSContextFactory";
```

```
String jmsURL = "file:/c:/JNDINamespace";

//connect to JNDI Namespace
Hashtable environment = new Hashtable();
environment.put(Context.INITIAL_CONTEXT_FACTORY, jmsICF);
environment.put(Context.PROVIDER_URL, jmsURL);

Context ctx = new InitialContext(environment);
```

The `InitialContext` constructor is passed a `java.util.Hashtable` that has at least two key properties defined. `Context.INITIAL_CONTEXT_FACTORY` specifies the name of the factory class for a specific JNDI service provider. The factory class is responsible for creating the `InitialContext`, and in our example we specify the file system factory class provided by Sun Microsystems. `Context.PROVIDER_URL` gives the factory class all the information it needs to successfully locate the namespace and establish a connection to it. In our example, since we are using the file system as our namespace, all that needs to be specified is the directory that hosts the namespace. Depending on the namespace used, the values for `Context.INITIAL_CONTEXT_FACTORY` and `Context.PROVIDER_URL` will vary. JNDI also specifies additional properties, if authentication is required, for passing security information. As an illustration, in order to connect to a namespace implemented in a Lightweight Directory Access Protocol (LDAP) server with simple authentication, we might specify the following:

```
String jmsICF =
"com.sun.jndi.ldap.LdapCtxFactory";
String jmsURL = "ldap://192.168.1.1/o=ibm,c=us";
String jmsAuth = "simple";
String jmsUser = "cn=Developer";
String jmsPass = "changeme";

//connect to JNDI Namespace
Hashtable environment = new Hashtable();
environment.put(Context.INITIAL_CONTEXT_FACTORY, jmsICF);
environment.put(Context.PROVIDER_URL, jmsURL);
environment.put(Context.SECURITY_AUTHENTICATION, jmsAuth);
environment.put(Context.SECURITY_PRINCIPAL, jmsUser);
environment.put(Context.SECURITY_CREDENTIALS, jmsPass);

Context ctx = new InitialContext(environment);
```

By specifying a default JNDI namespace to which J2EE components can refer, J2EE eliminates the need for J2EE components to refer explicitly to a particular JNDI service provider factory class. The namespace is used to retrieve a variety of resources, including EJB home interfaces, data sources, and JMS-administered objects. The namespace is implemented by the J2EE server, and the J2EE client application does not need to reference provider-specific factory classes. The base context (entry point) for the namespace is bound to `java:comp/env`. The specification recommends the use of subcontexts for various entities, such as `java:comp/env/ejb` for EJBs and `java:comp/env/jms` for JMS-administered objects. Thus, for J2EE-based clients, we can adopt a simplified approach to defining our `InitialContext`:

```
//connect to JNDINamespace
Context ctx = new InitialContext();
```

This binds us to the root of the default namespace and implies that we supply the full path-name when trying to retrieve a given object. such as `java:comp/env/jms/myQCF`.

A similar level of abstraction can be achieved with non-J2EE applications by defining the JNDI properties as JVM system properties (see the technical article "Specifying Environment Properties" in Appendix D). In this case we pass the factory class, URL, and other relevant properties as arguments to the JVM at startup, as shown:

```
java -Djava.naming.factory.initial=com.sun.jndi.fscon-
text.RefFSContextFactory -Djava.naming.provider.url= file:/c:/
JNDINamespace
```

The JMS client then simply creates an `InitialContext` without having to define the property `Hashtable`.

Retrieving the QueueConnectionFactory

Having obtained a `Context`, we can now retrieve the `QueueConnectionFactory`. This is done using the lookup method defined by `Context`. The lookup method takes as argument the name of the object to be retrieved. Depending upon how `InitialContext` was defined and where the objects are stored in the namespace, we may specify just the name of the `QueueConnectionFactory` or the name including the full path. We must cast the returned object to the required type. If the object does not exist, a `NamingException` is thrown.

```
//retrieve QueueConnectionFactory
QueueConnectionFactory factory =
(QueueConnectionFactory)ctx.lookup("jms.book.QCF");
```

In a J2EE client application our lookup would be bound to `java:comp/env`, as shown:

```
//retrieve QueueConnectionFactory
QueueConnectionFactory factory =
(QueueConnectionFactory)ctx.lookup("java:comp/env/jms/myQCF");
```

Create a QueueConnection

The `QueueConnection` defines an active connection to a provider. It is created by calling the `createQueueConnection` method of the `QueueConnectionFactory`:

```
//create QueueConnection
QueueConnection conn = factory.createQueueConnection();
```

An overloaded version of the `createQueueConnection` method allows the client to pass its credentials in the form of a user identifier and password with which it is authenticated by the provider. The user identifier and password are both defined as `Strings`. If no credentials are passed, as with our example, then the identity under which the client is running is used.

Once a `QueueConnection` is created, we can establish a session with the provider, which encapsulates the client's interaction. It is useful to note that the `QueueConnection` is a thread-safe object and can be used by multiple threads to create `QueueSessions`.

Create a QueueSession

The `QueueSession` encapsulates the interaction (sending and/or receiving of messages) between the client and the provider. It also defines the scope of transactions, enabling all interaction derived from the session to be defined as a single unit of work. The `QueueSession` is created by calling the associated create method on the `QueueConnection`. The method takes as argument a Boolean expression that defines if the session is transacted or not and an integer constant that defines how received messages are acknowledged.

```
//create QueueSession
QueueSession session = conn.createQueueSession(false,
Session.AUTO_ACKNOWLEDGE);
```

If it is desired to define the interaction based on the session as a transaction, then a transacted Boolean value of true is used. This implies that none of the operations will be committed until the `QueueSession`'s `commit` method is called; similarly, work can be rolled back by calling the rollback method. Note that this affects only resources under the provider's control and does not include updates to other resources such as databases (see section "Handling Local Transactions"). The `acknowledgeMode` specifies how the client will let the provider know that a message has been successfully received. This allows the provider to permanently remove the message from the queue and make it unavailable for redelivery. If the session is transacted, then acknowledgment is handled automatically by the commit call. For nontransacted sessions, three acknowledgment options are defined.

- `Session.AUTO_ACKNOWLEDGE`: This tells the session to automatically acknowledge the delivery of a message once the client has successfully returned from a receive call or its `MessageListener` that has been called to process the message successfully returns. This is by far the most common option used by JMS clients and it simplifies message handling.
- `Session.DUPS_OK_ACKNOWLEDGE`: This option instructs the session to acknowledge messages at some point in time that it deems suitable. This opens up the possibility of duplicate messages, as a message that has been successfully processed by the client may be redelivered by the provider if the provider happens to fail and then restart. Using this option requires the client to be tolerant of duplicate messages and supposedly offers the benefit of reduced overhead in the session due to the relaxed

approach taken to message acknowledgment. Such benefits must be carefully examined as it is dependent on how the underlying JMS provider is implemented. Thus, the overriding factor is whether the client can tolerate duplicate messages. If it can, then this is an acceptable option; if it can't, then this option should be ignored.

- `Session.CLIENT_ACKNOWLEDGE`: This places the responsibility for acknowledging message receipt firmly in the hands of the client. The client calls the JMS message acknowledge method when it wishes to acknowledge receipt. Note that this does not acknowledge the receipt of the message in isolation but rather the receipt of all messages that have been delivered by its session.

The creation of the `QueueSession` fully establishes the client's connection to the provider and enables the client to now interact with the provider as a sender and/or receiver of messages. The `QueueSession` and all other objects created from it are not thread-safe and should ideally not be accessed by multiple threads. If this is desired for some reason, then steps must be taken to synchronize thread access.

Sending Messages

In order to send a message, we need to create a `QueueSender`; however, before doing this, we typically retrieve a `Queue` object from the JNDI namespace that defines the destination to which the message will be sent:

```
//retrieve Queue
Queue outQ = (Queue)ctx.lookup("jms.book.Q");
```

As with retrieving the `QueueConnnectionFactory`, we cast the retrieved object to the expected type. JMS offers an alternative method to create a queue using the `QueueSession`'s `createQueue` method. This takes as argument a queue name defined as a `String`. The issue here is that the format of the name is provider-specific, as `Queues` created in this manner are referencing existing provider queues in much the same way the administered `Queue` object does. Thus, dependency on this approach renders the client nonportable.

Armed with a `Queue`, we can now use the `QueueSession` to create the `Queue-Sender` bound to the `Queue`:

```
//create QueueSender
  QueueSender sender = session.createSender(outQ);
```

In the case when we are sending a reply to a received request, we would use the `Queue` held in the `JMSReplyTo` field of the request message:

```
//create QueueSender
Queue replyQ = (Queue)requestMsg.getJMSReplyTo();
QueueSender sender = session.createSender(replyQ);
```

JMS does allow the `QueueSender` to be created if a null is passed instead of a defined Queue. This is known as an unidentified `QueueSender`, and the `Queue` must then be passed when sending the message.

To send the message, we simply invoke the `send` method, passing the `Message` object created from the `QueueSession` (see Chapter 3, "JMS Messages"):

```
//send Message with defaults
sender.send(msg);
```

This sends the message with the default values that have been specified for `JMSDesti-nationMode`, `JMSPriority`, and `timeToLive`, which sets `JMSExpiration`. The defaults are taken from the `QueueSender` (inherited from `MessageProducer`), and JMS defines them as `DeliveryMode.PERSISTENT` with a priority of 4 and a `timeToLive` of 0, which defines an unlimited lifespan. To have the message sent with different values set, we can update the `QueueSender` using defined setter methods or simply use the overloaded send method:

```
//send with options set
sender.send(msg,DeliveryMode.NON_PERSISTENT, 4, 0);
```

An alternative is to have the values overridden by the JMS administrator. As discussed in Chapter 3, with IBM JMS providers this is achieved by setting the values in the externally defined `Queue` object.

JMS defines two additional versions of the send method, which additionally take a `Queue` as argument. These are used when the `QueueSender` is unidentified, that is, created with a null argument for `Queue`.

Once the client, acting solely as message producer, has completed its processing, we need to clean up resources. We do this by calling the `close` method on the `QueueSender`, `QueueSession`, and potentially the `QueueConnection` if we are no longer going to use it to create `QueueSessions`. This disconnects the client from the provider and enables all objects to be garbage collected. The `close` methods of objects higher in the hierarchy trigger the `close` methods of objects created from them, so closing `QueueConnection` will clean up all resources:

```
//close connection
conn.close();
conn = null;
```

Receiving Messages

As with sending messages, before we can create a `QueueReceiver` to receive messages, we must instantiate the `Queue` that represents the destination from which messages will be retrieved. The `Queue` is typically retrieved from a JNDI namespace:

```
//retrieve Queue
Queue replyQ = (Queue)ctx.lookup("jms.book.replyQ");
```

In designing request-reply scenarios that involve a client sending a request and waiting for a reply, an issue that must be addressed is whether each runtime instance of the client has a dedicated queue for its replies or whether the runtime instances access a shared queue, selecting their specific reply message based on an appropriate attribute, such as the JMSCorrelationID. If multiple queues are required, then we need the ability to create a queue dynamically for use by the client, and JMS provides this facility using the concept of temporary queues. The TemporaryQueue is created on request by the QueueSession and exists until it is deleted or for the life of the QueueConnection (i.e., until the QueueConnection is closed). This means that although the TemporaryQueue is created by a specific QueueSession, it can be reused by any other QueueSessions created from the same QueueConnection to create a QueueReceiver.

The tradeoff between having a shared queue for replies or having individual temporary queues is influenced by the potential number of active client instances. With a shared-queue approach, at some provider-specific threshold, contention for access to the queue can become a concern. This has to be contrasted against the additional overhead associated with the provider creating queue storage at runtime and the impact on machine memory of having to host a potentially large number of temporary queues. If a temporary queue is to be used, it is created as shown:

```
//create temporary reply queue
Queue replyQ = (Queue)session.createTemporaryQueue();
```

The QueueReceiver is created by using QueueSession's createReceiver method to bind the QueueReceiver to the Queue:

```
//create QueueReceiver
QueueReceiver receiver = session.createReceiver(replyQ);
```

If we wish to receive messages based on a specific filter, we define a message selector (see Chapter 3) and associate it with the QueueReceiver at the time of creation. For instance, to retrieve reply messages from a shared queue based on JMSCorrelationID, we would do the following:

```
//set selector
String messageID = requestMsg.getJMSMessageID();
String selector = "JMSCorrelationID ='" + messageID + "'";

//create QueueReceiver
QueueReceiver receiver = session.createReceiver(replyQ,
selector);
```

Once a QueueReceiver has been created, its associated message selector cannot be changed. This poses a specific challenge for clients that might want to continuously send request messages and process replies based on JMSCorrelationID or any other property that varies between messages. You may recall that the JMSCorrelationID of the reply message is based on the JMSMessageID of the request message, which is automatically generated by the provider. We would thus need to change the selector to receive each reply, which requires that the QueueReceiver be closed and then re-created with the new selector. From a performance standpoint, the repeated closing and re-creation of the QueueReceiver is unattractive, and the use of a dedicated TemporaryQueue for the client to receive its replies is a better alternative.

Before messages can be received, the QueueConnection must be started. While this operation is not required in order to send messages, it must be executed before any messages can be received. JMS recommends that the QueueConnection be started after setup is complete, that is, after the QueueReceiver is created but prior to using the QueueReceiver to receive messages. The thought here is that the client starts the connection, signifying that it is fully configured to handle incoming messages. However, this sequence might not always be convenient, and there is no enforced restriction on when the call is made:

```
//start connection to enable receive
    conn.start();
```

The QueueReceiver uses the receive method to retrieve messages. The messages are retrieved using the root Message interface and must be cast to the expected type:

```
//receive next Message
    TextMessage msg = (TextMessage)receiver.receive();
```

The receive() method retrieves the next available message from the Queue. It is a blocking call and if no message is on the queue, it will wait indefinitely, only returning when a message is available. To specify a wait interval, use the overloaded receive() method, which takes the wait interval in milliseconds:

```
//receive next Message with timed wait: 5 secs
    TextMessage msg = (TextMessage)receiver.receive(5000);
```

Specifying 0 milliseconds similarly results in a indefinite wait. To retrieve the next message without waiting at all, use receiveNoWait():

```
//receive next Message with no wait
    TextMessage msg = (TextMessage)receiver.receiveNoWait();
```

When either receive with a wait interval or receiveNoWait are used, if no message is available in the allotted time, then a null is returned. Use of the receive calls is synchronous in nature, involving a blocked thread until a message is returned. JMS offers a facility to receive messages asynchronously by providing the MessageListener interface.

Receiving Messages Using JMS MessageListener

The MessageListener interface enables the client to define a message listener object that processes incoming messages while the client continues with other functions, enabling asynchronous message handling. The MessageListener interface defines a single method, onMessage, which is passed a Message object by the JMS provider:

```
package jms.book.sample;

import javax.jms.*;

/**
 * @author yusufk
 *
 * MessageListener implementation
 */
public class JMSMessageListener implements MessageListener {

    /**
     * Constructor for JMSMessageListener.
     */
    public JMSMessageListener() {
        super();
    }

    /**
     * @see javax.jms.MessageListener#onMessage(Message)
     */
    public void onMessage(Message msg) {
        try{
            if(msg instanceof TextMessage){
            TextMessage tMsg = (TextMessage)msg;
            System.out.println("message received");
System.out.println("message: " + tMsg.getText());
            }
        }catch(Exception e){
            System.out.println("Exception thrown " + e);
        }
    }

}
```

The onMessage method is used to implement the desired message processing; typically, the message type is confirmed and the message is unpacked and processed. In the example shown, the message is simply displayed. The MessageListener interface is the same interface implemented by MDBs. As discussed earlier in the chapter, the primary difference between using an MDB and using a message listener is that with the MDB, message retrieval services are provided by the J2EE container, while with a message listener they are supplied by the underlying JMS provider. Furthermore, use of MDBs offers superior transaction control and performance options when compared with a message listener.

To use a message listener (we explore the configuration of MDBs in Chapter 7, "JMS Implementation Scenarios"), we register the message listener with the target QueueReceiver:

```
//setup MessageListener
receiver.setMessageListener(new JMSMessageListener());

//start connection to enable receive
conn.start();
```

Once the message listener has been set, the provider will begin to pass it messages as long as the connection is started. This assumes that any resources that the message listener might need to access, such as a QueueSender, have been defined—hence the recommendation that the connection only be started after all setup is complete. In addition, if message listeners are to be associated with multiple QueueReceivers, this must be completed before the connection is started.

The message listener is invariably run by the provider on a separate delivery thread, which allows the JMS client thread to continue with application processing. With a message listener set, it is illegal for the client to call the receive method on the QueueReceiver associated with the message listener or indeed on any QueueReceiver associated with the QueueSession. It is also illegal for the client to use the session to send messages via a QueueSender, although the message listener may avail itself of this facility. This prevents multiple threads (client and message listener) from accessing the same session resource. The client is allowed, however, to call the session's close method.

From a message-handling perspective, the message listener is domain-independent, as the same message listener can be used unchanged with either the point-to-point, publish-subscribe, or common interfaces. This assumes, of course, that our logic in the onMessage method is strictly focused on processing the received message.

Additional Facilities

JMS offers some additional facilities in the point-to-point domain associated with request-reply scenarios and browsing messages on a Queue.

Using QueueRequestor

QueueRequestor condenses the act of sending a request message and receiving a reply into a single operation based on its request method. Consider the following code snippet:

```
//retrieve request Queue
Queue requestQ = (Queue)ctx.lookup("jms.book.requestQ");

//create temporary reply queue
Queue replyQ = (Queue)session.createTemporaryQueue();

//create QueueSender
QueueSender sender = session.createSender(requestQ);

//prepare request
```

```
TextMessage requestMsg = session.createTextMessage();
requestMsg.setText("This is the request");
requestMsg.setJMSReplyTo(replyQ);

//send request
sender.send(requestMsg);

//create QueueReceiver
QueueReceiver receiver = session.createReceiver(replyQ);

//receive reply
TextMessage replyMsg = (TextMessage)receiver.receive(0);
```

Here we retrieve a Queue for requests, create a TemporaryQueue for the reply, and create a QueueSender and QueueReceiver with which to send the request and receive the reply (note that the connection has been started earlier). The QueueRequestor allows us to condense the functions of the QueueSender and QueueReceiver into a single entity, as shown:

```
//retrieve request Queue
Queue requestQ = (Queue)ctx.lookup("jms.book.requestQ");

//create QueueRequestor
QueueRequestor requestor = new QueueRequestor(session,
requestQ);

//prepare request
TextMessage requestMsg = session.createTextMessage();
requestMsg.setText("This is the request");

//send request and receive reply
TextMessage replyMsg =
(TextMessage)requestor.request(requestMsg);
```

The QueueRequestor constructor takes as arguments the QueueSession and the request Queue. The QueueRequestor internally creates a TemporaryQueue with which it populates the JMSReplyTo field of the message passed via its request method. As part of the function of the request method, the QueueRequestor waits for a reply to be returned to the specified TemporaryQueue from which it retrieves the message and passes it back to the client. The QueueRequestor simplifies the act of making service calls; note, however, that only nontransacted sessions can be passed as argument and that the QueueConnection must be started prior to calling the request method. As with all other resources, the QueueRequestor has a close method, which can be explicitly called to clean up the object. It is relevant to note that calling QueueRequestor.close() actually calls close() on the associated QueueSession, which would close down any other resources (i.e., QueueSenders or QueueReceivers) that might be associated with the QueueSession.

Browsing Messages

QueueBrowser enables the client to browse the queue for messages. In contrast to using a QueueReceiver, a QueueBrowser does not remove the messages from the queue but rather returns a snapshot of its content. The QueueBrowser is created by the QueueSession and, as with the QueueReceiver, can be optionally passed a message selector at create time. The QueueBrowser provides a getEnumeration method, which returns a java.util.Enumeration variable containing all the messages browsed at the time. Remember that the Enumeration variable represents the state of the queue at a given point in time. New messages may arrive on the queue or browsed messages may expire during the time the Enumeration is being examined. Such changes would not be known until getEnumeration is issued again. To illustrate the use of QueueBrowser, consider:

```
//create QueueBrowser
QueueBrowser browser = session.createBrowser(inQ);

//start connection to enable receive
conn.start();

//browse Messages on queues
Enumeration cursor = browser.getEnumeration();
while(cursor.hasMoreElements()){
    TextMessage msg = (TextMessage)cursor.nextElement();
    System.out.println("message: " + msg.getText());
}
```

The Enumeration variable is handled in the familiar way, using hasMoreElements() to determine the extent of its contents and nextElement() to retrieve each message in turn. Note that the object retrieved is cast to the expected type.

Publish-Subscribe Interface

Publish-subscribe messaging is typically adopted when the message needs to be distributed to a varying number of recipients that can change dynamically (see Chapter 1). In contrast to the one-to-one relationship between a sender and receiver, a publisher may have zero or more subscribers interested in its publication. Common usage scenarios include publishing weather information, airline departure and arrival information, sensor readings such as metering data for billing, sports scores, and stock prices.

The exchange of messages between publishers and subscribers is bound by a common interest in a given topic that characterizes the message. The format that describes a given topic varies between providers, and as with queues, the actual details of the topic are hidden from the client by the Topic object. As we see, using the JMS publish-subscribe interface is similar to using the point-to-point interface. Indeed, you will recall from Table 2–1 in Chapter 2 that both extend the same base set of parent interfaces. However, certain semantics and concepts particular to publish-subscribe messaging are exposed by the publish-subscribe interface. We once again examine the API by considering the three basic phases our JMS client will experience: connecting to a provider, producing a message, and consuming a message.

Connecting to a Provider

Connectivity to the provider is based on the `TopicConnectionFactory`. Similar to the `QueueConnectionFactory`, it is typically retrieved from a JNDI namespace, so everything we previously discussed in the point-to-point interface about creating an `InitialContext` applies. Once a `TopicConnectionFactory` is retrieved, it is used to create a `TopicCon-nection`, and the `TopicConnection` is used to create a `TopicSession`. The arguments and method calls are identical in type and meaning to those used in the point-to-point interface except that the word *Queue* is replaced with the word *Topic*:

```
......

String jmsICF = "com.sun.jndi.fscontext.RefFSContextFactory";
String jmsURL = "file:/c:/JNDINamespace";

//connect to JNDINamespace

Hashtable environment = new Hashtable();
environment.put(Context.INITIAL_CONTEXT_FACTORY, jmsICF);
environment.put(Context.PROVIDER_URL, jmsURL);
Context ctx = new InitialContext(environment);

//retrieve TopicConnectionFactory
TopicConnectionFactory factory =
(TopicConnectionFactory)ctx.lookup("jms.book.TCF");

//create TopicConnection
TopicConnection conn = factory.createTopicConnection();

//create TopicSession
TopicSession session = conn.createTopicSession(false,
Session.AUTO_ACKNOWLEDGE);
```

The `createTopicConnection` method is similarly overloaded to accept the client's credentials for authentication, and the creation of the `TopicSession` defines our ability to interact with the provider. The `TopicSession`, like its peer the `QueueSession`, is not thread-safe by design. It is thus assumed that only a single thread will access the `TopicSes-sion` unless steps to synchronize thread access are taken.

Publishing Messages

Messages are published using a `TopicPublisher`, which is based on a `Topic`. The `Topic` is typically retrieved from the JNDI namespace and, as before, is cast to the specific object type:

```
//retrieve Topic
Topic topic = (Topic)ctx.lookup("jms.book.T");
```

We similarly have the option to create a `Topic` by passing a topic name as a string, using `TopicSession`'s `createTopic` method. As discussed earlier, the format of the name is provider-specific and thus dependency on this approach compromises the portability of the client. However, with publish-subscribe, where we might want to dynamically define the topic, it does provide additional flexibility.

The `TopicPublisher` is created by the `TopicSession` in the now familiar manner:

```
//create TopicPublisher
TopicPublisher publisher = session.createPublisher(topic);
```

We can similarly create an unidentified `TopicPublisher` by passing null instead of a defined `Topic`, in which case we pass the `Topic` when publishing the message.

To publish a message, we call the `publish()` method of the `TopicPublisher`, passing the created message as argument:

```
//publish message with defaults
publisher.publish(msg);
```

This publishes the message with the default values that have been specified for `JMSDestinationMode`, `JMSPriority`, and `timeToLive`, which sets `JMSExpiration`. The defaults are taken from the `TopicPublisher` (inherited from `MessageProducer`), and JMS defines them as `DeliveryMode.PERSISTENT` with a priority of 4 and a `timeToLive` of 0, which defines an unlimited lifespan. To publish the message with a different set of values, we can update the `TopicPublisher` using defined setter methods or simply use the overloaded publish method:

```
//publish with options set
publisher.publish(msg,DeliveryMode.NON_PERSISTENT, 4, 0);
```

By now you should be getting an idea of how similar the point-to-point and publish-subscribe APIs are. As should be expected, the alternative approach is to have the values overridden by the JMS administrator, which in the case of the IBM JMS providers is achieved by setting the values in the `Topic` object (see Chapter 3). As with the `send` method, the `publish` method is further overloaded to support unidentified `TopicPublishers`, allowing the `Topic` to be passed on the publish call.

Cleanup for the client acting as a publisher follows the familiar pattern of `close` methods being defined for all resources: `TopicPublisher`, `TopicSession`, and `TopicConnection`. As discussed earlier, the `close` methods of objects higher in the hierarchy trigger the `close` methods of objects created from them, so closing `TopicConnection` will clean up all resources.

```
//close connection
conn.close();
conn = null;
```

Creating Subscribers

A client interested in receiving publications creates a `TopicSubscriber`, which notifies the provider of the client's interest in a given topic. JMS defines two kinds of subscribers: nondurable and durable subscribers, which differ in the lifetime of their subscriptions.

Nondurable Subscribers

Nondurable subscribers are characterized by the fact that they do not wish to receive publications if they are not running. In other words, they are only interested in a published message when they are active. A typical usage scenario is a client that subscribes to messages about stock prices (the popular stock ticker tape). The nature of the data and the fact that it changes frequently suggests that when inactive, the client would not want publications piling up on its doorstep, so to speak. In essence the lifetime of a nondurable subscriber's subscription is its active state. Once inactive, the subscription (interest in the topic) is essentially deactivated by the provider, and any publications on that topic are no longer delivered. To create a nondurable subscriber, we obtain the `Topic` from the JNDI namespace and call the `createSubscriber` method of the `TopicSession`:

```
//retrieve Topic
Topic topic = (Topic)ctx.lookup("jms.book.T");
//create TopicSubscriber
TopicSubscriber subscriber = session.createSubscriber(topic);
```

JMS also supports the concept of temporary topics (analogous to temporary queues), which might be used to establish a context for conversational clients—for example, client A publishes a message to a well-known topic, including in the message's `JMSReplyTo` field a `TemporaryTopic`, which it subsequently subscribes to. Interested respondents then publish to the `TemporaryTopic`, and the `TemporaryTopic` can form the basis for the rest of the exchange, with each client publishing and subscribing to the `TemporaryTopic`. The `TemporaryTopic` is created by the `TopicSession` and, like the `TemporaryQueue`, exists for the lifetime of the `TopicConnection` or until explicitly closed:

```
//create TemporaryTopic
Topic topic = (Topic)session.createTemporaryTopic();

//create TopicSubscriber
TopicSubscriber subscriber = session.createSubscriber(topic);
```

If we are interested in the subscriber further qualifying its interest in receiving a particular message based on its content, then as with QueueReceiver, we create the TopicSubscriber, passing in addition a message selector:

```
//Set selector
String selector = "orderValue > 2500";

//create TopicSubscriber
boolean noLocal = false;
TopicSubscriber subscriber = session.createSubscriber(topic,
selector, noLocal);
```

This version of createSubscriber introduces an additional variable: the Boolean variable noLocal (set to false in the example). When noLocal is set to true, it instructs the provider not to deliver to the subscriber any publications on that topic that originate from a TopicPublisher using the same TopicConnection. To understand what this means in practice, consider a chat application that allows individuals to converse with each other. Each chat session is implemented by a JMS client that publishes and subscribes to a given topic (say "conversation"). Each time conversing parties publish a message, they want their partners to receive it but do not necessarily want their own message sent back to them. Hence, setting noLocal to true suppresses the sending party's own publications. If we want to set noLocal but do not want to specify a selector, then null should be passed for the selector variable:

```
//create TopicSubscriber suppress local publications
TopicSubscriber subscriber = session.createSubscriber(topic,
null, true);
```

In order to actually retrieve a published message sent to it, the TopicSubscriber provides the same options as the QueueReceiver, offering the various versions of the receive method, including receiveNoWait. Remember that before attempting to receive messages, the connection must be started:

```
//start connection
conn.start();

//receive message
TextMessage msg = (TextMessage)subscriber.receive();
```

Recall that receive() will block and wait indefinitely for a message, while receive with a time interval specified and receiveNoWait both block and wait for the specified time (in the case of receiveNoWait, that is no time at all). They both return a null if no message is available in the allotted time. We can also use a message listener to asynchronously receive messages. Indeed, this is one of my favored cases for using a message listener, particularly in applications where the data being subscribed to is to be processed in exactly the same way regardless of content, such as displaying sport scores. The message listener assigned to the TopicSubscriber is domain-independent and, as shown in our example, is the same message listener used previously with the `QueueReceiver` (see section "Receiving Messages Using the JMS Message Listener"):

```
//register listener
subscriber.setMessageListener(new JMSMessageListener());

//start connection
conn.start();
```

When the subscribing client wants to stop receiving publications, it simply closes the `TopicSubscriber`, or alternatively the `TopicSession` or `TopicConnection`, depending on application logic. This serves to deregister the client's interest in the given topic. Note that there is no unsubscribe method for the `TopicSubscriber`.

Durable Subscriber

The durable subscriber differs from the nondurable subscriber in one key respect: its subscription remains active even when the durable subscriber is inactive. Consequently, publications will be delivered whether the subscriber is running or not and held in storage by the provider until the subscriber retrieves them. For example, consider a back-office accounting application that subscribes to sales figures being published by a number of retail store branches. It is logical to expect that the application will want the publications to be delivered irrespective of whether or not it happened to be running at the time.

The creation and use of a durable subscriber follows the same pattern as that of the nondurable subscriber:

```
//retrieve Topic
Topic topic = (Topic)ctx.lookup("jms.book.T");

//create TopicSubscriber
TopicSubscriber durSubscriber =
session.createDurableSubscriber(topic, "DSUB_01");

//start connection
conn.start();
```

However, note that now we use the `createDurableSubscriber` method to create the `TopicSubscriber`. In addition to the `Topic`, the client passes a name that will be used to uniquely identify the subscription. In order for the durable `TopicSubscriber` to be successfully created, the `TopicConnection` must have a client identifier assigned. JMS introduces the concept of the client identifier as a means for the provider to associate the client's connection and its objects with state maintained on its behalf by the provider, in this case durable subscriptions. It is recommended by JMS that the client identifier be transparently assigned to connections based on the configuration of the provider-specific `ConnectionFactory` (we explore this configuration in Chapter 6). The client identifier defines the scope of uniqueness for subscription names. Thus, in our example the subscription name DSUB_01 must be unique among all `TopicConnections` having the same client identifier (i.e., created from the same `TopicConnectionFactory`).

The `createDurableSubscriber` method is overloaded in the same way as the `createSubscriber` method to allow a message selector and instructions for handling local publications to be set. We use the durable `TopicSubscriber` in exactly the same way as the nondurable `TopicSubscriber` to retrieve delivered publications:

```
//receive message
TextMessage msg = (TextMessage)durSubscriber.receive();
```

When the client is shut down by closing the `TopicSubscriber`, `TopicSession`, or `TopicConnection`, the subscription remains active and publications are received and stored by the JMS provider. When the client is restarted, it executes exactly the same code used initially. This means it is retrieving the same `TopicConnectionFactory` and creating a durable `TopicSubscriber` with the same name. Once setup is complete, the `TopicSubscriber` receives existing messages that arrived when it was inactive and new messages that are being published in much the same way.

To deregister a durable subscription, the `TopicSession`'s `unsubscribe` method must be used. It takes as argument the name of the durable subscription. Thus, in designing a durable subscriber, we could implement a termination block similar to the one shown:

```
//shut down
if(terminate){
    //unsubscribe durable subscriber
    durSubscriber.close();
    session.unsubscribe("DSUB_01");

    //close connection,
    conn.close();
    conn = null;
}else{
    //maintain subscription and close connection,
conn.close();
    conn = null;
}
```

Observe that when maintaining the subscription, I simply closed the `TopicConnection`, effectively closing all resources derived from it. However, when unsubscribing, I explicitly close the `TopicSubscriber` before issuing the unsubscribe call. This is because it is illegal to unsubscribe a durable subscription that has an active `TopicSubscriber`.

Additional Facilities

The publish-subscribe interface does not support the concept of topic browsing, but it does provide a `TopicRequestor`, which works in an identical fashion to its point-to-point counterpart, the `QueueRequestor`. The `TopicRequestor` facilitates the implementation of service calls in the publish-subscribe domain. For instance, a client publishes a message on a well-known `Topic`, and a subscribing respondent publishes a response to a `Temporary-Topic` created by the `TopicRequestor`. Given that `TopicRequestor` returns only a single message, thought must be given to the appropriateness of this facility if there is a potential for multiple responses to be received. The creation and use of the `TopicRequestor` parallels that of the `QueueRequestor`, as shown (note, the `TopicSession` must be nontransacted):

```
//create TopicRequestor
TopicRequestor requestor = new TopicRequestor(session, topic);
......

//publish message and receive reply
TextMessage replyMsg =
(TextMessage)requestor.request(requestMsg);
```

Handling JMS Exceptions

Having explored the use of the point-to-point and publish-subscribe interface APIs in some detail, it is now prudent to discuss how we handle exceptions. As with any Java application, exceptions are thrown on errors, and they must be caught and handled. The approach to handling exceptions is of course application-dependent, but it is useful to note the basic exceptions we can expect a JMS client to throw.

The use of JNDI invariably implies that `NamingException` must be handled. `NamingException` is the root exception from which all JNDI exceptions are extended, the most common one experienced by JMS clients being the `NameNotFoundException`. Similarly, all JMS exceptions inherit from `JMSException`, and it provides a generic way of handling all JMS-related exceptions. It exposes three methods of specific interest to the client: `getMessage()`, `getErrorCode()`, and `getLinkedException()`.

- `getMessage()` is inherited from `java.lang.Throwable` and returns a provider-specific string describing the error. It is closely related to `getLocalizedMessage()`, which if used returns the localized string describing the error.
- `getErrorCode()` returns a provider-specific error code associated with the error.
- `getLinkedException()` returns a reference to another exception, which can be viewed as the root cause of the `JMSException`. Given that messaging errors may easily occur in the provider-specific layers, it offers an easy way to surface provider-specific exceptions and is accessed in the following way:

```
try{
    //JMS calls
    .........
}catch(JMSException je){
```

```
      System.out.println("JMSException thrown " + je);
      Exception e = je.getLinkedException();
      if(e != null){
        System.out.println("JMS Linked Exception: " + e);
      }
    }
  }
```

JMS defines a number of standard exceptions, such as `IllegalStateException` and `MessageNotWritableException`, that extend `JMSException` and standardize the reporting of basic error conditions. However, JMS rarely mandates that a specific `JMSExcep-tion` must be thrown in response to an error condition, and application logic generally should not depend on a specific problem resulting in a specific `JMSException` being thrown. The rules that govern the throwing of a specific exception are reproduced for your convenience in Appendix A.

If a message listener is used, the client is faced with the unique problem of how it gets notified if errors occur during retrieval of the message. This is because (as you will recall) when a message listener is used, the client does not issue the receive call; rather, the message listener's `onMessage` method is simply passed a message when it is successfully retrieved by the provider. The question then is: How is the client notified if the provider experiences errors while receiving the message? To address this issue, JMS defines the `ExceptionListener` interface, which defines the `onException` method:

```
      package jms.book.sample;

      import javax.jms.ExceptionListener;
      import javax.jms.JMSException;

      /**
       * @author yusufk
       *
       * ExceptionListener Implementation
       */
      public class JMSExceptionListener implements ExceptionListener
      {

          /**
           * Constructor for JMSExceptionListener.
           */
          public JMSExceptionListener() {
            super();
          }

          /**
       * @see javax.jms.ExceptionListener#onException(JMSException)
           */
          public void onException(JMSException je) {
```

```
        //handle exception
        System.out.println("JMSException thrown " + je);
        Exception e = je.getLinkedException();
        if(e != null){
        System.out.println("JMS Linked Exception: " + e);
        }


    }


    }
```

The onException method is passed a JMSException by the provider, which is handled in accordance with the application logic. The JMS specification stresses the point that exceptions passed to the exception listener are those that have no other place to be reported. If a JMS exception arises from a JMS call, such as from createTopicSubscriber(), it is not passed to the exception listener but rather handled by the calling thread using a try-catch block or other appropriate construct.

The exception listener is registered by the client with the Connection. As with the message listener, the exception listener is domain-independent and can be reused in either domain:

```
    //setup MessageListener
    receiver.setMessageListener(new JMSMessageListener());

    //setup ExceptionListener
    conn.setExceptionListener(new JMSExceptionListener());

    //start connection to enable receive
    conn.start();
```

Handling Local Transactions

Transactions define atomic units of work—that is, a set of instructions that should be executed together—with every instruction either succeeding or the whole set being considered as having failed. Consider, for instance, a JMS client servicing requests. It is desirable to have the receipt of the request, its processing, and the sending of the reply defined as a single unit of work (transaction). This provides the benefit of ensuring that if any exception is thrown during processing, the transaction fails, and the act of receiving the request is effectively reversed, making the request available for receipt and reprocessing.

A transaction manager is that entity that coordinates a transaction, managing the state of the resources involved and ensuring that they remain consistent within the defined scope of the transaction. Scope in this context refers to the set of instructions associated with a given unit of work. JMS assigns the provider the role of transaction manager; however, the provider can only manage what are termed *local transactions* involving updates to resources under its control, that is, Queues and Topics. JMS does not support the concept of a provider managing global or

XA transactions, which involve the transaction manager using the XA protocol to coordinate a number of externally managed resources such as JMS and database (JDBC) resources. Rather, global/XA transactions are managed by the J2EE server. We examine the configuration of the IBM WebSphere Application Server in this role in Appendix B.

The scope of local transactions managed by the JMS provider is defined by the `Session`. As mentioned earlier in this chapter, we can create a transacted session by specifying true as the value of the transacted Boolean variable. With a transacted session, we can then define units of work and complete them or undo them using `Session.commit()` and `Session.roll-back()`:

```
//create QueueSession
QueueSession session = conn.createQueueSession(true,
Session.AUTO_ACKNOWLEDGE);

//retrieve Queue
Queue requestQ = (Queue)ctx.lookup("jms.book.requestQ");

//create QueueReceiver
QueueReceiver receiver = session.createReceiver(requestQ);

//start connection to enable receive
conn.start();

//start transaction
try{
   //receive request
   TextMessage requestMsg = (TextMessage)receiver.receive();

   //process request
   System.out.println("message: " + requestMsg.getText());

   //prepare response
   TextMessage replyMsg = session.createTextMessage();
   replyMsg.setText("This is the response");

   //set correlationID

replyMsg.setJMSCorrelationID(requestMsg.getJMSMessageID());

   //create QueueSender
   Queue replyQ = (Queue)requestMsg.getJMSReplyTo();
   QueueSender sender = session.createSender(replyQ);

   //send reply
   sender.send(replyMsg);

   //commit receive and send operations
```

```
        session.commit();

    }catch(JMSException te){
        //on exception rollback transaction
        session.rollback();
        ......
    }
```

The instructions that comprise the unit of work are defined within the try portion of the try-catch block. Of particular importance are the `receive` and `send` method calls. Because they are made within a transacted session, the following state changes occur:

1. On receive, a copy of the request message is returned but the state of the destination (`requestQ`) is not updated by the provider to reflect the removal of the request message.
2. On send, the reply message is sent to the identified destination (`replyQ`), but the state of the destination is not updated by the provider to reflect the placement of the reply message.
3. On commit, the `Session` acknowledges receipt of the request and confirms the sending of the reply, resulting in the provider updating the states of the destinations accordingly and making the changes permanent. At this point, the transaction is complete.
4. If any exceptions are thrown by the calls in the try block, they are caught by the catch block, which calls `session.rollback`. In response, the provider undoes any tentative state changes that may have been made in the try block, resulting in the request message remaining on the queue.

In the instance that an exception occurs and the session is rolled back, when the transaction is retried, the receive call returns the previously processed message. If the exception was thrown due to a problem with the message itself, then we can expect the exception to be thrown again and soon find ourselves in an infinite loop. In order to address this, a strategy must be defined for handling poison messages. Our first step would be to check JMSRedelivered and potentially JMSXDeliveryCount on receipt of the message to confirm if this message is being redelivered and indeed how many times it has been delivered. Based on the application design, we can then decide if this is within the reprocessing threshold we will allow or whether the message should be moved to some other destination for failed messages, where it can be examined by other processes. If the exception is due to a transient problem with the provider, a retry may prove sufficient, and consequently when defining our strategy thought should also be given to the question of having different reprocessing thresholds based on the nature of the exception.

Unified Interface

As we discussed in Chapter 2, the main modification introduced by JMS 1.1 is the unification of the point-to-point and publish-subscribe messaging domains. This allows JMS clients to use the parent (common) interfaces (see Chapter 2, Table 2–1) rather than their point-to-point–specific or publish-subscribe–specific counterparts, such as `Connection` rather than `QueueConnection` or `TopicConnection`. The common interface serves to further simplify the API and enables mixed-domain programming where messages can be moved between `Queues` and `Topics` in a single transaction.

To enable the use of the common interfaces, a number of new methods have been defined, as shown in Table 4–1.

Table 4–1 New Common Interface Methods: JMS 1.1

Interface	New Methods
ConnectionFactory	`createConnection()` `createConnection(String username, String password)`
Connection	`createSession(boolean transacted, int acknowledgeMode)`

MessageProducer*	`getDestination()`
	 `send(Message message)`
	 `send(Message message, int deliveryMode, int priority, long timeToLive)`
	 `send(Destination destination, Message message)`

Session	`createProducer(Destination destination)`
	 `createConsumer(Destination destination)`
	 `createConsumer(Destination destination, String messageSelector)`
	 `createConsumer(Destination destination, String messageSelector, boolean noLocal)`
	 `createDurableSubscriber(Topic topic, String name)`
	 `createDurableSubscriber(Topic topic, String name, String messageSelector, Boolean noLocal)`
	 `createBrowser(Queue queue)`
	 `createBrowser(Queue queue, String messageSelector)`
	 `createQueue(String name)` †
	 `createTopic(String name)` †
	 `createTemporaryTopic()`
	 `createTemporaryQueue()`
	 `unsubscribe()`

* `MessageConsumer` already has the `receive` methods defined.

† Name defined in provider-specific URI format.

While some of the methods are new and allow the client to be written in a domain-independent manner, some of the methods, for example, the createBrowser method, are simply exposed from the domain-specific versions. Exposing domain-specific methods at the common interface raises the possibility of domain-specific clients making illegal calls, since domain-specific interfaces extend the common interfaces. For example, since QueueSession extends Session, it consequently inherits the unsubscribe method. JMS specifies that an illegalStateException be thrown in such cases.

Everything we have discussed regarding the use of the JMS API remains true and the use of the unified domain adopts the familiar form:

```
//retrieve ConnectionFactory
ConnectionFactory factory =
(ConnectionFactory)ctx.lookup("jms.book.CF");

//create Connection
Connection conn = factory.createConnection();

//create Session
Session session = conn.createSession(true,
Session.AUTO_ACKNOWLEDGE);

//retrieve target and source destinations
Destination source =
(Destination)ctx.lookup("jms.book.Source");
Destination target =
(Destination)ctx.lookup("jms.book.Target");

//create MessageConsumer and MessageProducer
MessageConsumer consumer = session.createConsumer(source);
MessageProducer producer = session.createProducer(target);

//start connection to enable receive
conn.start();

//start transaction
try{
    //forward received message
    producer.send(consumer.receive());

    //commit receive and send operations
    session.commit();
}catch(JMSException te){
    //on exception rollback transaction
    session.rollback();
    ......
}
```

Here we implement a client that forwards messages from a source to target destination within a unit of work. The beauty of the unified interface is that it enables the client to receive a message from a `Queue` and publish it to a `Topic` and interested subscribers in one transaction, which is not achievable if the domain-specific APIs are used. The nature of the `MessageConsumer` and `MessageProducer` are determine by the nature of the `Destination` (`Queue` or `Topic`) passed to their respective `create` methods.

Summary

In this chapter we focused on the mechanics of messaging using the JMS API. We began by considering the choices available for implementing the JMS client, the entity that utilizes the JMS API. The JMS client can be implemented by any Java artifact, ranging from standalone Java applications to J2EE components. For J2EE components, we considered the suitability of applets, servlets and portlets, and EJBs. We determined that applets, because they are clientside components, are least suited to the role of JMS clients. On the other hand, EJBs—specifically, session EJBs and MDBs—offer some distinct advantages when used to implement JMS clients. These advantages stem from the facilities and services provided by the EJB container, such as transaction services and performance tuning options.

We devoted the rest of the chapter to examining the JMS API in detail. For each interface point-to-point, publish-subscribe, and the unified interface, we discussed how the JMS client connects to the provider, produces messages, and consumes messages. We also discussed approaches to handling exceptions and executing local transactions.

We have now completed our basic introduction to JMS, and in the following chapters we review the JMS providers supplied by IBM and how we use them.

Using JMS with IBM WebSphere

In the second part of this book (Chapters 5 to 8), we examine IBM JMS implementations and explore their use and configuration in support of JMS solutions. We build on the generic knowledge gained in Part 1 to implement real-world solutions based on IBM WebSphere.

CHAPTER 5

IBM JMS Providers

A s we have now seen, JMS defines an API for which software vendors implement support in a JMS provider. JMS client applications subsequently interact with the JMS provider via the JMS API. We have examined in detail the JMS API and its use and are now ready to examine a vendor-specific implementation of the JMS provider, specifically that provided by IBM. We begin by introducing the IBM WebSphere Software Platform, which encapsulates the software components with which we are concerned. We then review the software components that constitute JMS providers: WebSphere MQ, WebSphere MQ Everyplace, WebSphere Business Integration Message Broker, and the WebSphere Application Server. The review undertaken here is by no means exhaustive and is primarily aimed at understanding the components from the perspective of JMS rather than at discussing each component itself. In Appendix D further reading material is detailed, which will prove useful for anyone installing and configuring these components.

The WebSphere Software Platform

The IBM WebSphere Software Platform is a comprehensive software platform that addresses through its integrated product families the *middleware* infrastructure needs for the enterprise. The WebSphere Software Platform is modular in nature, enabling parts to be used standalone to provide specific solutions while providing a broad platform from which end-to-end solutions can be built. The WebSphere Software Platform is described by a pyramid (Figure 5–1); each side of the pyramid represents distinct but complementary functionality.

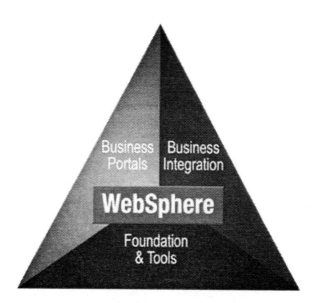

Figure 5-1 The WebSphere Software Platform

Foundation and Tools provides the runtime and tooling infrastructure for developing and executing open standards-based business applications. It is made up of the WebSphere Application Server and WebSphere Studio family of products. The WebSphere Application Server is a high-performance, scalable J2EE server that provides a J2EE execution environment for J2EE components such as servlets, Java Server Pages (JSP), and EJBs. It additionally provides an execution environment for Web services. The WebSphere Studio family offers a suite of development tools useful to both the J2EE and non-J2EE developer. The WebSphere Studio tools are themselves based on an open standards tooling framework called Eclipse (*http:// www.eclipse.org/*).

Business Portals focuses on the infrastructure required to support the integration of the user's environment with other users to enable real-time collaboration. It is also concerned with ensuring that the user has access to the right information when needed in a manner tailored to the user's needs. Furthermore, it includes the infrastructure required to extend the user environment to any given type of device or interaction mechanism, facilitating the user's ability to access and utilize information. These needs are met by the WebSphere Portal and WebSphere Commerce families, which together enable the implementation of business portals. Business portals enable people to interact in a personalized way with diverse business resources. Both WebSphere Portal and WebSphere Commerce are implemented as J2EE applications, and they are hosted by the WebSphere Application Server. The WebSphere Everyplace and Voice families provide software components that extend the reach of business applications to pervasive mobile devices and enable natural voice interactions with applications and data.

Business Integration addresses the integration of diverse business resources in support of given business functions. It addresses this at two levels: first at the lower level of the application and then at the higher level of the business process. At the level of the application, we are concerned with application connectivity, focusing on the infrastructure required to connect diverse systems together so that information from different business applications can be shared and used across and beyond the enterprise. At the level of the process, we are concerned with business process integration, from modeling how the business runs to managing the business activities once the process is in place.

It is with application connectivity that we are primarily concerned in this book, as our focus is on the use of messaging as a means to communicate between business applications. The WebSphere Business Integration family addresses the issue of connectivity management, isolating applications from concerns with network protocols and platform dependencies. Additionally, it addresses message delivery management, providing routing, distribution (publish-subscribe or point-to-point), and transformation functions with varying levels of quality of service. The core of this functionality is delivered by WebSphere MQ, which functions as a high-performance communications transport, enabling reliable and secure application communication. WebSphere MQ Everyplace extends that integration to users with mobile devices, enabling secure and reliable exchange of information in the mobile environment. Finally, the WebSphere Business Integration Message Broker enhances message delivery by enabling transformation of information and intelligent routing to the right set of business applications as events occur. The WebSphere Business Integration family also offers a suite of adapters that bridge between popular off-the-shelf business applications, such as SAP or PeopleSoft, and WebSphere MQ. Note that most of the adapters utilize JMS as the means of interfacing with WebSphere MQ.

Business process integration focuses on the control and coordination of applications and their users in support of business processes. The realm of business process integration spans the spectrum ranging from fully automated processes to those that involve human activity or a mix thereof. It provides a basis for capturing, managing, and executing business rules that affect the process, and it utilizes application connectivity as the means to interact with the applications that are being coordinated. This integration capability is rendered by the WebSphere Business Integration Server, which provides a wealth of services concerned with state management, transactions, compensation, and staff resolution in support of its functions. The integration solution is extended to cover business-to-business (B2B) transactions by WebSphere Business Integration Connect, which extends business integration beyond the enterprise, orchestrating the interaction between business partners in fulfillment of business functions. The solution is rounded out by the WebSphere Business Integration Modeler and Monitor, which provide sophisticated tools for modeling business processes and subsequently monitoring them once implemented in the Web-Sphere Business Integration Server.

From a JMS perspective, the WebSphere Software Platform impacts us in a number of ways. First, it provides the operating environment in the guise of the WebSphere Application Server and Portal Server for components such as servlets, EJBs, and portlets with which we might implement JMS clients. Second, it provides the underlying JMS provider, implemented by the WebSphere Business Integration family with which our JMS client interacts. In the rest of this chapter we examine relevant members of the WebSphere Business Integration family and the WebSphere Application Server, specifically in terms of their support for JMS.

WebSphere MQ

WebSphere MQ is quite simply a messaging provider, the entity that provides message-based communication services to applications. First released by IBM in 1993 under the brand name MQSeries, it was rebranded in 2001 to WebSphere MQ. It is the market share leader, owning about 81 percent of the message-oriented middleware market, and is considered the de facto standard in terms of messaging provider implementations. A major factor in its adoption is that it is available on more than 35 different platforms (operating systems) and supports communication across numerous network protocols. In addition, it supports both JMS and non-JMS applications, providing a native API that is rendered in all the major languages. Coupled with this is its ability to deliver mission-critical levels of service in terms of assuring the delivery of messages and providing once-and-once-only delivery semantics. It thus provides a firm foundation for enabling application connectivity between business applications that exist in the enterprise.

System Components

Figure 5–2 depicts the main components of a WebSphere MQ network and provides a basis for understanding the technical architecture of WebSphere MQ.

MQ Queue Manager

The queue manager is the base entity that supplies the messaging facilities used by the application. It provides access to MQ queues, which store MQ messages, and is responsible for maintaining the queues and ensuring messages are delivered to the right queue destination with the defined qualities of service. From the JMS perspective, it is that entity with which the JMS client interacts: the JMS provider.

Applications interact with the queue manager using either JMS, the native API (MQI), or one of a number of other APIs. The application may establish either a local or client connection to the queue manager. A local connection requires that the application run on the same physical machine as the queue manager and uses interprocess memory to communicate with the queue

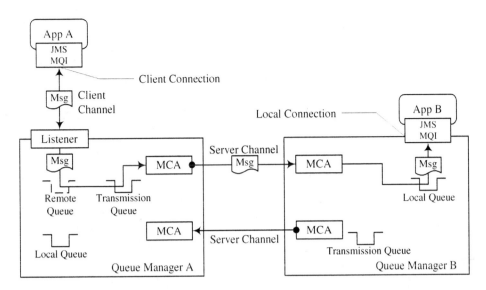

Figure 5-2 WebSphere MQ

manager. A client connection allows the application to run on a machine that is remote from the queue manager and, in contrast, employs a protocol exchange over the network to invoke messaging facilities. The client connection uses a network abstraction called a client channel, which is bidirectional, being designed to pass both API calls and results. Communication over a client channel can be optionally authenticated and secured using the inbuilt Secure Socket Layer (SSL) support. The choice of connection type is driven by topology considerations, which we discuss in Chapter 8, "Enterprise Deployment." However, it has no impact from an API perspective, as its selection is based on externally configurable properties. As we see in Chapter 6, "IBM JMS–Administered Objects," for JMS this is done via the `ConnectionFactory`-administered object.

While communication between applications can be based on a single queue manager, most typical implementations involve more than one queue manager, with applications and associated queue managers potentially running on different physical machines and different operating systems. A queue manager is a named entity, and generally this name is unique among a network of interconnected queue managers so that a queue manager can be unambiguously identified when a message is to be sent to a queue it manages. Queue managers are connected to each other by server channels, which, like client channels, are network abstractions that isolate the queue managers and, by extension, the applications from the different network protocols that may be in use in the enterprise (e.g., TCP/IP, SNA LU.62). Server channels are typed, the most common being a sender channel and a receiver channel. In contrast to client channels, server channels are unidirectional, so a sender/receiver pair are required by a given queue manager to enable bidirectional communication. Transmission and receipt of messages across channels is managed by an internal component called the Message Channel Agent (MCA), and this communication can be similarly authenticated and secured using the inbuilt SSL support.

The queue manager is an XA-compliant resource manager, and thus updates to its queues can be coordinated with updates to another XA-compliant resource, such as a database, by an external transaction coordinator such as the WebSphere Application Server. Rather uniquely, the queue manager can also act as a transaction coordinator, coordinating updates to itself as well as to some other XA-compliant resource, typically a database. Queue managers can also be grouped together in clusters to provide load balancing or high-availability configurations.

MQ Message

The MQ message is the unit of exchange and contains the data that is to be communicated between applications. It thus defines the physical implementation of the JMS message. In its most basic form, the MQ message consists of a message header called the MQ message descriptor (MQMD) and a body that contains data. Additional headers may be used to convey specific information; for example, the rules and formatting header v2 (RFH2) can convey topic associations for publish-subscribe–based distribution. In all cases when additional headers are used, they are placed within the message body in front of the message data. The MQMD contains fields which, based on our discussion in Chapter 3, "JMS Messages," are familiar to you. The fields include identification attributes such as message identifiers and correlation identifiers; destination attributes such as reply-to-queue, and behavioral attributes such as message persistence and expiry.

The message body is opaque in that it contains no specific references to the actual physical representation of the data being transported (unlike the JMS message) but rather handles all data as a sequence of bytes. However, a format field in the MQMD allows the sender of a message to associate with it a name that indicates the nature of the message to the receiver (by default this is set to MQFMT_NONE, which means "no format name"). In the instance when the message contains additional headers, these headers are arranged in a chain. Each header typically includes a format field that describes the format of the header that follows. The last header in the chain optionally describes the format of message data. The relevance of this to JMS will become apparent when we examine communicating between JMS and non-JMS clients in Chapter 7. Currently, the maximum size of an MQ message is 100 MB; this can be extended by defining a logical message that comprises a number of physical segments (messages) or by creating a number of physical messages that are defined as belonging to a group.

MQ Queue

The MQ queue is the ultimate destination of the message; messages are sent to, received from, and moved between queues in fulfillment of the communication process. Hence it defines the underlying implementation of the JMS Destination. A queue belongs to a queue manager, which is responsible for maintaining the queue. The queue is a named entity and must be unique within the queue manager that owns it. The queue acts as a storage medium, accumulating messages that are later removed by the queue manager for transmission or by the application for processing. Message storage on the queue is based on FIFO (first in, first out), with messages being added to the end and messages (by default) being removed from the front. The messages may also be stored based on priority, with messages of higher priority being moved (in FIFO order) to the front of the queue. The queue manager additionally supports specific messages being retrieved from the queue based on identifiers. MQ queues have a controllable depth allowing the maximum number of messages that can be stored at any given time to be defined.

MQ queues are rendered as storage in process memory but are associated with a directory structure on the hard disk. If allowable memory storage (which is configurable) is exceeded, the messages (persistent or nonpersistent) temporarily spill over to the hard disk. Persistent messages are additionally logged by the queue manager to file-based logs, which enables message recovery in the event that the queue manager process fails. WebSphere MQ types queues based on their function; examples include local queues that represent an application's inbox or outbox, remote queues that are definitions on one queue manager of queues that exist on another, and transmission queues that serve as storage for outbound messages. Queues can either be statically defined by an administrator or created dynamically by an application, enabling, for instance, on-the-fly creation of a dedicated queue for a given application's replies.

JMS Support

There are two kinds of JMS providers: those that were developed strictly to support only JMS and those that predate JMS and were extended to support JMS. WebSphere MQ clearly falls into the second of these categories, having been in use since 1993. Consequently, WebSphere MQ implements support for JMS as a set of Java classes that implement the JMS interface and translate the JMS API to the native MQ API (MQI). At the time of writing, WebSphere MQ 5.3 supports JMS 1.0.2b.

The Java classes and supporting infrastructure are packaged as follows:

- `com.ibm.mqjms.jar`, which packages the JMS implementation classes.
- `com.ibm.mq.jar` packages the Java MQI classes.
- `rmm.jar` provides support for multicast-based distribution, discussed later in the chapter.
- `mqjbnd`*xx*, where *xx* signifies a version number, is a system library (e.g., DLL on Windows) used by the Java MQI to effect a local connection to the queue manager.
- Additional system libraries, such as `mqjbdf`*xx* and `maxai`*xx*, provide internal functions.
- Various supporting jars—`jms.jar`, `jndi.jar`, `connector.jar`, `providerUtil.jar`, `fscontext.jar`, `ldap.jar`, and `jta.jar`—are shipped as a convenience to the user and could be alternately downloaded from the Java

home page *(http://java.sun.com/)*. They are also typically packaged as part of a J2EE environment.

• `jmsadmin` is a command line-based tool for creating MQ JMS-administered objects.

These components are packaged as part of a WebSphere MQ installation image and can be found distributed under the `<installation_directory>\java\` subdirectory. Prior to WebSphere MQ 5.3, JMS support was packaged as a standalone product extension called the MQSeries classes for Java and JMS, popularly known by its assigned designation MA88. Users requiring JMS support would have to install the queue manager, then download MA88 and install it. Separate packaging also meant that users would have to upgrade their versions of MA88 and MQSeries (as it was then known) independently while remaining aware of potential dependencies. WebSphere MQ 5.3 eliminated these issues by making the JMS support part of a standard queue manager install. It is also possible to install only the JMS support on a given machine without the queue manager, as would be the case for a client application that is running remotely from its queue manager.

The glue that binds the JMS client to the WebSphere MQ environment is the JMS-administered objects. As we see in Chapter 6, the administered objects basically contain as attributes arguments for MQI calls. Thus, in order to further our understanding of how WebSphere MQ implements support for JMS, we briefly examine how the JMS API maps to the MQI and how the JMS message is transformed to the MQ message.

Mapping the JMS API to the MQI

The Message Queue Interface (MQI) defines a simple set of verbs that are rendered as a set of procedural calls or object method calls in a variety of languages, including C/C++, COBOL, Java, REXX, RPG, Perl, PL1, and Visual Basic. There are 13 verbs in total; six are typically used by communicating applications:

• `MQCONN` connects the application to the named queue manager.
• `MQOPEN` accesses a named queue.
• `MQPUT` sends messages to an opened queue.
• `MQGET` retrieves messages from an opened queue.
• `MQCLOSE` closes access to a previously opened queue.
• `MQDISC` disconnects the application from the queue manager.

Each verb takes a varying set of mandatory and optional arguments that influence its function. The other verbs are associated with command optimizations, administrative tasks such as setting or inquiring about a queue or queue manager attribute, and executing transaction semantics: begin, commit, and rollback.

Figure 5–3 annotates the previously seen application flow for sending a JMS message using the point-to-point interface with the associated MQI calls.

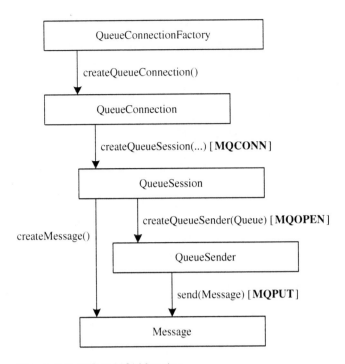

Figure 5-3 JMS to MQI Mapping

As shown, the JMS client actually connects to the queue manager via an MQCONN when the QueueSession is created. This makes sense when you consider that the QueueSession defines the scope of transactions for the JMS client, and the corresponding WebSphere MQ construct is the connection to the queue manager that is returned by the MQCONN. Creation of a QueueSender or QueueReceiver results in an MQOPEN being issued for the MQ queue identified by the Queue-administered object passed on the create call. Sending or receiving messages then map to MQPUT or MQGET calls. Overloaded calls, such as receive with a wait interval, conveniently map to a MQGET with a wait option specified. Similarly, message selectors based on JMSMessageId or JMSCorrelationId take advantage of the fact that the MQI provides options for the MQGET that match the equivalent fields in the MQMD of the MQ message. However, the MQI does not support selecting MQ messages based on their contents (remember, it treats the message body as a sequence of bytes). Thus, selectors based on application-specific properties generally require the JMS implementation to browse the MQ messages using MQGET with the browse option and then on ascertaining that the message is the one the client wants destructively retrieve it with a standard MQGET. This, as would be expected, attracts some performance overhead.

As resources are closed, the corresponding MQCLOSE call is issued. When QueueSession is closed, if connection pooling is enabled, the queue manager connection it encapsulates is returned to a connection pool maintained by the JMS implementation. If the queue manager connection is returned to the connection pool, then MQDISC is not issued at the time. The connection can then be reused the next time a QueueSession is created. The use of pooling is based on the configuration of the MQQueueConnectionFactory (see Chapter 6). When the QueueConnection is closed, any open sessions are closed. The connection pool is flushed once the number of active QueueConnections drops to zero. At this point, MQDISC calls are issued against any open queue manager connections, which disconnects the JMS client from the queue manager.

If the JMS client is using the publish-subscribe interface, the JMS calls map in much the same way to the MQI calls. The additional information associated with publish-subscribe is carried in a special command header that is populated and placed in the MQ message by the JMS implementation. These are processed by the message broker associated with the queue manager, which provides the subscription list and subscription-matching functions that publish-subscribe requires. Thus, the effect of using the publish-subscribe interface is simply a slightly differently formatted MQ message and some additional interaction (we discuss this in detail in the section "WebSphere Business Integration Message Broker").

Mapping JMS Messages to MQ Messages

Figure 5–4 depicts the basic philosophy associated with the way the WebSphere MQ JMS implementation maps JMS messages to MQ messages, and vice versa. In essence, JMS message header properties that have equivalent attributes in the MQMD of the MQ message are simply mapped. Those that do not, particularly application-specific properties, are copied to the RFH2 header. The JMS message body is copied to the MQ message body and placed after the RFH2 header.

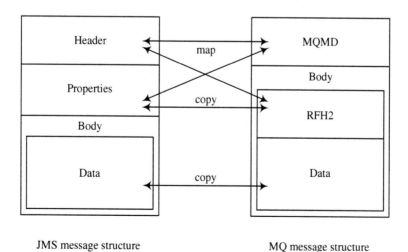

JMS message structure   MQ message structure

Figure 5-4 JMS Message to MQ Message Mapping

The RFH2 header is a WebSphere MQ header that is used to carry specific information about an MQ message. It is not only used for JMS-specific information, but also carries meta-data information about the physical format of the message body and command data for publish-subscribe commands, which are both used by the message broker. Its structure comprises a fixed portion and a variable portion. The fixed portion contains a number of fields which include identifier and data encoding information, and it is rendered as a record oriented structure. The variable portion contains a number of folders that define attributes using an XML-like syntax. An RFH2 created by the JMS implementation typically contains the following folders.

The <mcd> Folder   The <mcd> folder contains attributes that describe the structure of the message data contained in the MQ message. Though this information is not used by the queue manager, it is of great importance to the message broker because it identifies the location of physical format definitions in the broker's message repository, which the broker uses to parse retrieved messages. It contains four attributes that uniquely identify the location of the metadata: message service domain, message set, message type, and message format. The JMS implementation by default populates only the message service domain with the JMS message type: Text, Bytes, Stream, Map, or Object. This folder is always present in the RFH2 created by the JMS implementation.

If a BytesMessage or a TextMessage object is being sent and the JMS client knows that the message is destined for the message broker, it can choose to override the values set by default in the <mcd> folder with metadata identification attributes. It does this by setting the JMSType attribute of the message header using setJMSType (see Chapter 3). This takes as argument a provider-specific URL, as shown:

```
//set message repository attributes
//url: "mcd://domain/[set]/[type][?format=fmt]"
msg.setJMSType("mcd://mrm/setvalue/messageType?format=CWF");
```

The <jms> Folder   This folder is also always present in the JMS-created RFH2 and is used to transport JMS header fields and JMS standard properties (JMSX) that do not have a corresponding attribute in the MQMD.

The <usr> Folder   When application-specific properties are defined, they are transported in the <usr> folder. In the absence of any application-specific properties, the <usr> folder is not included in the JMS-created RFH2.

The <psc> Folder   The <psc> folder is used to convey publish-subscribe command messages and is only created and populated when the publish-subscribe interface is used.

The WebSphere MQ user guide "Using Java" referenced in Appendix D offers a detailed breakdown on how fields are mapped and how transformations are performed. There is no need to reiterate that information here, as quite frankly, a JMS developer need not understand the specifics to successfully develop JMS programs. The MQ message is created automatically by the JMS implementation, and the underlying structure is not exposed to the JMS developer. That is, after all, a big part of the value proposition of using the JMS API. However, as we see in Chapter

7, if the JMS client is going to knowingly communicate with a non-JMS client, then the understanding gained here of message structure and mapping relationships can be crucial.

WebSphere MQ Everyplace

WebSphere MQ Everyplace (WMQe) is a messaging provider that extends the functions of WebSphere MQ to mobile devices. It addresses the unique needs for pervasive devices offering a very small footprint and optimizations for unreliable networks. WebSphere MQ Everyplace was first introduced in October 1999 as MQSeries Everyplace and was similarly rebranded with the release of version 2.0 in December 2002 to WebSphere MQ Everyplace. It supports the same messaging semantics and quality of service delivery options as WebSphere MQ, but additionally introduces facilities peculiar to a mobile messaging environment. For instance, it supports the use of dial-up connections and unreliable wireless networks. However, it not only enables secure and reliable messaging between mobile applications, but also provides integration into WebSphere MQ messaging networks. For example, one of the fastest growing usage scenarios of WebSphere MQ Everyplace involves using it on point-of-sale systems in retail stores to pass sales transaction data to business applications connected to WebSphere MQ.

WebSphere MQ Everyplace is implemented differently from WebSphere MQ. WebSphere MQ provides an external component, the queue manager, which is configured and run independently of the application that uses its services. In contrast, WebSphere MQ Everyplace is implemented as a toolkit with which you develop messaging capabilities for your application, in effect embedding a personal queue manager in an application. The toolkit is implemented as a set of classes written in Java and provides an extensive framework for building queue managers, defining queues and channels, and creating and exchanging messages. The toolkit is also offered as a native C implementation for Windows Pocket PC platforms. Unfortunately, the scope and nature of the toolkit is such that a discussion of the framework and associated APIs is outside the scope of this book, so we do not delve any further into it here. However, we briefly examine the level of JMS support that is offered.

JMS Support

Though WebSphere MQ Everyplace provides an extensive class library for developing messaging applications, its use obviously requires detailed knowledge of the framework. The provision of a JMS implementation enables the messaging aspects of the application to be developed using a standard API. Support for JMS was thus introduced in WebSphere MQ Everyplace 2.0.

The JMS support is implemented as an extension to the existing WMQe class library, implementing the JMS API using the appropriate classes and methods in the underlying framework. As with WebSphere MQ, the glue lies in the implementation of the WMQe-administered objects. The JMS implementation is packaged as follows:

• MQeJMS.jar packages the JMS implementation classes.

- MQeBase.jar packages the WMQe toolkit.
- MQeJMSAdmin is a command line–based tool for creating JMS-administered objects.

The various supporting jars. such as jms.jar and jndi.jar, are not included in the package and can be obtained from a WebSphere MQ installation or alternatively downloaded from the Java home page (*http://java.sun.com/*).

At the time of this writing, the JMS implementation supports only the point-to-point interface. It also does not implement the MapMessage or StreamMessage interfaces, though as you recall from our discussion in Chapter 3, these were defined to address provider-specific compatibility issues with non-JMS clients and are implemented differently by each provider. In addition, there is no implementation of the TemporaryQueue interface, which means the JMS client cannot use QueueRequestor in request-reply scenarios (see Chapter 4). Finally, as would be expected' WebSphere MQ Everyplace does not implement the optional Application Server Facilities (ASF), since it is designed to be used in mobile devices rather than in J2EE components.

WebSphere Business Integration Message Broker

The WebSphere Business Integration Message Broker extends the connectivity and transport capabilities of the messaging providers by providing message brokering facilities. These take the form of message-processing services, including message transformation, message warehousing, and content-based routing. Message Broker also performs the role of a publish-subscribe broker, managing subscription requests and matching publications to interested subscribers. The publish-subscribe capabilities of Message Broker are also packaged in a separate offering called the WebSphere Business Integration Event Broker. This is aimed at customers who want to use only the publish-subscribe services offered by Message Broker and provides a subset of the functionality of Message Broker at a lower price point.

The brokers trace their lineage to January 2000 when MQSeries Integrator 2.0 first became available. MQSeries Integrator was rebranded to WebSphere MQ Integrator when version 2.1 was released in December 2001. The Integrator Broker packaging was released shortly after, and the Event Broker was released in July 2002. The brokers were rebranded again with the release of version 5 in June 2003 to their current name. The brokers lead the market in terms of market share and, as we see shortly, offer a flexible framework for the definition and execution of message-processing services. From a JMS perspective, we are primarily interested in the broker's support for publish-subscribe, as this rounds out the capability we require from the JMS provider. However, we will also see how a JMS client can directly take advantage of message processing services offered by the broker.

System Components

The technical architecture for both Event Broker and Message Broker is shown in Figure 5–5. For all intents and purposes, Event Broker and Message Broker are identical components except that Event Broker provides only a subset of Message Broker's function. The broker architecture can be thought of as comprising a broker runtime and definition tools.

Broker Runtime

A broker is a named entity that provides the operating environment that hosts and runs message-processing services. Message-processing services are defined as message flows, which are directed graphs (akin to flowcharts) that define a sequence of actions executed on receipt of a message by the broker. The actions that are orchestrated by the message flow are rendered in components called message-processing nodes. Message-processing nodes are prebuilt function libraries packaged as either system libraries (e.g., DLLs on the Windows platform) or jar files. The brokers ship with a number of supplied message-processing nodes that can be categorized as follows:

- Transport Access: Includes nodes that are capable of accessing the messaging transports that the broker supports for the retrieval and distribution of messages—for example, `MQInput` and `MQOutput` nodes for accessing WebSphere MQ.

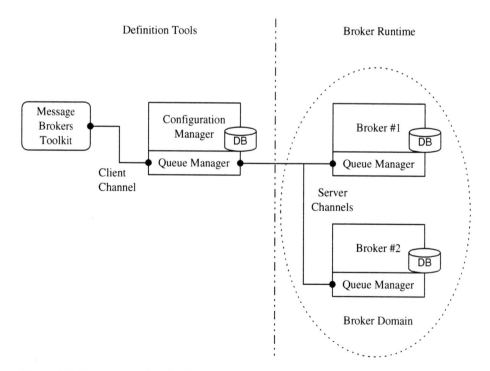

Figure 5-5 Message Broker Architecture

- Database Access: Nodes for inserting, updating, and deleting data from databases as well as a warehouse node, which warehouses all or part of a message received, typically with a timestamp, in a database table.
- Routing/Transformation: Nodes that effect the transformation of messages from one physical format to another and provide routing logic for messages based on content— for example, the Compute node, Mapping node, and Filter node.

Message-processing nodes are generally configured using property editors. A scripting language for computation, called ESQL, is also provided. Users additionally have the capability to write their own custom message-processing nodes and include them in message flows. Message flows run in the broker in runtime engines called execution groups; an execution group can host a number of message flows, and a broker can manage a number of execution groups. In addition, multiple instances of a given message flow can run in an execution group, providing excellent performance and scalability characteristics.

Message flows generally require access to one or more fields in a message, be it in the message headers or message body. The brokers provide message-parsing services, including parsers that can parse the WebSphere MQ headers. In addition, Message Broker includes a message repository that contains metadata (templates) called message sets, which describe the physical format of a given message. This metadata can be used to parse, validate, and indeed transform messages from one physical format to the other.

The broker is hosted by an MQ queue manager, which provides the broker with access to other components via WebSphere MQ. The broker also uses database tables to persist its configuration information. In general, applications invoke message flows by sending messages to the message flow over any of the transports that the message flow is capable of accessing. For instance, a message flow monitoring an MQ queue is triggered by the arrival of a message on that queue.

Definition Tools

The Message Brokers Toolkit for WebSphere Studio is a GUI tool that supports the creation of message flows and message sets (Figure 5–6). Through its interactions with the configuration manager, it also enables the configuration and control of the broker runtime. The configuration manager, as the name suggests, is responsible for storing and managing configuration data used to configure brokers that make up its broker domain. The configuration manager is hosted by an MQ queue manager, and the Toolkit communicates with the configuration manager using WebSphere MQ. The Toolkit uses a client connection to connect to the queue manager, allowing it to be sited on a machine remote from the configuration manager. The configuration manager also uses WebSphere MQ to communicate with the broker it is configuring. The use of WebSphere MQ as the communications transport enables the configuration manager to configure brokers in the same way regardless of the actual platform (operating system) the broker might be installed on. Currently, the broker runtime is supported on AIX, HP-UX, Linux, Solaris, Windows, and zOS, while the configuration manager and Toolkit are both Windows-based.

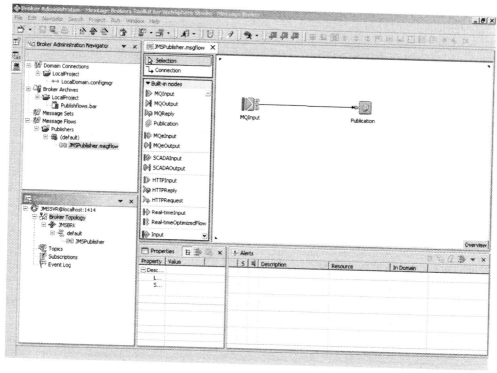

Figure 5-6 Message Brokers Toolkit for WebSphere Studio

A user's typical interaction with the Toolkit involves developing message flows and message sets, packaging developed assets into broker archive files, and then deploying the archive files to the broker. On deployment, the configuration manager creates and sends a configuration message to the broker, describing the message flows and message sets that are to be hosted by the broker runtime. The broker, on receipt of the message, updates its environment and acknowledges successful deployment by sending a reply back to the configuration manager. Once deployment is complete, the broker and configuration manager do not interact until the configuration manager initiates conversation again.

JMS Support

From a JMS perspective, our main interest in the broker is for its publish-subscribe capability. Coupled with the queue manager, the broker provides the JMS client with a JMS provider that supports both the point-to-point and publish-subscribe messaging domains. In fulfilling its publish-subscribe function, the broker allows publishers and subscribers to exchange messages over a number of messaging transports. In addition to WebSphere MQ, these include (Figure 5–7):

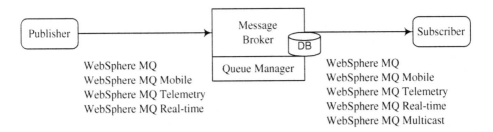

Figure 5-7 Publish-Subscribe Transport Protocols

- WebSphere MQ Mobile Transport, implemented by WebSphere MQ Everyplace for connecting applications running on mobile and wireless devices.
- WebSphere MQ Telemetry Transport for connecting remote devices through low-bandwidth communications.
- WebSphere MQ Real-time Transport for connecting messaging clients across the Internet and intranet.
- WebSphere MQ Multicast Transport, which extends the MQ Real-time Transport, optimizing network bandwidth when broadcasting messages to clients.

At the time of this writing, in addition to WebSphere MQ, the MQ Real-time and the MQ Multicast transports provide JMS implementations for the publish-subscribe interface and are thus accessible to the JMS client.

The MQ Real-time transport is a high-volume, high-performance transport that does not use queuing but rather provides a lightweight transport based on IP sockets. Its origins lie in work done by IBM Research in the efficient distribution of messages across wide area networks. This was done in support of sports-casting events such as the Olympics. It is thus an ideal transport for applications in which high-performance and large volumes are most important and transport robustness is noncritical, such as for online quotes and trading. The MQ Real-time Transport is accessible to JMS clients via the publish-subscribe interface only, and its implementation classes are packaged as part of the WebSphere MQ JMS implementation (in com.ibm.mqjms.jar).

Use of the MQ Real-time Transport by the JMS client does not involve any special programming considerations beyond the fact that since the MQ Real-time Transport has no queuing facilities, it cannot be used by durable subscribers. In addition, it does not support transactions or persistent messages. The choice of transport used by the JMS client (WebSphere MQ or MQ Real-time) is based on configuration attributes in the MQTopicConnectionFactory-administered object (see Chapter 6).

The MQ Multicast Transport optimizes the transmission of messages to subscribers using the MQ Real-time Transport. It allows the same message to be sent to multiple subscribers in one transmission (as opposed to sending the message to each subscriber separately). This can potentially save network bandwidth and is thus well suited to applications in which the same message is being received by a large number of subscribers. Once again, the JMS client takes advantage of this feature based on configuration attributes set in the MQTopicConnection-Factory-administered object. Its implementation classes are similarly packaged as part of the WebSphere MQ JMS implementation (in rmm.jar).

The broker's ability to publish messages—that is, to match publications to interested subscribers and subsequently deliver these messages to them—is encapsulated in the Publication node. The Publication node can be included in any message flow. However, a simple publish flow (such as would be deployed to Event Broker) contains an input node for the transport that is being published on and the Publication node. Figure 5–8 illustrates the process for a number of interacting JMS clients.

1. In the broker, we deploy a message flow in support of publications over WebSphere MQ comprising an MQInput node and a Publication node. The MQInput node is configured to monitor the queue on which the broker will receive publications (PUBQ). We also deploy a message flow in support of publications over the MQ Real-time Transport. The MQ Real-time Transport publication message flow contains a single node called the Real-timeOptimizedFlow node. This is provided as a performance optimization, combining the Real-timeInput node and Publication node into a single entity. The Real-timeOptimizedFlow node is configured to monitor a specified port for incoming transmissions.

2. JMS client S1 communicates with the broker using WebSphere MQ. When it issues TopicSession.createSubscriber(Topic), a subscription request message

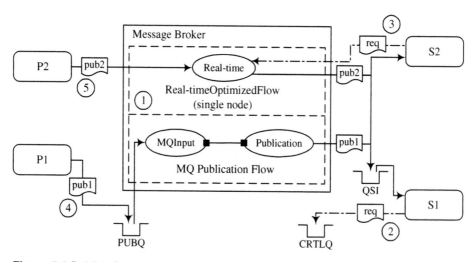

Figure 5-8 Publish-Subscribe

containing the topic string (T) and the queue (QS1) to which publications should be delivered is sent to the broker's control queue (CTRLQ). The broker processes the subscription request and stores the subscription in its database. The broker then sends a positive acknowledgment message back to client S1, and the message is processed by the JMS implementation. At this point, client S1 returns from the `createSubscriber` method call. Client S1 then monitors QS1 for arriving messages using, for instance, a `receive` call.

3. JMS client S2 communicates with the broker using the MQ Real-time Transport. Its API calls are identical to client S1's, but its subscription request is passed over IP to the hostname and port specified in the `MQTopicConnectionFactory`. The hostname and port correspond to the machine on which the broker is running and the port on which the `Real-timeOptimizedFlow` node is listening. The `Real-timeOptimizedFlow` node recognizes the incoming message as a subscription request and passes it to the broker for processing. Once the subscriber is successfully created, client S2 monitors the attached socket for incoming publications via a receive call.

4. JMS Client P1 creates a publisher and publishes a message on topic T, using WebSphere MQ. The act of publishing results in a message being sent to the publication queue (PUBQ), which is being monitored by the `MQInput` node of the publication message flow. The `MQInput` node retrieves the message and passes it to the publication node. The publication node ascertains that clients S1 and S2 are subscribed to topic T and sends a message to queue QS1 via WebSphere MQ for client S1 and to client S2 using the MQ Real-time Transport.

5. JMS client P2 similarly publishes a message on topic T, but this time using the MQ Real-time Transport. The message is received by the `Real-timeOptimizedFlow` node and similarly sent to clients S1 and S2.

By default, the broker discards a publication once it has sent the publication to all interested subscribers. However, the broker supports a publisher specifying that it wants the broker to keep or retain a copy of the publication (termed a retained publication). The publication is then sent to new subscribers who register an interest in the topic, ensuring that the subscriber does not have to wait for information to be published again before it receives it. For instance, with a retained publication, a subscriber registering an interest in a certain stock price would receive the current price straightaway without having to wait for the stock price to change and hence be republished. Unfortunately, JMS does not support the concept of retained publications, and thus this facility is not available to the JMS client. The broker additionally supports the concept of subscription points, which allow publications on the same topic to be differentiated by subscribers; for example, subscribers subscribing to a stock price could receive it in US dollars or in UK pounds. However, once again, JMS does not support this feature and it is thus not directly available to the JMS client.

Brokers can be grouped in entities called collectives. Brokers in a collective share their subscriptions, which enables publishers and subscribers to be connected to different brokers and still exchange publications. In addition, brokers can be cloned, allowing subscribing clients to be serviced by a secondary broker in the case of broker failure (see Chapter 8).

Besides acting as a publish-subscribe broker, Message Broker offers additional support for JMS in terms of providing parsers for JMS `MapMessage` and JMS `StreamMessage`. You may recall that with WebSphere MQ, the message bodies of map and stream messages are rendered using an XML format (see Chapter 3). Message Broker provides direct support for parsing such message bodies. In addition, if a JMS client wishes to associate its message content with metadata stored in Message Broker's message repository, it can do this by using the `setJM-SType` method and specifying a specifically formatted URL (see "Mapping JMS Messages to MQ Messages").

WebSphere Application Server

The WebSphere Application Server is a J2EE server that provides a highly extensible and scalable operating environment for J2EE components such as servlets, JSPs and EJBs. It also offers extensive support for Web services–based applications, implementing associated standards and extensions. First introduced in 1999, version 5 of the Application Server was released in October 2002 and is compliant with J2EE 1.3. It is offered in a number of packages to meet the needs of different users:

- *WebSphere Application Server Express* is focused on Web application development where the programming model does not include the use of EJBs. It provides the lowest cost of entry and supplies an operating environment for servlets and Java Server Pages (JSPs), but excludes support for EJBs.
- *WebSphere Application Server* supports the full J2EE environment, hosting servlets, JSPs, and EJBs. It is fully compliant with J2EE 1.3, providing support for message-driven beans (MDBs) and an embedded JMS provider implementation. It supports only a single server configuration.
- *WebSphere Application Server Network Deployment* adds additional quality of service features to the application server. It enables the creation of advanced deployment topologies, such as application server clusters. It also provides workload management and distributed administration functions.
- *WebSphere Application Server Enterprise* extends the application server with a number of programming extensions that enable very sophisticated applications to be built. These range from service-oriented architecture frameworks to process choreography for J2EE components and advanced transaction coordination models.

The WebSphere Application Server, as the operating environment for our J2EE-based JMS client, plays an important role in both the development and subsequent deployment of the JMS client. It implements a number of facilities and services, which we examine next.

JMS Support

We have already discussed the services a JMS client can expect from a J2EE 1.3–compliant server (see Chapter 4). These include support for MDBs and transaction management services, which the WebSphere Application Server implements. J2EE 1.3 additionally requires that a J2EE server provide an embedded JMS provider that can be installed as part of the J2EE server installation and managed by the J2EE server environment. WebSphere Application Server meets this requirement using the WebSphere JMS Provider, which is based on technology from WebSphere MQ and WebSphere Business Integration Event Broker. In addition, WebSphere Application Server provides JMS administrative facilities to WebSphere MQ and any generic JMS provider that implements the ASF component of the JMS specification. WebSphere Application Server Enterprise further extends the application server's JMS support by providing a programming framework that simplifies the development of J2EE-based JMS client applications.

Transaction Management and MDB Support

The WebSphere Application Server provides transaction management services, coordinating updates to JMS providers with other resource managers. It supports any JMS provider that implements ASF support, which defines the XA variants of the JMS interfaces. As discussed in Chapter 2, the J2EE server obtains the XA resource handle (encapsulated in the XASession) from the JMS client. WebSphere Application Server 5.0 uses a connection manager runtime component to provide the required services. Prior to version 5, version 4 of the application server provided a specific solution for WebSphere MQ in the form of a specific XAConnectionFactory type (more in Chapter 6) that included the necessary functions for the application server environment.

MDB support is implemented by the application server as a message listener service. The message listener service comprises a listener manager that manages a number of listeners. Each listener monitors a JMS destination (Queue or Topic) for incoming messages and notifies an identified MDB when a message arrives. The listener is associated with a listener port, which specifies the ConnectionFactory that is used to connect to the provider and the Destination that is to be monitored. Besides triggering the MDB, the listener is responsible for starting a transaction, if one is associated with the retrieval of the message. It also has automatic recovery features for handling JMS provider failures.

WebSphere JMS Provider (Embedded JMS Server)

The WebSphere JMS Provider meets the J2EE 1.3 requirement that a JMS provider be supplied as an integral part of the J2EE server. In contrast, WebSphere MQ would be considered an external JMS provider because it is installed, configured, and managed independently from the J2EE server. The WebSphere JMS Provider is based on WebSphere MQ and Event Broker, using WebSphere MQ to provide point-to-point distribution services, while the Event Broker handles publish-subscribe, supporting WebSphere MQ and the MQ Real-time Transport discussed earlier. In addition, it uses the same JMS implementation classes provided by WebSphere MQ. However, it has a reduced footprint, and as we see, less functionality than the individual products on which it is based.

The provider is installed and managed as part of the application server, with all configuration and administration being done via the application server's administration console or scripting tool. None of the administration tools associated with WebSphere MQ and Event Broker are installed, and from a usage perspective, none of the underlying technology is exposed to the user. The provider is implemented by a component called the JMS server, which hosts the broker runtime and manages the queue manager processes. It is responsible for stopping and starting the broker and queue manager, and also controls the creation and deletion of WebSphere MQ resources such as MQ queues. As shown in Figure 5–9, the JMS server runs in the application server Java Virtual Machine (JVM) in a single server configuration. In a network deployment configuration (involving multiple servers) the JMS server runs in its own dedicated JVM.

The WebSphere JMS Provider is designed to support communication between JMS clients only. JMS servers run standalone and cannot be configured to communicate with each other or interoperate with WebSphere MQ. This obviously limits the topologies that can be implemented to support distributed messaging. Because it insulates the user from the underlying technology, it provides preconfigured services, facilitating ease of use. The flipside to this is that little or no access is provided to performance-tuning options for the underlying broker or queue manager.

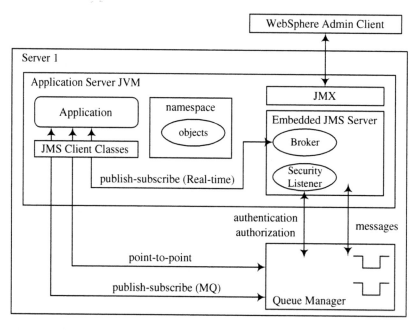

Figure 5-9 JMS Server: Single Server Configuration

With these restrictions in mind, in WebSphere Application Server 5.0, the WebSphere JMS Provider is best suited to unit test environments or for small projects with limited scope. It has the advantage of requiring no separate installation or configuration and is tightly integrated into the application server management environment, utilizing the same security model and problem determination infrastructure as other J2EE components. It thus provides an ideal messaging engine for a developer with no WebSphere MQ or Event Broker experience, or for a user new to messaging with a simple project. Enterprise messaging infrastructure, however, generally requires the flexibility and robustness offered by WebSphere MQ-based and Message/Event Broker-based solutions, including their ability to support both JMS and non-JMS clients. In the instance when the WebSphere JMS Provider is used for a unit test environment, and WebSphere MQ is used for system test and production environments. It is important to remember that the JMS client application can be deployed unchanged to the new JMS provider. The only difference is in the type of administered object it ultimately retrieves, which as you will recall from our discussion in Chapter 4 is completely transparent to the JMS client.

JMS Administration Facilities

The WebSphere Application Server, through its administration console, enables the creation of JMS-administered objects in the application server's federated namespace. This facility is extended to three defined JMS providers:

- **WebSphere JMS Provider:** This is the embedded JMS server, and the console supports the creation and configuration of WebSphere JMS-administered objects in the WebSphere namespace. It is useful to note that WebSphere JMS-administered objects can be stored only in the WebSphere namespace. No other JNDI namespace is supported.
- **WebSphere MQ JMS Provider:** This refers to the WebSphere MQ JMS implementation, and the console similarly supports the creation and configuration of WebSphere MQ JMS-administered objects. It additionally exposes WebSphere Application Server-specific properties for XA, security, and resource pool configuration. It provides a ready alternative to using jmsadmin, the command line-based tool included with WebSphere MQ. However, unlike jmsadmin, the console stores administered objects only in the WebSphere namespace.
- **Generic JMS Provider:** This can be any JMS provider that implements ASF support. In this case, the administration console does not directly create provider-specific administered objects in the WebSphere namespace. Instead, it creates local JNDI aliases for the JMS-administered objects, which are stored in an external namespace. This allows applications to still use the namespace provided by the application server, with the application server taking responsibility for accessing the external namespace where the real objects are stored. This facility provides a useful alternative in the case where we have decided to store our WebSphere MQ JMS–administered objects in a

different name space, such as in an LDAP server. We populate the LDAP server using WebSphere MQ–supplied tools (jmsadmin) and then access them from within the WebSphere namespace by registering WebSphere MQ as a generic JMS provider.

In Chapter 6 we examine JMS-administered objects and explore the use of these tools in more detail.

Extended Messaging Service

WebSphere Application Server Enterprise 5.0 provides a programming model called Extended Messaging Service for implementing messaging applications based on EJBs. The programming model combines a number of tooling and runtime extensions to simplify and automate the creation of messaging applications based on the messaging interaction patterns we discussed in Chapter 1: message producer, message consumer, and request-reply. It also implements approaches to dealing with the implementation considerations we discussed in Chapters 1 and 4, such as implementing request-reply and handling late replies. It essentially encapsulates the JMS API, automating the creation of JMS code.

Extended Messaging Service introduces two types of messaging beans: the sender bean and the receiver bean. The sender bean is a session EJB that implements either the message producer pattern or the request-reply pattern variation, where the requester waits for its own replies. The receiver bean is implemented using either an MDB or a session EJB, which can be called by an application to receive messages (called an *application callable receiver bean*). Extended messaging also introduces message-handling facilities, which reduce the burden of message definition when communicating between JMS clients written to the model. It allows the application to call a sender bean with a sequence of objects, which are then written to a JMS StreamMessage. The StreamMessage is tagged with a format tag (stored in JMSType) and sent. On receipt of the message, the receiver bean unpacks the StreamMessage based on the associated format definition identified by JMSType and passes the appropriate set of objects to the target application. Extended messaging also introduces some additional definition constructs called input and output ports, which encapsulate JMS provider and destination information used by the messaging beans (similar to listener ports used by MDBs).

WebSphere Application Server Enterprise is required to take advantage of extended messaging runtime services. Associated tooling, including resource wizards, are packaged in WebSphere Studio Application Developer Integration Edition 5.0. A number of useful references on using this programming model to implement messaging applications are included in Appendix D.

Summary

JMS specifies an API, which messaging providers implement. In this chapter we examined a number of JMS providers implemented by the IBM WebSphere software platform. We began by reviewing the WebSphere software platform, which addresses through its constituent product families the middleware infrastructure needs for the enterprise. We then examined a number of software components, with particular focus on their support for JMS.

WebSphere MQ is a messaging provider that enables communication between disparate applications, on disparate platforms, across disparate network protocols. We detailed its JMS implementation, noting that because it predates JMS, its implementation is built as an extension to its existing services. We then examined WebSphere MQ Everyplace, which extends WebSphere MQ to mobile devices, and similarly reviewed its JMS implementation. We rounded out our review of messaging infrastructure with a review of the WebSphere Business Integration Message Broker and Event Broker, which provide message brokering services, including publish-subscribe, message transformation, and content-based routing facilities.

We completed our discussions with a detailed examination of the operating environment provided for the J2EE-based JMS client by the WebSphere Application Server. We detailed its support for transaction management and MDBs, examined its implementation of a native JMS provider, and considered its support for external JMS providers such as WebSphere MQ. We also reviewed a programming model provided by the application server for implementing EJB-based messaging applications.

Now that we have a general understanding of the JMS provider implementations offered by IBM WebSphere, in the next chapter we examine the administered objects that enable the JMS client to avail itself of the services of these providers.

CHAPTER 6

IBM JMS–
Administered
Objects

A dministered objects, first discussed in Chapter 2, "Java Message Service," contain provider-specific information that allows the JMS client to access the services of the JMS provider. Defined by the `ConnectionFactory` and `Destination` objects, administered objects provide the glue that binds the JMS client to the provider's environment. In this chapter, we focus on the administered objects associated with two IBM JMS providers: the WebSphere JMS Provider and the WebSphere MQ JMS Provider. The WebSphere JMS Provider is supplied as an integral part of the WebSphere Application Server, while the WebSphere MQ JMS Provider comprises WebSphere MQ and WebSphere Business Integration Message Broker (see Chapter 5, "IBM JMS Providers"). We examine the `ConnectionFactory` and `Destination` objects associated with these providers and review tools available for the creation and population of these objects in JNDI namespaces.

Administered Objects Revisited

Administered objects provide the basis for the JMS client to access the services of the JMS provider. As shown in Table 6–1, they are defined for each of the interfaces specified by JMS.

Table 6–1 Administered Objects

Common (Parent)	Point-to-Point	Publish-Subscribe
ConnectionFactory	QueueConnectionFactory	TopicConnectionFactory
Destination	Queue	Topic

The `ConnectionFactory` contains the attributes that enable a connection to the provider to be established, and as you recall from Chapter 4, "Using the JMS API," one of the first things the JMS client does is retrieve a `ConnectionFactory` from a JNDI namespace, as shown:

```
//connect to JNDINamespace
Context ctx = new InitialContext();
...
//retrieve QueueConnectionFactory
QueueConnectionFactory factory =
(QueueConnectionFactory)ctx.lookup("jms.book.QCF");
```

In this example, `jms.book.QCF` references a provider-specific `ConnectionFactory` (in this case, `QueueConnectionFactory`) stored in a JNDI namespace. To protect the JMS client's portability, we do not explicitly handle the provider-specific `ConnectionFactory` type but rather cast the retrieved object to the generic interface `QueueConnectionFactory`, which the provider-specific object extends. A similar process is undertaken for the `TopicConnectionFactory`.

Before it can process messages, the JMS client retrieves a `Destination` object (`Queue` or `Topic`), which specifies a location to which messages can be sent or from which they can be retrieved:

```
//retrieve Queue
Queue outQ = (Queue)ctx.lookup("jms.book.Q");
```

Once again, the retrieved provider-specific object is cast to the parent interface, in this case a `Queue`.

The objects retrieved represent provider-specific implementations of the administered objects and are stored in JNDI namespaces using provider-specific tools. In the following sections we examine these provider-specific implementations defined for the WebSphere JMS and WebSphere MQ JMS Providers.

WebSphere JMS Provider (Embedded JMS Server)

Recall from our discussions in Chapter 5 that the WebSphere JMS Provider is supplied as an integral part of the WebSphere Application Server in accordance with J2EE 1.3. Though based on WebSphere MQ and Event Broker, it has less functionality than the software components on which it is based. Most importantly, it does not expose its underlying implementation to the user. Thus, administration tools normally associated with these components are not made available, and creation of all resources, such as MQ queues, is handled internally by the implementation. This is reflected in the attributes exposed in its administered objects, as they define a relatively simple set of attributes that require no detailed knowledge of the JMS provider implementation.

WebSphere QueueConnectionFactory

The WebSphere `QueueConnectionFactory` provides the basis for the JMS client to establish a connection to the WebSphere JMS Provider using the point-to-point interface. It defines a relatively simple set of attributes, listed in Table 6–2.

Table 6–2 Properties: WebSphere QueueConnectionFactory

Attributes	Description
Name	Specifies the name used to display the `QueueConnectionFactory` in the admin console.
JNDI Name	Specifies the name used by the JMS client to retrieve the object definition.
Description	Defines an optional description string, which can be used to document the purpose of the `QueueConnectionFactory`.
Category	An optional string that classifies or groups the `QueueConnectionFactory`.
Node	Specifies the location of the JMS server that this `QueueConnectionFactory` represents. The value corresponds to the name of the WebSphere node (machine) where the JMS server is installed and defaults to `localhost`. All connections based on this `QueueConnectionFactory` will connect to the JMS server at the location specified. Note that the JMS server provides a TCP/IP port for incoming client connections. This port is not specified in the `QueueConnectionFactory` but rather is part of the JMS server configuration.
Component-Managed Authentication Alias	Lists an optional J2C Authentication Data entry, which defines a user ID and password. The user ID and password are used by the application to authenticate the creation of a connection. The use of this option is dependent on global security being switched on in the application server. In addition, the authentication setting for the resource reference in the EJB or servlet that specifies this `QueueConnectionFactory` must be set to `application`. The use of this option is clearly tied to the security model adopted for applications running in the application server, and further details can be found in the references listed in Appendix D.
Container-Managed Authentication Alias	Similarly lists an optional J2C Authentication Data entry, which defines a user ID and password. It has the same usage constraints as the Component-Managed Authentication Alias. However, in this case the entry is referred to only if the authentication setting for the resource reference is set to `Container`. As might be expected, authentication is carried out by the `Container`.
XA-Enabled	If set, connections created from this factory can be enlisted as part of an XA global transaction. By default, it is set to `enabled`.
Connection Pools	Exposes settings for configuring the connection pool associated with the `QueueConnections` derived from this factory.
Session Pools	Exposes settings for configuring the session pool associated with the `QueueSessions` derived from this factory.

From the perspective of the JMS client, a number of attributes merit further discussion. In order to locate the `QueueConnectionFactory`, the JMS client must specify the value represented by JNDI Name or some other variable that eventually resolves to that value. As we see in Chapter 7, "JMS Implementation Scenarios," the WebSphere Application Server allows resource references to be defined for the application, which refer to the JNDI names of objects in its namespace. This provides a layer of indirection as the application searches the namespace using the name of the resource reference, and the container resolves the resource reference to the actual JNDI name. This allows the administered object retrieved by the JMS client to be changed without changing the actual client code. The resource reference additionally provides a basis for defining authentication controls.

The Node attribute is critical to establishing the location of the JMS server and defaults to `localhost`, which assumes the client is running on the same machine as the provider. The JMS server defines a single TCP/IP port for incoming client connections, and thus the TCP/IP port value is not exposed in the administered object.

Runtime properties such as XA-Enabled and the Connection Pool settings allow the appropriate transaction context and performance characteristics to be set. Related to the `QueueConnectionFactory` object definition is a set of optional J2C authentication data entries, which are used to define authentication aliases.

WebSphere TopicConnectionFactory

JMS clients using the publish-subscribe interface utilize the WebSphere `TopicConnection-Factory` to establish their connection to the WebSphere JMS Provider. It contains the same attributes as the WebSphere `QueueConnectionFactory` (Table 6–2), but has additional attributes, listed in Table 6–3, specific to the provider's support for publish-subscribe.

Table 6–3 Properties: WebSphere TopicConnectionFactory

Attributes	Description
Name	Specifies the name used to display the `TopicConnectionFactory` in the admin console.
JNDI Name	Specifies the name used by the JMS client to retrieve the object definition.
Description	Defines an optional description string, which can be used to document the purpose of the `TopicConnectionFactory`.
Category	An optional string that classifies or groups the `TopicConnectionFactory`.
Node	Specifies the location of the JMS server that this `TopicConnectionFactory` represents. The value corresponds to the name of the WebSphere node (machine) where the JMS server is installed and defaults to `localhost`.
	All connections based on this `TopicConnectionFactory` will connect to the JMS server at the location specified. Note that the JMS server provides a TCP/IP port for incoming client connections. This port is not specified in the `TopicConnectionFactory` but rather is part of the JMS server configuration.

Table 6–3 Properties: WebSphere TopicConnectionFactory (*continued*)

Attributes	Description
Port*	Refers to the transport (and thus TCP/IP port) that will be accessed by publishers or subscribers on connection to the provider. Its value (QUEUED or DIRECT) corresponds to the transports supported by the underlying Event Broker for publish-subscribe:WebSphere MQ and the MQ Real-time Transport. The default value for Port is QUEUED.
ClientID*	This is required if the TopicConnectionFactory is used to define durable subscribers.
Clone Support*	Normal JMS behavior allows only one active durable subscriber to a subscription. In an application server environment that is cloned, setting this attribute to ENABLED allows cloned durable subscribers to share the same durable subscription; i.e., a given publication will be sent to only one of them, facilitating workload balancing. It is set to DISABLED by default.
Component-Managed Authentication Alias	Lists an optional J2C authentication data entry, which defines a user ID and password. The user ID and password are used by the application to authenticate the creation of a connection. The use of this option is dependent on global security being switched on in the application server. In addition, the authentication setting for the resource reference in the EJB or servlet that specifies this TopicConnectionFactory must be set to application. The use of this option is clearly tied to the security model adopted for applications running in the application server, and further details can be found in the references listed in Appendix D.
Container-Managed Authentication Alias	Similarly lists an optional J2C authentication data entry, which defines a user ID and password. It has the same usage constraints as the Component-Managed Authentication Alias. However, in this case the entry is only referred to if the authentication setting for the resource reference is set to Container. As might be expected, authentication is carried out by the Container.
XA-Enabled	If set, connections created from this factory can be enlisted as part of an XA global transaction. By default, it is set to enabled.
Connection Pools	Exposes settings for configuring the connection pool associated with the TopicConnections derived from this factory.
Session Pools	Exposes settings for configuring the session pool associated with the TopicSessions derived from this factory.

* Unique to WebSphere TopicConnectionFactory.

A JMS client that uses a TopicConnectionFactory with Port set to DIRECT cannot define a durable subscriber because the MQ Real-time Transport does not provide a queuing mechanism or support for persistent messages. The actual machine port associated with each transport is defined as part of the JMS server configuration.

Inline with JMS recommended practice, the WebSphere `TopicConnectionFactory` is used to store the client identifier attribute. Recall from Chapter 4 that JMS introduces the concept of the client identifier as a means for the provider to associate durable subscriptions with related connections.

A similar set of related properties for pool configuration and authentication data are defined for the `TopicConnectionFactory`.

WebSphere Queue

The WebSphere `Queue` implements the `Queue`-administered object, defining a message destination for the point-to-point interface. It defines a simple set of attributes, shown in Table 6–4.

Table 6–4 Properties: WebSphere Queue

Attributes	Description
Name	Specifies the name used to display the `Queue` object in the tooling. This is a required property.
JNDI Name	Specifies the name used by the JMS client to retrieve the object definition. This is a required property.
Description	Defines an optional description string, which can be used to document the purpose of the `Queue` object.
Category	An optional string that classifies or groups the `Queue` object.
Persistence	Specifies whether the messages sent to this destination are persistent, nonpersistent, or have their persistence defined by the client application. It defaults to `APPLICATION DEFINED`.
Priority	Defines whether the priority of the message is specified by the application or by the Specified Priority attribute. It defaults to `APPLICATION DEFINED`.
Specified Priority	If Priority is set to `SPECIFIED`, then the value here defines the priority of the message. It takes as value an integer ranging from 0 to 9, where 0 is the lowest and 9 the highest priority.
Expiry	Defines if the message expiry is specified by the application by the associated attribute, Specified Expiry, or is `UNLIMITED` (messages on this queue never expire). It similarly defaults to `APPLICATION DEFINED`.
Specified Expiry	If Expiry is set to `SPECIFIED`, then the value here specifies the number of milliseconds after which messages on this queue expire. Valid values are any long value greater than zero.

The WebSphere JMS Provider uses the WebSphere Queue to override values for persistence, priority, and expiry that are specified by the client when sending the message. This allows JMS administrators to enforce company policy, ensure adopted best practice, or change the behavior of the client without having to change code (see Chapter 3).

Once the WebSphere Queue has been defined, it must be added to the JMS server's list of queues. This involves modifying the application server's configuration file and enables the JMS server to create the underlying queue that the administered object represents. We see how this is done in Chapter 7.

WebSphere Topic

The WebSphere Topic bears a close resemblance to the WebSphere Queue and has the same attributes. However, it introduces one new attribute related to its publish-subscribe function, as shown in Table 6–5.

Table 6–5 Properties: WebSphere Topic

Attributes	Description
Name	Specifies the name used to display the Topic object in the tooling. This is a required property.
JNDI Name	Specifies the name used by the JMS client to retrieve the object definition. This is a required property.
Description	Defines an optional description string, which can be used to document the purpose of the Topic object.
Category	An optional string that classifies or groups the Topic object.
Topic*	Contains the topic name that serves to bind publishers and subscribers together.
Persistence	Specifies whether the messages sent to this destination are persistent, nonpersistent, or have their persistence defined by the client application. It defaults to APPLICATION DEFINED.
Priority	Defines whether the priority of the message is specified by the application or by the Specified Priority attribute. It defaults to APPLICATION DEFINED.
Specified Priority	If Priority is set to SPECIFIED, then the value here defines the priority of the message. It takes as value an integer ranging from 0 to 9, where 0 is the lowest and 9 the highest priority.
Expiry	Defines if the message expiry is specified by the application by the associated attribute. Specified Expiry, or is UNLIMITED (messages never expire). It similarly defaults to APPLICATION DEFINED.

Table 6–5 Properties: WebSphere Topic (*continued*)

Attributes	Description
Specified Expiry	If Expiry is set to SPECIFIED, then the value here specifies the number of milliseconds after which messages at this destination expire. Valid values are any long value greater than zero.

* Unique to WebSphere Topic

JMS does not specify the format of the topic name, and thus the string format associated with the Topic attribute is provider-specific. The WebSphere JMS and WebSphere MQ JMS providers adopt a tree-like hierarchy for topic names, enabling categories and subcategories to be defined. A forward slash (/) is used to separate levels in the tree: for example, London/Temp/Celsius and London/Temp/Fahrenheit define two valid topic names.

Topic names specified for subscribers have the option of including wildcards, defined by # and +. The # wildcard matches multiple levels in a topic; the + wildcard matches a single level. Continuing with our previous example, if a subscriber wishes to receive publications on London's temperature in both Celsius and Fahrenheit, its topic could specify London/Temp/+. Note that publishers cannot publish on a Topic whose name contains wildcards.

The design of the Topic name hierarchy, and the design decisions that go into deciding how information is categorized, is probably one of the most underestimated efforts associated with utilizing publish-subscribe messaging. It is highly application-dependent and should be undertaken as early as possible in the project.

WebSphere MQ JMS Provider

WebSphere MQ and WebSphere Business Integration Message Broker (or Event Broker) together provide the JMS client with a JMS provider that supports both the point-to-point and publish-subscribe messaging domains. As discussed in Chapter 5, their support for JMS is implemented by a set of Java classes that essentially translate JMS API calls to the appropriate set of proprietary API calls defined by WebSphere MQ and the other Message Broker transports (MQ Real-time and Multicast).

Consequently, you will note that the attributes associated with the WebSphere MQ–administered objects expose terms and options specific to the underlying implementation and thus require some knowledge of WebSphere MQ and Message Broker to be appropriately configured. It is also important to remember that the administered objects are referring to external resources such as queue managers, queues, or message flows, which have to be defined using the supplied provider-specific administration tools. With this in mind, I would argue that in enterprise projects the WebSphere MQ system administrator should be responsible for creating the JMS-administered objects, especially in situations where the JMS client developer does not know WebSphere MQ. That being said, it is useful to note that since the WebSphere MQ–administered objects supply useful defaults for most of their attributes, configuring them can be fairly simple, as we see shortly.

MQQueueConnectionFactory

The `MQQueueConnectionFactory` defines a factory object for creating connections to WebSphere MQ via the point-to-point interface. It encapsulates a wealth of configuration options for connecting to an MQ queue manager, which to facilitate our discussion I have split into basic and advanced properties.

The basic properties shown in Table 6–6 define all that is required to successfully connect to an MQ queue manager. The default values supplied mean that the only property you are explicitly required to define is the name of the `MQQueueConnectionFactory`. Using the resulting `MQQueueConnectionFactory` object (accepting all defaults) results in a local connection to the default MQ queue manager on the machine where the JMS client runs.

Table 6–6 Basic Properties: MQQueueConnectionFactory

Attributes	Description
NAME	Specifies the name of the object. This is the name used to retrieve the factory from the JNDI namespace.
DESCRIPTION	Defines an optional description string, which can be used to document the purpose of the `QueueConnectionFactory`.
QMANAGER	Specifies the name of the MQ queue manager to which a connection will be established. If left blank, which is its default, the default queue manager on the machine will be used.
TRANSPORT	Defines the type of connection that will be established with the queue manager: a client or local connection. It has two valid values, `BIND` and `CLIENT`. `BIND`, which is the default value, results in a local connection being created, which requires that the JMS client run on the same physical machine as the queue manager. `CLIENT` creates a client connection, allowing the JMS client to run on a machine remote from the queue manager. When `CLIENT` is specified, then the `HOSTNAME`, `PORT`, and `CHANNEL` attributes become mandatory.
HOSTNAME	This is only relevant if `TRANSPORT` is set to `CLIENT` and takes a machine name or IP address as value. By default it is set to `localhost`.
PORT	Specifies the TCP/IP port on which the queue manager listens for incoming client connections. The port specified should match the listener port configured for the target queue manager. It defaults to 1414, which is the default port for the queue manager listener.

Table 6–6 Basic Properties: MQQueueConnectionFactory (*continued*)

Attributes	Description
CHANNEL	Specifies the name of the server connection channel (SVRCONN), which is the WebSphere MQ network abstraction used by the client connection to communicate with the queue manager. It defaults to a standard SVRCONN channel defined by all queue managers: SYSTEM.DEF.SVRCONN.
LOCALADDRESS	Defines the local address to be used by the outbound client connection (TRANSPORT = CLIENT). It defaults to null. Typically, you allow this to be assigned automatically when the socket is created, but should you need to have the socket bound to a specific address and port, you specify it here. This might be required when the client connection needs to go out through a firewall that only accepts connections originating from defined ports. It takes as argument an IP address or hostname and optionally a port or range of ports. Specifying a range of ports is recommended for MQ JMS clients to allow for connections required internally by the implementation: e.g., 9.123.4.56(3000, 4000).

Certain dependencies exist among the attributes; for example, if TRANSPORT is set to CLIENT, then HOSTNAME, PORT, and CHANNEL must be specified. Table 6–7 details the relatively straightforward dependencies among these attributes:

Table 6–7 Transport Dependencies: MQQueueConnectionFactory

Transport	QMANAGER	HOSTNAME	PORT	CHANNEL
BIND (default)	–	n/a	n/a	n/a
CLIENT	–	–	–	–

Even though default values are specified, it must be remembered that they refer to resources that must physically exist in the underlying provider. Thus, the value of QMANAGER must match the name of an existing MQ queue manager, and if left blank, an MQ queue manager defined as the default queue manager must exist on that machine. Similarly, if using a client connection, the value of PORT and CHANNEL must match settings and resources already specified for the target MQ queue manager. Note that the default value for CHANNEL maps to a resource that is automatically created by the queue manager on its creation.

Table 6–8 lists what I have termed advanced properties for the MQQueueConnectionFactory. These attributes further configure the behavior of the connection, exploiting a number of WebSphere MQ-specific features as well as exposing certain details about how JMS behavior is implemented. Note that an in-depth understanding of some of the listed properties requires a deeper understanding of WebSphere MQ than can be contained in this book. Useful references are listed in Appendix D; they provide further insight into the workings of Web-Sphere MQ.

Table 6–8 Advanced Properties: MQQueueConnectionFactory

Attributes	Description
USECONNPOOLING	If set to yes, connections to the queue manager (encapsulated in JMS Session objects) are pooled. Alternative value is no. It is, however, set to yes by default.
POLLINGINT	When MessageListeners are used, this controls how often the receivers are checked (polled) for incoming messages. The interval is specified in milliseconds and defaults to 5000.
MSGBATCHSZ	Used to specify the maximum number of messages that can be retrieved from a queue in one packet by the asynchronous delivery mechanism, which supports the use of message listeners. It defaults to 10.
MSGRETENTION[*]	It controls whether unwanted messages are kept on the queue by the ConnectionConsumer and takes as value yes or no. The default is yes.
RESCANINT	Selection of messages using a message selector typically requires the implementation to browse the queue and then get the matching message. Because it is possible for new messages to arrive behind the browse cursor, RESCANINT defines the interval in milliseconds when the browse cursor gets reset to the beginning of the queue. It defaults to 5000 milliseconds.
TEMPMODEL[*]	The creation of MQ queues dynamically (as is required when using the TemporaryQueue object) is based upon a model queue. The model queue provides a template for queue creation, detailing desired configuration options. Specify here the name of the MQ model queue that should be used. Its value defaults to one created automatically by the queue manager: SYSTEM.DEFAULT.MODEL.QUEUE.
TEMPQPREFIX[*]	This prefix is applied to the name of any temporary MQ queues that are created dynamically in support of JMS temporary queues. It defaults to AMQ.* (CSQ.* on z/OS) and can be any string. It must, however, end in an asterisk (*) and must be no more than 33 characters including the asterisk.
FAILIFQUIESCE	A queue manager cannot execute a controlled shutdown if applications are connected to it. Setting this option to yes allows the queue manager to deny service to the client application once it has started shutting down. This is done in response to a service call made by the client, and on receipt, the client disconnects from the queue manager, allowing it to shut down. If set to no, the queue manager will not shut down until the client disconnects of its own free will. By default it is set to yes.
SSLCIPHERSUITE	Specifies the cipher suite to be used for securing the client connection. This property is only relevant if the TRANSPORT property is set to CLIENT.

Table 6–8 Advanced Properties: MQQueueConnectionFactory (*continued*)

Attributes	Description
SSLPEERNAME	Defines a distinguished name, which must match that specified for the queue manager. Its value is only significant if SSLCIPHERSUITE has been set.
SSLCRL	Specifies the LDAP server that should be used for SSL certificate revocation checking. Its value is only significant if SSLCIPHERSUITE has been set.
CCSID	The default coded-character set that should be used for MQ messages resulting from this connection. It defaults to 819, which is ASCII.
SYN-CPOINTALLGETS	If set to yes, then messages are retrieved under local transaction control, irrespective of what the JMS client actually specifies.
CLIENTID	While exposed by the MQQueueConnectionFactory, it has little relevance here, as it is only used by the MQTopicConnectionFactory for durable subscribers.
VERSION	Internal version number for the implementation. It is currently set to 2. This attribute can be ignored.
RECEXIT	WebSphere MQ supports a number of exits that can be called when using a client connection. This defines the fully qualified class name of the receive exit, which is called after data is received over the client connection.
RECEXITINIT	An initialization string for the receive exit, passed to the class constructor for the exit.
SECEXIT	The fully qualified class name of the security exit. This was the only option available to authenticate the client connection prior to the introduction of SSL support.
SECEXITINT	An initialization string for the security exit, passed to the class constructor for the exit.
SENDEXIT	The fully qualified class name of the send exit, which is called before data is sent over the client connection.
SENDEXITINIT	An initialization string for the send exit, passed to the class constructor for the exit.

* Unique to MQQueueConnectionFactory.

As you can see, quite a few additional properties are exposed ranging from performance tuning to security configuration. We discussed how the connection pooling facility works in Chapter 5, when we examined the mapping of the JMS API to the MQI. The Session object encapsulates the connection to the MQ queue manager, and when it is closed the queue manager connection is pooled by the JMS implementation and reused if a new `Session` is requested. Note that the properties of the pool itself, such as its size, are not exposed.

With the `FAILIFQUIESCE` property set to yes, the JMS client will catch a JMS exception in response to its service call if the queue manager is executing a controlled shutdown. Handling the exception, the JMS client should then close the `Session` and `Connection` to disconnect from the queue manager.

In Chapter 7, "JMS Implementation Scenarios," we examine the use of SSL to secure client connections in some detail and discuss appropriate values for the SSL-related properties then.

MQTopicConnectionFactory

The JMS client, using the publish-subscribe interface, retrieves the `MQTopicConnection-Factory`, which provides access to all the transports supported by Message Broker for publish-subscribe: WebSphere MQ, MQ Real-time, and MQ Multicast. As might be expected, it shares quite a few properties with the `MQQueueConnectionFactory` and introduces a number of properties unique to the publish-subscribe messaging domain. Once again, I have split these into basic (Table 6-9) and advanced properties to facilitate our discussion.

Table 6-9 Basic Properties: MQTopicConnectionFactory

Attributes	Description
NAME	Specifies the name of the object. This is the name used to retrieve the factory from the JNDI namespace.
DESCRIPTION	Defines an optional description string, which can be used to document the purpose of the `TopicConnectionFactory`.
QMANAGER	Specifies the name of the MQ queue manager to which a connection will be established. If left blank, the default queue manager on the machine will be used.
TRANSPORT[*]	Defines the type of connection that will be established with the queue manager or message broker: a client or local connection. It has four valid values: BIND, CLIENT, DIRECT,[†] and DIRECTHTTP.[†]
	BIND, which is the default value, results in a local connection to the queue manager being created, which requires that the JMS client run on the same physical machine as the queue manager.
	CLIENT creates a client connection, allowing the JMS client to run on a machine remote from the queue manager. When CLIENT is specified, then the HOSTNAME, PORT, and CHANNEL attributes become mandatory.
	DIRECT[†] connects the client to the Message Broker via the MQ Real-time Transport. It does not use any WebSphere MQ resources, but requires HOSTNAME and PORT to be set.
	DIRECTHTTP[†] tunnels over the MQ Real-time Transport using HTTP. It connects to the Message Broker at the location identified by HOSTNAME and PORT.

Table 6–9 Basic Properties: MQTopicConnectionFactory (*continued*)

Attributes	Description
HOSTNAME	This is only relevant if TRANSPORT is set to CLIENT, DIRECT, or DIRECTHTTP. It takes a machine name or IP address as value. By default it is set to localhost.
PORT	Specifies the TCP/IP port on which the queue manager listens for incoming client connections. If TRANSPORT is set to CLIENT, the port specified should match the listener port configured for the target queue manager. It defaults to 1414, which is the default port for the queue manager listener. If TRANSPORT is set to DIRECT or DIRECTHTTP, the port specified should match the port specified in the Real-timeInput node (or Real-timeOpti-mizedFlow node) running in the Message Broker. It defaults to 1506, which is the default port for the Real-timeInput node (or Real-timeOptimized-Flow node)
CHANNEL	Specifies the name of the server connection channel (SVRCONN), which is the WebSphere MQ network abstraction used by the client connection to communi-cate with the queue manager. It defaults to a standard SVRCONN channel defined by all queue managers: SYSTEM.DEF.SVRCONN.
LOCALADDRESS	Defines the local address to be used by the outbound client connection (TRANS-PORT = CLIENT), it defaults to null. Typically, you allow this to be assigned automatically when the socket is created, but should you need to have the socket bound to a specific address and port, you specify it here. This might be required when the client connection needs to go out through a firewall that only accepts connections originating from defined ports. It takes as argument an IP address or hostname, and optionally a port or range of ports. Specifying a range of ports is recommended for MQ JMS clients to allow for connections required internally by the implementation: e.g., 9.123.4.56(3000, 4000). If TRANSPORT = DIRECT, this property is only used if MULTICAST is enabled. In this case only an IP address can be specified; there should be no port specified.
MULTICAST†	This activates the MQ Multicast Transport. As it extends the MQ Real-time Trans-port, it is relevant only when TRANSPORT is set to DIRECT. It takes as value DISABLED, ENABLED, NOTR (not reliable), and RELIABLE, and defaults to DISABLED. Note that this distribution optimization only affects subscribers based on this TopicConnectionFactory; publishers do not utilize the MQ Multi-cast Transport.
PROXYHOSTNAME†	This property applies only if TRANSPORT = DIRECT. It defines the location of a proxy via which connections will be made to the Message Broker at HOSTNAME. The Internet protocol defined in RFC 2817 is used to request that the proxy for-ward the connection to the Message Broker. It defaults to null.

Table 6–9 Basic Properties: MQTopicConnectionFactory (*continued*)

Attributes	Description
PROXYPORT†	The port number of the proxy, it defaults to 443.
BROKERVER†	Controls the version of the command header used to convey publish-subscribe commands. It provides backwards compatibility with broker technology that existed prior to the introduction of Event and Message Broker. It takes as value V1 or V2, defaulting to V1. While Event or Message Broker will accept a V1 command header, I recommend setting BROKERVER to V2, which uses their native header format described in Chapter 5.
BROKERQMGR†	If TRANSPORT is set to BIND or CLIENT, this defines the name of the queue manager that is hosting Event or Message Broker. This may be the same or different from the name specified in QMANAGER. If different, then there must exist MQ connectivity (server channels) between the two queue managers. By default it is empty, which is interpreted as having the same value as QMANAGER.
BROKERCONQ†	Defines the control queue on BROKERQMGR to which subscription requests should be sent. It defaults to SYSTEM.CONTROL.BROKER.QUEUE, which is created by the broker on its hosting queue manager.
BROKERPUBQ†	The queue on BROKERQMGR to which publications are sent. It should correspond to a queue being monitored by a publication message flow. It defaults to SYSTEM.BROKER.DEFAULT.STREAM.
BROKERSUBQ†	The queue on QMANAGER from which nondurable subscriptions are retrieved. It defaults to a single queue, SYSTEM.JMS.ND.SUBSCRIBER.QUEUE, which all nondurable subscribers based on this connection factory share. If it is desired that individual queues be created dynamically for each subscriber, then a queue name specified ending in *: e.g., SYSTEM.JMS.ND.MYSUBS.* The dynamic queues created will all have the same prefix, defined by the characters prior to *, followed by a system-generated unique identifier. Note that in either case your queue name must start with SYSTEM.JMS.ND.
CLIENTID	This is required if the MQTopicConnectionFactory is used to define durable subscribers.

* Includes additional valid values for publish-subscribe.

† Unique to MQTopicConnectionFactory.

Once again the basic properties listed in Table 6–9 address the basic connectivity needs of a JMS client using the publish-subscribe interface. Useful default values similarly means that the only attribute that must be set is the name of the MQTopicConnectionFactory; however, the configuration of the underlying provider is somewhat more involved than in the point-to-point case (see Appendix C).

New transport options are introduced in support of the MQ Real-time Transport, and this updates the transport dependencies for the MQTopicConnectionFactory, as shown in Table 6–10.

Table 6–10 Transport Dependencies: MQTopicConnectionFactory

Transport	MQ NAMES*	HOSTNAME	PORT	CHANNEL	MCAST	PROXY Settings
BIND (default)	–	n/a	n/a	n/a	n/a	n/a
CLIENT	–	–	–	–	n/a	n/a
DIRECT	n/a	–	–	n/a	–	–
DIRECTHTTP	n/a	–	–	n/a	n/a	n/a

* Queue Manager and Queue names

As with the WebSphere TopicConnectionFactory, a JMS client that uses an MQTopicConnectionFactory with TRANSPORT set to DIRECT cannot define a durable subscriber, since the MQ Real-time Transport does not provide a queuing mechanism or support for persistent messages.

Use of the MQ Multicast Transport is dependent on the MQ Real-time Transport being selected; however, the multicast distribution option is only applicable to subscribers. Publishers based on the same MQTopicConnectionFactory will not have their messages sent via multicast. This makes sense when you consider that the publisher's message goes directly to the broker, and it is from the broker that the message is then distributed to multiple subscribers.

If the WebSphere MQ Transport is being used—that is, TRANSPORT is set to BIND or CLIENT—then the default MQ resources specified are created by a command script, MQJMS_PSQ.mqsc, which is included as part of the installation of WebSphere MQ. With the WebSphere MQ Transport, you additionally have the option of using a single queue for all non-durable subscribers based on this ConnectionFactory object or having each subscriber access its own dynamically created queue. In general, the shared queue approach offers a modest performance benefit and also reduces the number of MQ queues that must be administered. However, considerations such as the potential accumulation of messages, contention, and the associated capacity of the queue might make individual queues more attractive. Individual queues also allow the behavior of each subscriber to be monitored more easily.

The MQTopicConnectionFactory similarly hosts a client identifier (CLIENTID), which is used to associate durable subscriptions with related Connections (see Chapter 4, "Using the JMS API"). Consequently, it is mandatory if durable subscribers are to be defined based on the `MQTopicConnectionFactory`. Its absence will result in an exception being thrown.

Table 6–11 lists the advanced properties for the `MQTopicConnectionFactory`. As with the `MQQueueConnectionFactory`, they reflect further configuration options for both JMS behavior and the underlying provider. A number of properties are shared with the `MQQueueConnectionFactory`, while others are unique.

Table 6–11 Advanced Properties: MQTopicConnectionFactory

Attributes	Description
SUBSTORE*	Defines where persistent data used to resume durable subscriptions and cleanup after failed nondurable subscribers is stored. It takes as value BROKER, QUEUE, or MIGRATE.
	The values reflect that broker technology that existed prior to Event and Message Broker could not handle this information, and thus it was stored by the JMS implementation in MQ queues. However, Event and Message Broker can be used to store this persistent data, and the default setting of MIGRATE dynamically detects this fact and causes data to be stored at the broker. In general, you should not have to change this property.
PUBACKINT*	The interval, in number of messages, between publish requests that require an acknowledgment from the broker. It defaults to 25, which means after 25 publications, the next publication will request the broker to send back an acknowledgment.
	This allows you to optimize the traffic between the client and the broker; note, however, that the acknowledgments are handled by the implementation; the JMS client remains unaware.
STATEREFRESHINT*	Controls the refresh rate of the transaction used to detect failed subscribers if SUBSTORE is set to QUEUE. It defaults to a value of 60,000 milliseconds.
CLEANUP*	With SUBSTORE set to BROKER or MIGRATE, a cleanup utility runs at specified intervals. This property controls the cleanup level and takes as value NONE, SAFE, or STRONG. It defaults to SAFE.
	An additional valid value, ASPROP, specifies that the value of CLEANUP should be taken from a system property, com.ibm.mq.jms.cleanup, which is queried at JVM startup. This allows the cleanup level to be changed without updating every TopicConnectionFactory in use and is useful for applications or application servers where multiple factories are in use.
CLEANUPINT*	With SUBSTORE set to BROKER or MIGRATE, a cleanup utility runs at specified intervals. This property specifies the intervals between background executions of the cleanup utility. Defined in milliseconds, it defaults to 60,000.

Table 6–11 Advanced Properties: MQTopicConnectionFactory (*continued*)

Attributes	Description
MSGSELECTION*	The JMS subscriber can define content-based subscriptions by subscribing to a specific topic and further defining a message selector against which matching publications are checked.
	This attribute defines who handles the additional matching based on the message selector and takes as value CLIENT or BROKER. If set to CLIENT, then the broker only matches the Topic, and the JMS client implementation checks the message selector. If set to BROKER, then the broker matches the publication based on the Topic as well as its content.
	It defaults to a value of CLIENT, reflecting limitations in broker technology that existed prior to Event and Message Broker. With the current brokers, a value of BROKER can be used. Note that if the value is set to BROKER, then BROKERVER must be set to V2.
	For the MQ Real-time Transport (TRANSPORT = DIRECT), all matching is done at the broker and this property is ignored.
SPARSESUBS*	Takes as value yes or no and marks resulting subscriptions as being ones that do or do not receive infrequent matching messages. It defaults to no.
CLONESUPP*	Normal JMS behavior allows only one active durable subscriber to a subscription. In an application server environment that is cloned, setting this attribute to ENABLED allows cloned durable subscribers to share the same durable subscription; i.e., a given publication will be sent to only one of them, facilitating workload balancing. It is set to DISABLED by default.
BROKERCCSUBQ*	The name of the queue from which nondurable subscriptions are retrieved by a ConnectionConsumer. It defaults to SYSTEM.JMS.ND.CC.SUBSCRIBER.QUEUE.
	ConnectionConsumers are part of Application Server Facilities (ASF) and are used in support of MDBs.
USECONNPOOLING	If set to yes, connections to the queue manager (encapsulated in JMS Session objects) are pooled. Alternative value is no. It is, however, set to yes by default.
POLLINGINT	When MessageListeners are used, this controls how often the receivers are checked (polled) for incoming messages. The interval is specified in milliseconds and defaults to 5000.
MSGBATCHSZ	Used to specify the maximum number of messages that can be retrieved from a queue in one packet by the asynchronous delivery mechanism, which supports the use of message listeners. It defaults to 10.

Table 6–11 Advanced Properties: MQTopicConnectionFactory (*continued*)

Attributes	Description
RESCANINT	Selection of messages using a message selector typically requires the implementation to browse the queue and then get the matching message. Because it is possible for new messages to arrive behind the browse cursor, RESCANINT defines the interval in milliseconds when the browse cursor gets reset to the beginning of the queue. It defaults to 5000 milliseconds.
FAILIFQUIESCE	A queue manager cannot execute a controlled shutdown if applications are connected to it. Setting this option to yes allows the queue manager to deny service to the client application once it has started shutting down. This is done in response to a service call made by the client, and on receipt, the client disconnects from the queue manager, allowing it to shut down.
	If set to no, the queue manager will not shut down until the client disconnects of its own free will. By default it is set to yes.
SSLCIPHERSUITE	Specifies the cipher suite to be used for securing the client connection, i.e., authentication and encryption. This property is relevant only if the TRANSPORT property is set to CLIENT.
DIRECTAUTH	Defines authentication level for the MQ Real-time Transport (TRANSPORT = DIRECT). It takes as value BASIC (the default) or CERTIFICATE, which uses SSL to authenticate the connection.
SSLPEERNAME	Defines a distinguished name, which must match that specified for the queue manager or broker. Its value is only significant if SSLCIPHERSUITE has been set.
SSLCRL	Specifies the LDAP server that should be used for SSL certificate revocation checking. Its value is only significant if SSLCIPHERSUITE has been set.
CCSID	The default coded-character set that should be used for MQ messages resulting from this connection. It defaults to 819, which is ASCII.
SYNCPOINTALLGETS	If set to yes, then messages are retrieved under local transaction control, irrespective of what the JMS client actually specifies.
VERSION	Internal version number for the implementation. It is currently set to 2. This attribute can be ignored.
RECEXIT	WebSphere MQ supports a number of exits that can be called when using a client connection. This defines the fully qualified class name of the receive exit, which is called after data is received over the client connection.
RECEXITINIT	An initialization string for the receive exit, passed to the class constructor for the exit.

Table 6–11 Advanced Properties: MQTopicConnectionFactory (*continued*)

Attributes	Description
SECEXIT	The fully qualified class name of the security exit. This was the only option available to authenticate the client connection prior to the introduction of SSL support.
SECEXITINT	An initialization string for the security exit, passed to the class constructor for the exit.
SENDEXIT	The fully qualified class name of the send exit, which is called before data is sent over the client connection.
SENDEXITINIT	An initialization string for the send exit, passed to the class constructor for the exit.

*Unique to MQTopicConnectionFactory.

The DIRECTAUTH property extends SSL support to the MQ Real-time Transport. However, it differs from the WebSphere MQ SSL support (SSLCIPHERSUITE) in one key respect. It addresses authentication of the connection only. With WebSphere MQ, the SSL support additionally provides encryption services for data passed over the connection. Both SSL implementations, however, utilize SSLPEERNAME and SSLCRL to specify checking options.

You will have noticed that quite a few of the unique properties address the handling of nondurable subscribers that fail to close down, that is, fail to call the close method on the TopicConnection object. This might occur due to the unexpected termination of the client application or its connection to the MQ queue manager. Recall that a nondurable subscriber expects its subscription to be canceled when it shuts down, and the failure to properly close down can result in the client's subscription not being appropriately deregistered from the broker. The cleanup utility implemented by the WebSphere MQ JMS implementation addresses this by monitoring the state of subscriptions and deregistering orphaned subscriptions as required. A detailed discussion of the internal workings of the cleanup utility is outside the scope of this book, but it is adequately covered in product manuals referenced in Appendix D.

MQXAQueueConnectionFactory and MQXATopicConnectionFactory

MQXAQueueConnectionFactory and MQXATopicConnectionFactory implement the JMS XAQueueConnectionFactory and XATopicConnectionFactory. As discussed in Chapter 2, the XA variants are defined as part of ASF and are used by the Transaction Manager (i.e., the J2EE server) to access the XA resources used to coordinate the transaction. As they extend MQQueueConnectionFactory and MQTopicConnectionFactory, they essentially expose the same properties.

For a JMS client that takes part in a global XA transaction, these are the versions of the ConnectionFactory objects that must be ultimately retrieved. We explore the use of these administered objects in Appendix B.

JMSWrapXAQueueConnectionFactory and JMSWrapXATopicConnectionFactory

These are specialized versions of MQXAQueueConnectionFactory and MQXATopicConnectionFactory, defined for WebSphere Application Server 4.0 only. If you are running a JMS client in WebSphere Application Server 4.0 that takes part in XA global transactions, then these are the ConnectionFactory objects that you must use. Their properties are ultimately inherited from MQQueueConnectionFactory and MQTopicConnectionFactory, and thus their configuration does not differ in any way. They are supplied as part of the WebSphere Application Server 4.0 installation and are packaged in <installation_directory>\lib\resources.jar.

WebSphere Application Server Runtime Properties

MQQueueConnectionFactory and MQTopicConnectionFactory can be created in the WebSphere Application Server 5.0 JNDI namespace for use by JMS clients running in the J2EE server. When they are created in the application server namespace, they gain a number of additional configuration options specific to the application server runtime environment (Table 6–12).

Table 6–12 WebSphere Application Server Runtime Properties: MQQueueConnectionFactory and MQTopicConnectionFactory

Attributes	Description
XA-Enabled	If set, this marks the ConnectionFactory as being of the XA variant, signifying that the JMS provider can be enlisted as part of an XA global transaction. It essentially results in the creation of an MQXAQueueConnectionFactory or an MQXATopicConnectionFactory.
Component-Managed Authentication Alias	Lists an optional J2C authentication data entry, which defines a user ID and password. The user ID and password are used by the application to authenticate the creation of a connection. The use of this option is dependent on global security being switched on in the application server. In addition, the authentication setting for the resource reference in the EJB or servlet that specifies this ConnectionFactory must be set to application. The use of this option is clearly tied to the security model adopted for applications running in the application server, and further details can be found in the references listed in Appendix D.
Container-Managed Authentication Alias	Similarly lists an optional J2C authentication data entry, which defines a user ID and password. It has the same usage constraints as the Component-Managed Authentication Alias. However, in this case the entry is only referred to if the authentication setting for the resource reference is set to Container. As might be expected authentication is carried out by the Container.
Connection Pools	Exposes settings for configuring the connection pool associated with the connections derived from this factory.
Session Pools	Exposes settings for configuring the session pool associated with the sessions derived from this factory.

These properties are the same properties exposed by the WebSphere JMS Provider for the WebSphere `QueueConnectionFactory` and WebSphere `TopicConnectionFactory`, which we reviewed earlier. Note that the use of the XA-enabled attribute eliminates the need to explicitly create the XA variants of the `ConnectionFactory` objects. The connection and session pool settings shown here are independent of and additional to the connection pooling implemented by the WebSphere MQ JMS Provider, which is controlled by the `USECONNPOOL-ING` attribute of the `ConnectionFactory` objects (see Tables 6–8 and 6–11). The connection pools defined as part of the application server environment are configurable, exposing settings such as pool size and timeouts. Recall that with the MQ `ConnectionFactory` objects, the pool can simply be enabled or disabled, but not configured in any way.

As with, the WebSphere `ConnectionFactory` objects, we can in the application server environment optionally relate a set of J2C authentication data entries to the MQ `ConnectionFactory` objects. These are then used to define authentication aliases.

MQQueue

`MQQueue` details the destination with which the JMS client will interact via the point-to-point interface. It represents a specific MQ queue hosted on a given MQ queue manager and defines the properties shown in Table 6–13.

Table 6–13 Properties: MQQueue

Attributes	Description
NAME	Specifies the name of the object. This is the name used to retrieve the factory from the JNDI namespace.
DESCRIPTION	Defines an optional description string, which can be used to document the purpose of the Queue object.
QUEUE*	The name of the MQ queue that this object represents.
QMANAGER*	The name of the MQ queue manager, which hosts the queue defined in QUEUE. If left blank, the value of QMANAGER in the MQQueueConnectionFactory is used.
PERSISTENCE	The persistence of messages sent to this destination. It takes as value APP, QDEF, PERS, or NON. APP is the default value and states that persistence is defined by the application. QDEF states that the persistence of the message is defined by the MQ queue definition. PERS states that all messages sent to this destination should be marked persistent. NON states that all messages sent to this destination should be marked nonpersistent.

Table 6–13 Properties: MQQueue (*continued*)

Attributes	Description
PRIORITY	The priority of messages sent to this destination. It takes as value APP, QDEF, or an explicit integer value. APP is the default value and states that priority is defined by the application. QDEF states that the priority of the message is defined by the MQ queue definition. An integer ranging from 0 to 9 can be specified, where 0 is the lowest and 9 the highest priority.
EXPIRY	The period after which messages sent to this destination will expire. It takes as value APP, UNLIM, or an explicit integer value. APP is the default value and states that expiry is defined by the application. UNLIM sets the message to an unlimited expiry, hence no expiry occurs. Alternatively, a positive integer representing the expiry in milliseconds can be specified.
CCSID	The coded-character set that should be used for MQ messages at this destination. It overrides the value specified in MQQueueConnectionFactory and defaults to 1208, which is Unicode.
ENCODING	The encoding scheme used for messages at this destination. It defaults to NATIVE, which sets appropriate encoding values for the Java platform. Alternatively, the encoding scheme can be specified based on three subproperties. Integer encoding: normal (N) or reversed (R) Decimal encoding: normal (N) or reversed (R) Floating-point encoding: IEEE normal (N), IEEE reversed (R), or z/OS (3) The encoding scheme is then specified as a three-character string, e.g., NNR or RR3.
TARGCLIENT	It takes as value JMS or MQ and defines whether or not the recipient of the message is a JMS client. If the value is set to MQ, then the RFH2 header, which carries JMS-specific information, is not included in the MQ message. It defaults to JMS.
FAILIFQUIESCE	Overrides the setting on the MQQueueConnectionFactory for a specific destination. It similarly defaults to yes.
VERSION	Internal version number for the implementation. It is currently set to 1. This attribute can be ignored.

* Unique to MQQueue

The WebSphere MQ JMS Provider similarly uses the Destination object MQQueue to override the settings for persistence, priority, and expiry that are specified by the JMS client when sending the message. Note that values for PRIORITY and PERSISTENCE can additionally be taken from the underlying MQ queue definition. This is a particularly useful feature that allows the behavior of the provider to be defined completely outside the application layer—that is, without changes to JMS code or object definitions—further facilitating the enforcement of company policy or adopted best practice (see Chapter 3).

The MQ resources specified in the `MQQueue` object must, of course, match existing MQ resources defined in the underlying provider. Note that the names specified can be MQ aliases to the actual MQ queue or queue manager.

The property `TARGCLIENT` is of particular importance because it facilitates communication between JMS and non-JMS clients. As discussed in Chapter 5, the JMS implementation uses folders in the RFH2 header to store JMS-specific information, such as standard and application properties. Since these attributes would not be understood by a non-JMS client, `TARGCLIENT` allows the entire RFH2 header to be suppressed and omitted from the MQ message when it is sent to the configured destination.

MQTopic

`MQTopic` defines the destination used by the publish-subscribe JMS client. It shares a number of properties with `MQQueue`, and as you would expect, includes a number of unique properties relevant to the publish-subscribe paradigm (Table 6–14).

Table 6–14 Properties: MQTopic

Attributes	Description
NAME	Specifies the name of the object. This is the name used to retrieve the factory from the JNDI namespace.
DESCRIPTION	Defines an optional description string, which can be used to document the purpose of the `Topic` object.
TOPIC*	Contains the topic name that serves to bind publishers and subscribers together.
MULTICAST*	This overrides the settings for the multicast transport in the `MQTopicConnectionFactory` for this specific destination. It is set by default to ASCF, which states that the value should be taken from the `ConnectionFactory`. Alternatively, the value can be explicitly set using any of the valid values: DISABLED, ENABLED, NOTR, and RELIABLE.
BROKERVER*	Similarly overrides the value in `MQTopicConnectionFactory` for this specific destination, controlling the version of the command header used to communicate with the broker. It similarly takes as value V1 or V2, defaulting to V1.
BROKERDURSUBQ*	Specifies the name of the queue on QMANAGER (defined in `MQTopicConnectionFactory`) from which durable subscriptions are retrieved. It defaults to a single queue, SYSTEM.JMS.D.SUBSCRIBER.QUEUE, which is shared by all durable subscribers defined from the same connection. Individual queues can be created dynamically for each durable subscriber by specifying a queue name ending in *, e.g., SYSTEM.JMS.D.MYSUBS.*. The dynamic queues created will all have the same prefix, defined by the characters prior to *, followed by a system-generated unique identifier. Note that in either case your queue name must start with SYSTEM.JMS.D.

Table 6–14 Properties: MQTopic (*continued*)

Attributes	Description
BROKERCCDSUBQ[*]	The name of the queue from which durable subscriptions are retrieved by a Con-nectionConsumer. It defaults to SYSTEM.JMS.D.CC.SUB-SCRIBER.QUEUE. ConnectionConsumers are part of ASF and are used in support of MDBs.
PERSISTENCE	The persistence of messages sent to this destination. It takes as value APP, QDEF, PERS, or NON. APP is the default value and states that persistence is defined by the application. QDEF states that the persistence of the message is defined by the MQ Queue defi-nition. PERS states that all messages sent to this destination should be marked persistent. NON states that all messages sent to this destination should be marked nonpersis-tent.
PRIORITY	The priority of messages sent to this destination. It takes as value APP, QDEF, or an explicit integer value. APP is the default value and states that priority is defined by the application. QDEF states that the priority of the message is defined by the MQ Queue defini-tion. An integer ranging from 0 to 9 can be specified, where 0 is the lowest and 9 the highest priority.
EXPIRY	The period after which messages sent to this destination will expire. It takes as value APP, UNLIM, or an explicit integer value. APP is the default value and states that expiry is defined by the application. UNLIM sets the message to an unlimited expiry, hence no expiry occurs. Alternatively, a positive integer representing the expiry in milliseconds can be spec-ified.
CCSID	The coded-character set that should be used for MQ messages at this destination. It overrides the value specified in MQTopicConnectionFactory and defaults to 1208, which is Unicode.
ENCODING	The encoding scheme used for messages at this destination. It defaults to NATIVE, which sets appropriate encoding values for the Java platform. Alternatively, the encoding scheme can be specified based on three subproperties. Integer encoding: normal (N) or reversed (R) Decimal encoding: normal (N) or reversed (R) Floating-point encoding: IEEE normal (N), IEEE reversed (R), or z/OS (3) The encoding scheme is then specified as a three-character string, e.g., NNR or RR3.

Table 6–14 Properties: MQTopic (*continued*)

Attributes	Description
TARGCLIENT	It takes as value JMS or MQ and defines whether or not the recipient of the message is a JMS client. If the value is set to MQ, then the RFH2 header that carries JMS-specific information is not included in the MQ message. It defaults to JMS. Note that if the value of BROKERVER is set to V2, the value of this property is ignored, as the RFH2 header is then required for publish-subscribe.
FAILIFQUIESCE	Overrides the setting on the MQTopicConnectionFactory for a specific destination. It similarly defaults to yes.
VERSION	Internal version number for the implementation. It is currently set to 1. This attribute can be ignored.

* Unique to MQTopic

The MQTopic TOPIC property uses the same string format as that used by WebSphere Topic's Topic attribute. They do, after all, utilize the same broker technology. The string format is provider-specific, as JMS does not specify one. A treelike hierarchy for topic names is adopted, which uses a forward slash (/) to separate levels in the tree—for example, Stocks/Trades/IBM. As discussed earlier, topic names specified for subscribers have the option of including wildcards, defined by # and +. The # wildcard matches multiple levels in a topic; the + wildcard matches a single level. Publishers, however, cannot publish on topic names that include wildcards.

The MQ queue used by the durable subscriber is defined here rather than in the MQTopicConnectionFactory, providing a more granular level of control. It is much more likely that an individual rather than shared-queue approach will be adopted for durable subscribers, as by definition they are more likely to accumulate messages. Remember that they are sent publications even when they are not running, and therefore must be stored. Thus, with a large number of subscribers, the shared-queue approach might not prove the most efficient.

With publish-subscribe, setting the TARGCLIENT property to MQ has an effect only if BROKERVER is set to V1. In this case publish-subscribe commands are carried in the RFH header, and thus the RFH2 header can be dropped. With BROKERVER set to V2 (recommended when using Event/Message Broker), settings for TARGCLIENT are ignored, as in this case the RFH2 header (discussed in Chapter 5) is required and cannot be omitted. It is also useful to note that the PERSISTENCE, PRIORITY, and EXPIRY attributes are only relevant if the WebSphere MQ Transport is being used to publish the message; that is, if the associated MQTopicConnectionFactory's TRANSPORT property is set to CLIENT or BIND.

Creating Administered Objects

Administered objects for the WebSphere JMS Provider and the WebSphere MQ JMS Provider can be created using one of two tools: the WebSphere Application Server administration console or JMSAdmin, supplied as part of WebSphere MQ. In both cases the tools enable you to connect to the supported JNDI namespace and subsequently insert, update, or delete administered objects.

The administration console supports the WebSphere Application Server 5.0 persistent namespace, while JMSAdmin supports a file-based or LDAP-based namespace. In addition, JMSAdmin supports the WebSphere Application Server 4.0 namespace; it does not, however, at the time of writing, support the persistent namespace implemented by WebSphere Application Server 5.0.

If it is required that the administered objects be stored in some other namespace—for instance, the namespace provided by another J2EE server—consider crafting a custom tool. Such a custom tool would use JNDI to interact with the namespace of choice and use the published interfaces of the administered objects to create and define their properties.

We briefly examine the administration console and JMSAdmin, and we use them in Chapter 7, where we implement a number of scenarios.

WebSphere Application Server Administration Console

The administration console facilitates the configuration of the WebSphere Application Server and associated resources. It is a J2EE application hosted by the target application server and is accessed via a Web browser. Of particular relevance to us is the resources panel that enables us to configure the administered objects for the WebSphere JMS Provider, the WebSphere MQ JMS Provider, and the generic JMS provider. Selecting any of the provider links loads the resource page for administered objects for that provider (Figure 6–1).

Each administered object type can then be accessed and appropriate instances defined and created. As you might expect, creating and editing objects is all based on forms, and being GUI-driven, is rather intuitive (Figure 6–2).

If you are defining administered objects for the WebSphere MQ JMS Provider, you will notice what I call GUI beautification. For instance, attributes are fully spelled out with spaces inserted for readability: QMANAGER becomes Queue Manager. You will also notice that not all of the properties we identified for the MQ JMS–administered objects are listed. For instance, you will not see attributes for SSL configuration detailed or properties such as MQTopicConnectionFactory's MSGSELECTION property. The simple truth is that at the time of writing, the administration console does not expose all the attributes defined for the MQ JMS–administered objects. However, careful inspection of the properties that are listed shows that all the basic connectivity attributes are defined, which is generally more than adequate for most JMS client configurations. I expect that the administration console will be updated over time, but

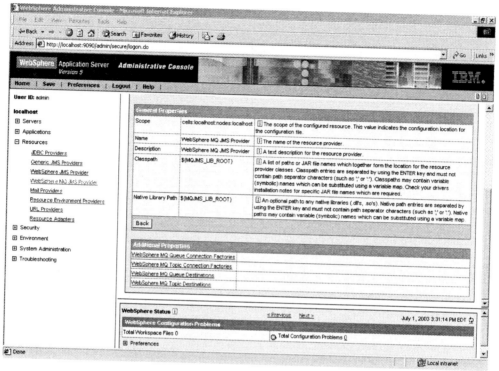

Figure 6-1 Administration Console: WebSphere MQ JMS Administered Objects

it is important not to view it as a full replacement for JMSAdmin; rather, it is a ready alternative that provides access to the most common set of attributes that you would usually need to configure. WebSphere Application Server additionally provides a scripting tool (wsadmin) that allows all the functions of the administration console to be scripted.

If you need to set a property for an MQ JMS–administered object that is not exposed by the administration console, you must use JMSAdmin. However, you are faced with a slight problem. Given that JMSAdmin does not support the application server's namespace, where will you store the objects, and how will your J2EE-based JMS client access them? A ready solution lies in the application server's support for generic JMS providers. Using JMSAdmin, you create and store your administered objects in an external namespace such as a file system. Then, using the administration console, you reference the external namespace as part of a generic JMS provider definition. Finally, in the generic JMS provider, you create local JNDI aliases for the JMS-administered objects that are stored in the external namespace. This allows the JMS client to still use the namespace provided by the application server, with the application server taking responsibility for accessing the external namespace where the real objects are stored. We undertake this process ourselves in Chapter 7.

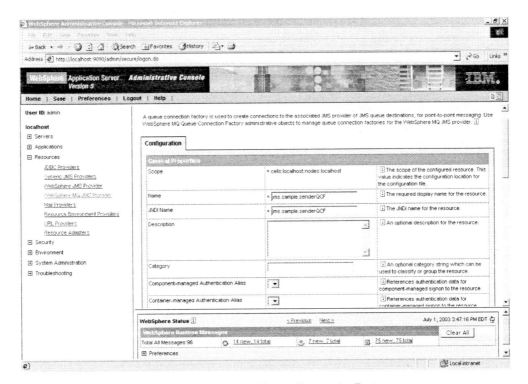

Figure 6-2 Administration Console: Editor, MQQueueConnectionFactory

JMSAdmin

JMSAdmin is a command-line tool for creating MQ JMS–administered objects only and is supplied as part of WebSphere MQ. It supports the use of file systems or LDAP servers as JNDI namespaces, and at the time of writing, only supports the namespace implemented by WebSphere Application Server 4.0.

JMSAdmin runs in a command prompt and connects to the namespace based on properties defined in its configuration file. The default configuration file is called `JMSAdmin.config`, but you can define others if desired. The properties in the configuration file bear a close resemblance to the properties we defined while trying to establish an initial context for our JMS client in Chapter 4. They similarly represent the JNDI provider's factory class, a URL that defines the location of the namespace and appropriate security attributes. The configuration file contains a set of supported values for each property defined, and setting up JMSAdmin generally involves removing the comment mark from desired property/value sets and supplying details such as the actual URL. For example, to set up access to a file-based namespace, I specify the following in the configuration file:

```
//excerpt from JMSAdmin.config
INITIAL_CONTEXT_FACTORY=com.sun.jndi.fscontext.RefFSContextFac
tory
PROVIDER_URL=file:/C:/JNDINamespace
SECURITY_AUTHENTICATION=none
```

A number of additional properties are defined, providing additional support for LDAP and other configuration options. But in many cases the properties shown are all you need specify. Once launched, JMSAdmin should connect to the namespace (in this case the directory C:\JNDINamespace) and present a prompt ready for you to enter commands (Figure 6–3).

The prompt represents the initial context (starting point) for the namespace, and JMSAdmin defines a number of commands for creating and navigating subcontexts. It also defines a basic set of verbs for creating and editing the administered objects. If you are using a file-based namespace, you will note that the namespace is contained in a single file called .bindings, which is created at the location you specified: PROVIDER_URL. This file is human-readable and can be moved or copied to another location should you need to make this namespace available to some other application.

Using JMSAdmin consequently involves invoking commands based on verbs with appropriate arguments. Verbs, objects, and their attributes can be invoked using either their full name or an associated keyword that reduces the amount of typing required. In addition, commands can be typed into a file and passed as input to JMSAdmin, enabling object generation to be scripted.

Table 6–15 lists verbs, administered objects, and associated keywords defined by JMSAdmin.

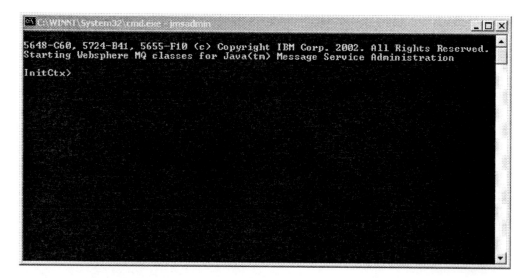

Figure 6-3 JMSAdmin: Initial Context

Table 6–15 JMSAdmin: Verbs and Administered Objects

Verb	Keyword	Object	Keyword
ALTER	ALT	MQQueueConnectionFactory	QCF
DEFINE	DEF	MQTopicConnectionFactory	TCF
DISPLAY	DIS	MQQueue	Q
DELETE	DEL	MQTopic	T
COPY	CP	MQXAQueueConnectionFactory	XAQCF
MOVE	MV	MQXATopicConnectionFactory	XATCF
END		JMSWrapXAQueueConnectionFactory	WSQCF
		JMSWrapXATopicConnectionFactory	WSTCF

Thus, to create an `MQQueueConnectionFactory` object with NAME MYQCF (Figure 6–4), I can type at the prompt:

```
DEF QCF(MYQCF)
```

I can then display its properties to view the default settings:

```
DIS QCF(MYQCF)
```

and then update the properties I choose:

```
ALTER QCF(MYQCF) QMANAGER(TESTMGR) TRANSPORT(CLIENT)
```

```
5648-C60, 5724-B41, 5655-F10 (c) Copyright IBM Corp. 2002. All Rights Reserved.
Starting Websphere MQ classes for Java(tm) Message Service Administration

InitCtx> DEF QCF(MYQCF)

InitCtx> DIS QCF(MYQCF)

    FAILIFQUIESCE(YES)
    QMANAGER()
    USECONNPOOLING(YES)
    TEMPMODEL(SYSTEM.DEFAULT.MODEL.QUEUE)
    MSGBATCHSZ(10)
    TRANSPORT(BIND)
    SYNCPOINTALLGETS(NO)
    MSGRETENTION(YES)
    RESCANINT(5000)
    POLLINGINT(5000)
    VERSION(2)

InitCtx> ALTER QCF(MYQCF) QMANAGER(TESTMGR) TRANSPORT(CLIENT)

InitCtx>
```

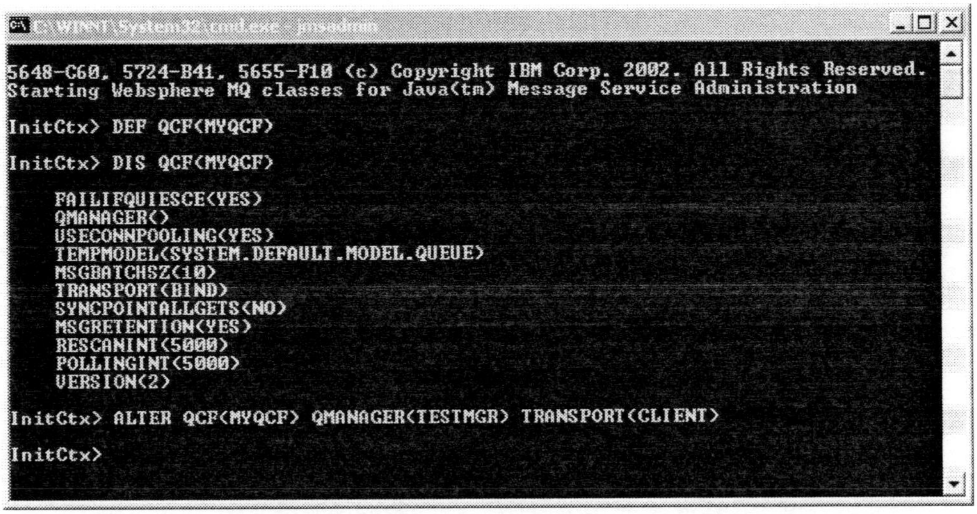

Figure 6-4 JMSAdmin: Creating Administered Objects

Once finished, the session is terminated by typing the verb END.

Summary

In this chapter we extensively reviewed the administered objects and their associated properties, defined by the WebSphere JMS and WebSphere MQ JMS providers. Administered objects form the glue that binds the JMS client to a particular JMS provider, and as we learned, the attributes exposed in the administered object tend to reflect the provider's underlying implementation and concepts. We observed that the administered objects defined for the WebSphere JMS Provider are relatively sparse in the properties they exposed, reflecting that the WebSphere JMS Provider, supplied as an integral part of the WebSphere Application Server, exposes little of its underlying implementation. In contrast, the administered objects associated with the WebSphere MQ JMS Provider expose a wealth of configuration options that give access to the underlying facilities in WebSphere MQ and WebSphere Business Integration Message Broker. We did note, however, that in most cases only a few properties need to be set for the MQ JMS–administered objects, as they define useful defaults for most attributes.

We reviewed two tools for creating administered objects: the application server's administration console and JMSAdmin. The administration console supports the creation of both WebSphere JMS–administered and WebSphere MQ JMS–administered objects in the application server namespace, while JMSAdmin supports the creation of only MQ JMS–administered objects in a number of supported namespaces. We considered approaches to and the limitations of working with each tool.

We have now rounded out the knowledge we have been acquiring since the beginning of this book, first developing an understanding of JMS, then examining a number of JMS providers, and finally detailing a set of administered objects that essentially enable the JMS client to function. In the next chapter we implement a number of scenarios using the knowledge we have gained.

JMS Implementation Scenarios

In the previous chapters, we explored messaging concepts and patterns, reviewed the JMS specification, detailed its use, and examined IBM JMS Provider implementations. In this chapter, we put the knowledge to use by implementing a number of JMS scenarios. We do this using a hands-on tutorial approach, which walks you through implementing the scenario to create a functional prototype. As you might expect, the scenarios are designed so that we can explore areas of general interest, and they illustrate useful implementation approaches. They are deliberately bare-boned, focusing on the messaging aspects rather than on the entire business application. The issues we discuss and the detailed instructions will provide helpful guidance as you undertake your own JMS implementations.

The first scenario focuses on exchanging messages between two J2EE applications using EJBs (session beans and message-driven beans, or MDBs). The second scenario extends the first scenario into the realm of publish-subscribe, reimplementing entities as publishers and durable and nondurable subscribers. The third scenario considers communication between JMS and non-JMS clients. The fourth and final scenario explores how communication between the JMS client and the JMS provider can be secured using technologies such as SSL. The scenario implementations are all based on the IBM WebSphere software platform and are designed to be executed in sequence. While the sequential order need not be strictly adhered too, as the only real dependency is that you complete scenario 1 before attempting scenario 3 or scenario 4, the instructions in later scenarios tend to assume that you have established a certain level of familiarity with the tools based on earlier scenarios.

The chapter commences with a review of the development environment required to execute the hands-on tutorials and then discusses and implements the four scenarios.

Development Environment

The development environment required to execute the hands-on tutorials is designed to enable the implementation of basic JMS scenarios with a minimal amount of software that is readily available. Consequently, it has the following software installed:

- Windows 2000 + SP3
- WebSphere Studio Application Developer 5.0 + FP1
- WebSphere MQ 5.3 + CSD04
- OpenSSL toolkit (installed as part of the Cygwin toolset)

Application Developer is the primary development tool with which we work. It facilitates, among other things, the development of J2EE components and provides a unit test environment based on WebSphere Application Server 5.0. The unit test environment provides all the basic runtime services we'd expect from a J2EE 1.3 server, including a native JMS provider. We thus use the unit test environment as the operating environment for the artifacts we create. The unit test WebSphere JMS Provider is the JMS provider used for the basic JMS scenarios (1 and 2), which cover both the point-to-point and publish-subscribe domains.

WebSphere MQ is the JMS provider used in the advanced JMS scenarios (3 and 4), which focus on communicating with non-JMS applications and securing JMS communications. These scenarios require facilities not available in the WebSphere JMS Provider, and thus WebSphere MQ is introduced into the development environment. Its introduction also enables us to explore how we might move JMS clients tested against the embedded WebSphere JMS Provider to the enterprise-level WebSphere MQ JMS Provider with minimal impact on the actual application.

Note that WebSphere Business Integration Event/Message Broker is not included in the development environment. This is in keeping with the objective of specifying the simplest environment required to implement and demonstrate JMS concepts. However, in Appendix C an extension to the publish-subscribe scenario is documented, which uses Message Broker rather than the unit test WebSphere JMS Provider.

The OpenSSL toolkit *(http://www.openssl.org/)* is used to generate self-signed digital certificates, which we use when implementing scenario 4 (securing JMS communications). It is installed as part of the Cygwin toolset *(http://www.cygwin.com/)*, which provides a Windows-based Linux-like environment for running UNIX-based utilities. Should you not wish to install the Cygwin toolset, you can alternatively download the OpenSSL source code and compile it for the Windows platform (see *http://www.openssl.org/*).

It goes without saying that in order to replicate this development environment and undertake the hands-on tutorials, you need appropriate licenses for all software. The OpenSSL and Cygwin toolkits are open-source initiatives and are thus freely available under the GNU General Public License. If you're new to IBM software, you may find the WebSphere Evaluation Download Center useful *(http://www7b.software.ibm.com/wsdd/downloads/)*; it provides access to trial licenses for the software specified. You may also want to consider a developer's toolbox subscription, which provides development licenses for over 1,000 IBM software products (see *http://www-106.ibm.com/developerworks/toolbox/*). Should you be unable to create the development environment, you should still find the tutorial useful in terms of the implementation stages it defines and the considerations discussed.

Please pay particular attention to the service levels associated with each software product. The listed service and fix pack levels reflect the current level of product code at the time of writing and are the code levels on which the tutorials are based. To minimize unforeseen errors, I strongly recommend that you use these or later code levels. The tutorials assume that you have installed the identified software and commence with the configuration of required resources, such as the unit test environment or MQ queue manager. Installation steps are documented in associated product documentation and for the most part are wizard driven. Links to these documents are included in Appendix D.

Scenario 1: Exchanging Messages Using EJBs

We start with a simple scenario that focuses on the exchange of data between two J2EE applications. Application A provides a Web-based interface through which authorized personnel can create and update employee records. It is required to communicate using messaging with Application B, which front-ends an employee "system of record." The system of record could be implemented by a database, off-the-shelf component, or some other suitable entity. Once in production, both applications will be hosted in different J2EE servers running on different physical machines.

Figure 7–1 depicts the messaging solution architecture for the scenario; Application A uses a JMS client implemented by a session bean to send the employee record to Application B. Application B uses an MDB to process incoming messages. The data in the message is then passed to a session bean, which invokes the business logic required to update the system of record. If the system of record supports XA global transactions, then message retrieval and system updates are handled as a single global transaction.

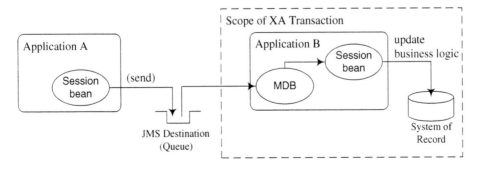

Figure 7-1 Employee Record Exchange: Point-to-Point

The solution architecture illustrates the classic roles performed by the different types of EJBs. Session beans are task-oriented and are used here to send messages and provide a façade for business logic. If the system of record is implemented by a database, then this business logic might be implemented using entity beans. From a messaging standpoint, however, we are insulated from the nature of the system of record.

The MDB allows the business logic to be driven by the receipt of a message. Note that the MDB does not access the system of record directly, but rather passes the data to a session bean. This is in keeping with the best practice recommendation that MDBs should not contain business logic but should focus on message handling and pass the data retrieved to session beans for subsequent processing. Configured appropriately, the MDB can retrieve the message as part of a transaction. This transaction is then propagated to the session bean that the MDB calls. If the resource that the session bean invokes is XA-compliant, we are then able to effect a global transaction.

The messaging interaction described here defines a basic point-to-point message distribution scenario, with Application A implementing the message producer pattern and Application B the message consumer pattern (see Chapter 1, "Enterprise Messaging"). Both applications are linked by a common destination (queue) to which messages are sent and retrieved.

As you will recall from Chapter 5, "IBM JMS Providers," the messaging infrastructure used to support this interaction could be physically implemented using WebSphere MQ in a number of ways. We review these deployment topologies in Chapter 8, "Enterprise Deployment," since they only affect how we configure the administered objects, and not how we implement JMS client code. Thus, for now, we focus on the creation and deployment of the JMS components. To implement the scenario, we use Application Developer to create a sender session bean and a receiver MDB, and test them in the unit test environment using the unit test WebSphere JMS Provider.

Create the Sender Session Bean

We begin by creating the session bean, which we use to implement the JMS client. We then create administered objects for the JMS client in the WebSphere namespace and deploy the session bean to the application server.

Create the Session Bean

The session bean is packaged as part of an enterprise application project, which represents Application A.

1. Launch Application Developer from the Start menu, then open or select the **J2EE** perspective.
2. In the J2EE Hierarchy Panel, right-click on the **Enterprise Applications Folder** and select **New ➡ Enterprise Application Project** (Figure 7–2).

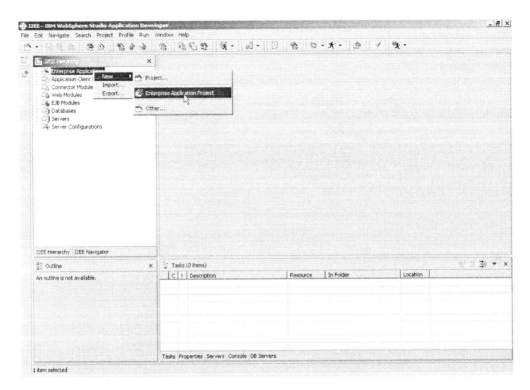

Figure 7-2 J2EE Perspective: J2EE Hierarchy Panel

3. In the resulting wizard select the radio button **Create J2EE 1.3 Enterprise Application Project**. Then click **Next** to display the **Enterprise Application Project** page.
4. Supply the name **EmpRecordSender** for the project. Note that the names for the modules are automatically generated. Uncheck **Application Client Module** and **Web Module**, as we wish only to create an EJB module (Figure 7–3).
5. Click **Finish**. The Enterprise Application Project and EJB Module will now be listed in the J2EE Hierarchy Panel.
6. In the J2EE Hierarchy Panel, expand the EJB Modules folder, then right-click on **EmpRecorderSenderEJB** and select **New ➡ Enterprise Bean**.
7. In the resulting wizard check that **EmpRecorderSenderEJB** is selected as the project for the EJB. Click **Next**.
8. On the next page select **session bean** as the EJB type and supply the name **EmpRecordSender** and package **jms.book.sample.ejb** for the EJB (Figure 7–4). Because we are building a J2EE 1.3 application, the EJB version defaults to version 2.0. Click **Next**.
9. Accept the defaults on the following two pages and press **Finish**. This creates our session bean. Note that we have created a stateless session bean with remote interfaces.

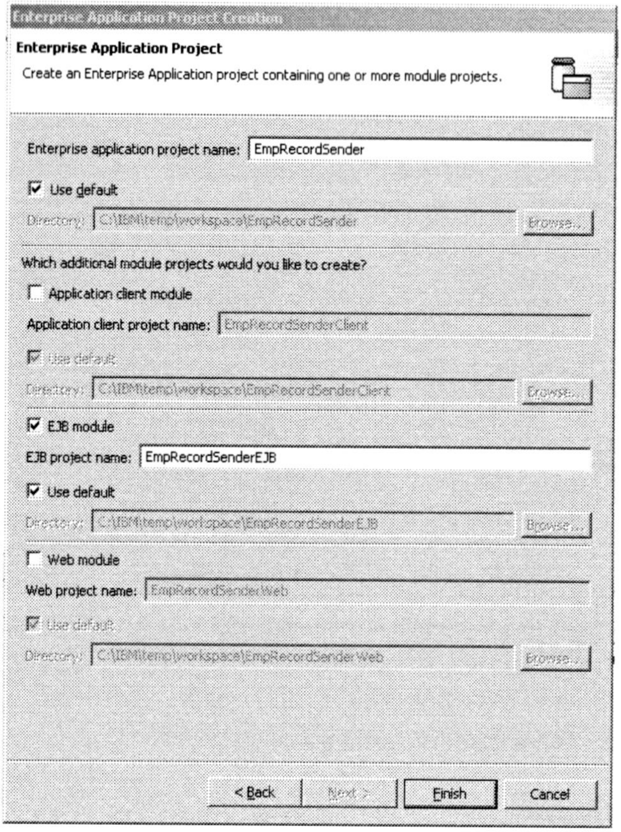

Figure 7-3 Enterprise Application Project Page

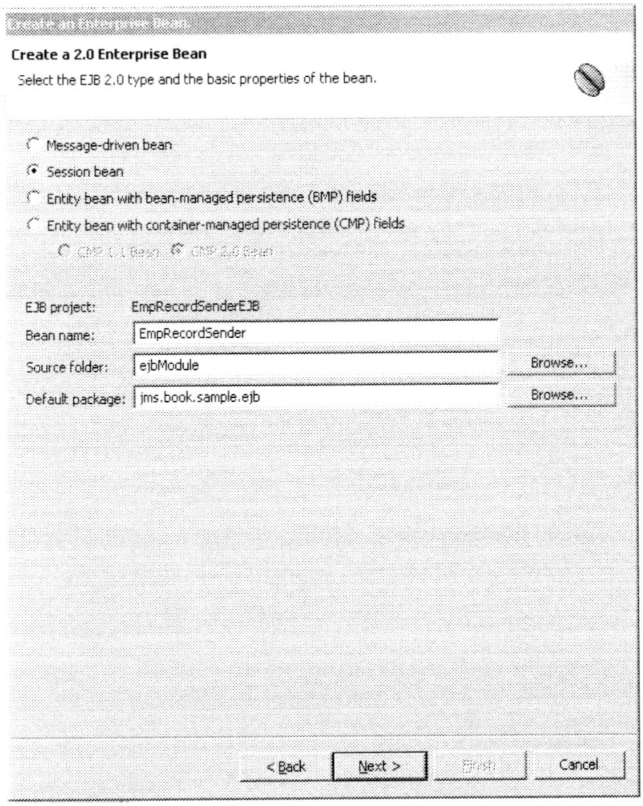

Figure 7-4 Create Session Bean

Implement the JMS Client

With our session bean (**EmpRecordSender**) now created, we can implement the JMS client. We use the `ejbCreate` method to establish a session with the JMS provider. As `ejbCreate` is called once in the lifecycle of the EJB, it allows us to handle the overhead of establishing a `QueueSession` when the EJB is being initialized. Placing the code in our service method would incur the overhead for every invocation of the EJB. This is neither desirable nor required. By placing all initialization code in `ejbCreate`, we improve the performance of client applications that subsequently invoke the EJB instance after it is created by the first client application. Remember that the J2EE server typically pools the EJB instances created, and they are used repeatedly by multiple clients during the course of the application's lifetime. Since we are sending messages to a static destination (all updates are sent to the same location), we also create the `QueueSender` in `ejbCreate`.

When the EJB `Container` is ready to discard the EJB instance, it calls `ejbRemove`. This occurs once in the lifetime of the EJB, and we use this method to implement required cleanup code (i.e., close connections, and so on). Finally, we implement a single service method called `submit`, which is responsible for actually sending the message.

Import Packages and Define Class Variables

1. In the J2EE Hierarchy Panel, expand the newly created EJB, **EmpRecordSender**. Note that the EJB implementation files are listed.
2. Double-click on **EmpRecordSenderBean.java**. This is the bean implementation class that opens in the Java editor.
3. Add the following import statements for JMS and JNDI packages. As these are packaged by the J2EE environment, you do not need to specify any additional class path settings:

```
import javax.jms.*;                    // JMS classes
import javax.naming.*;                 // JNDI imports
```

4. Add the following variables to the class definition. We need these in our method implementations:

```
//attributes
private QueueConnectionFactory factory = null;
private QueueConnection conn = null;
private QueueSession session = null;
private Queue queue = null;
private QueueSender sender = null;
```

5. Save your work—you can use the keyboard shortcut Ctrl-s. Right-click in the editor to launch a context menu or the File toolbar.

Modify ejbCreate and ejbRemove

1. Modify the `ejbCreate` method to retrieve a `QueueConnectionFactory` and Queue, then establish a `QueueConnection` and a `QueueSession` with the provider. Thereafter, use the `QueueSession` to create the `QueueSender`:

```
public void ejbCreate() throws javax.ejb.CreateException {
//on create retrieve administered objects, establish session
and sender
try{
        //bind to container namespace
        InitialContext context = new InitialContext();

        //lookup factory and queue
    factory = (QueueConnectionFactory)context.lookup("java:comp/
    env/jms/SenderQCF");
```

```
queue = (Queue)context.lookup("java:comp/env/jms/SenderQ");

    //create connection, session, and sender
    conn = factory.createQueueConnection();
session = conn.createQueueSession(false,
Session.AUTO_ACKNOWLEDGE);
    sender = session.createSender(queue);
}catch(NamingException ne){
    System.out.println("NamingException thrown in ejbCreate "
+ ne);
    throw new javax.ejb.CreateException(ne.getMessage());
}catch(JMSException je){
    System.out.println("JMSException thrown in ejbCreate " +
je);
    Exception e = je.getLinkedException();
    if(e != null){
      System.out.println("JMS Linked Exception: " + e);
    }
    throw new javax.ejb.CreateException(je.getMessage());    }
}
```

Observe that we bind the JMS client to the namespace provided by the J2EE server. We subsequently specify JNDI names of `java:comp/env/jms/SenderQCF` and `java:comp/env/jms/SenderQ` for the `QueueConnectionFactory` and `Queue` respectively. As discussed in Chapter 4, "Using the JMS API," `java:comp/env` reflects our starting point in the namespace, and in keeping with best practice, we have specified administered objects located in a subcontext called `jms`. Prior to deployment, we use the qualified names of the administered objects, `jms/SenderQCF` and `jms/SenderQ`, to define resource references that we will associate with **EmpRecordSender** and bind to the actual objects in the JNDI namespace. We use a simple, nontransacted `QueueSession` because the session bean does not invoke any local transactions.

2. Modify `ejbRemove`, adding code to close the `QueueConnection`. This will have a cascading effect on all other open JMS resources derived from it.

```
public void ejbRemove() {
//clean up resources
try{
      conn.close();
}catch(JMSException je){
System.out.println("JMSException thrown in ejbRemove " + je);
      Exception e = je.getLinkedException();
      if(e != null){
System.out.println("JMS Linked Exception: " + e);
      }
}
}
```

Implement the Submit Method   The submit method sends employee data and is called with employee data as argument. In reality we probably would have defined an employee object, but for simplicity we assume that employee data is passed to the session bean as a number of string variables. We package the passed data in a `TextMessage` object using a tagged/ delimited format, with each field being delimited using a semicolon (;). The tagged/delimited format was similarly selected for simplicity.

1. Add the implementation for the submit method to **EmpRecordSenderBean.java**:

```
public void submit(String employeeID, String firstName, String
lastName, String email) throws javax.ejb.EJBException
{
    try {
        TextMessage msg = session.createTextMessage();
        //message created as a delimited text string
msg.setText(employeeID + ";" + firstName + ";" + lastName +
";" + email);
        sender.send(msg);
    }catch (JMSException je){
System.out.println("JMSException thrown in submit " + je);
        Exception e = je.getLinkedException();
        if(e != null){
        System.out.println("JMS Linked Exception: " + e);
        }
    throw new javax.ejb.EJBException(je.getMessage());
    }
}
```

Note that we send the message, accepting default values for delivery mode, priority, and time-to-live. This results in a JMS message marked as persistent, with a priority of 4 and no expiry.

2. Check the EJB implementation files listed for **EmpRecordSender**, and open (double-click) **EmpRecordSender.java**. This defines the remote interface for the session bean and tells the client application what methods it can invoke.

3. Add a method definition for the submit method:

```
public void submit(
    String employeeID,
    String firstName,
    String lastName,
    String email)
throws javax.ejb.EJBException,java.rmi.RemoteException;
```

4. Save your work and fix any compilation errors if they occur.

Define Administered Objects

The JMS client retrieves a `QueueConnectionFactory` and `Queue` object from the application server's namespace. We must thus create appropriate definitions for the administered objects. First, we create and configure the unit test environment in Application Developer, which includes initialization of the embedded WebSphere JMS Provider. Then we start the test application server, and using the administration console, define our administered objects.

Set Up a Unit Test Environment

1. In Application Developer, select **File ➡ New ➡ Other**.
2. In the resulting wizard select **Server** in the left-hand pane and **Server and Server Configuration** in the right-hand pane (Figure 7–5). Click **Next**.

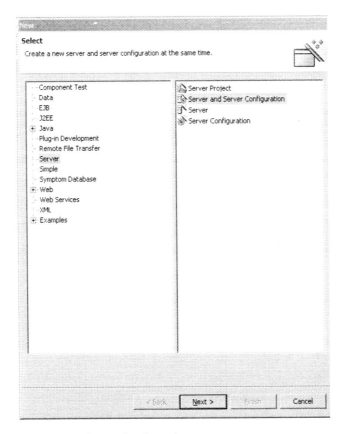

Figure 7-5 Create Server and Server Configuration

3. On the following page supply the name **TestSrv** for the server. Ensure that WebSphere 5.0 Test Environment is selected for server type (Figure 7–6). Click **Next**.

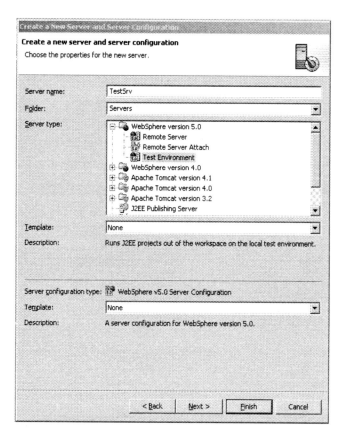

Figure 7-6 Server Configuration Details

4. Accept the **defaults** on the last page and click **Finish**. A test server is created.

5. If it is not already open, open the **Server** perspective (**Window ➡ Open Perspective**).

6. Double-click on **TestSrv** in the Server Configuration panel. This opens the server configuration file.

7. In the server configuration file, select the **Configuration** tab and ensure that the **Enable Administration Console** and **Enable Universal Test Client** options are selected (Figure 7–7).

We enable the administration console, as we will use it to create administered objects and other resources. The universal test client will be used to test the sender session bean.

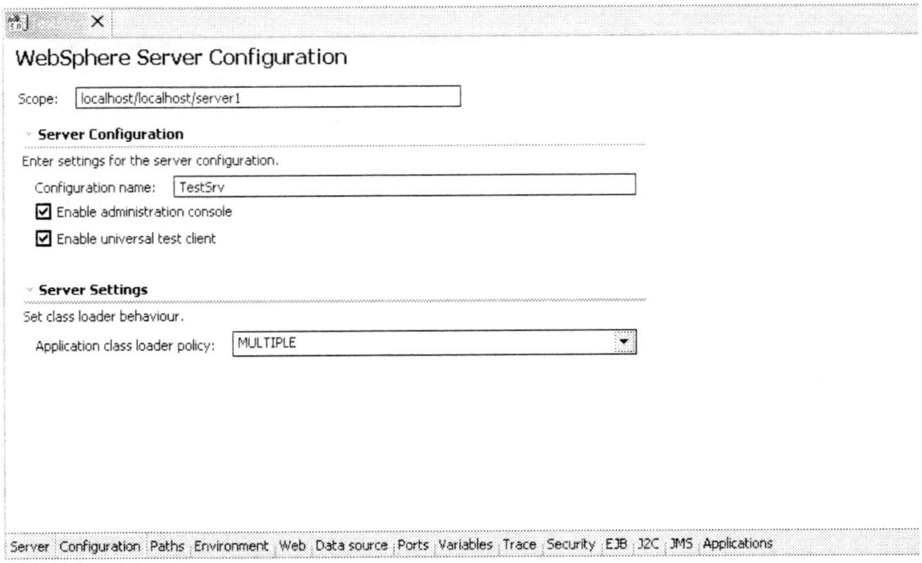

Figure 7-7 Server Configuration File: Configuration Tab

8. Switch to the **JMS** tab and change the initial state of the embedded JMS Server to **START** (Figure 7–8).

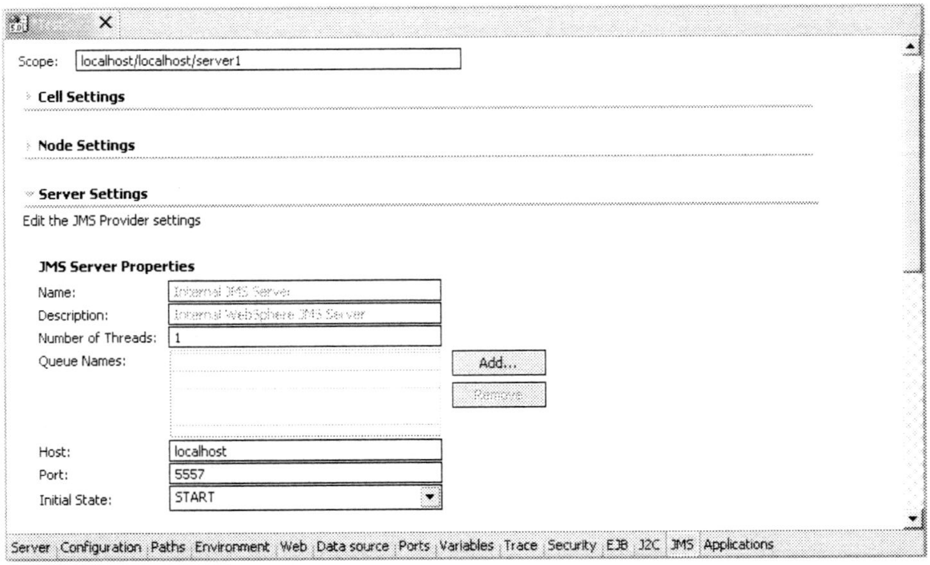

Figure 7-8 Server Configuration File: JMS Tab

9. Save the configuration file.

10. Move to the Servers panel, right-click on **TestSrv**, and select **Start**. The panel should automatically switch to the **Console** tab, which displays startup messages. You should see a message saying that the MQJD JMS Provider has started. This is the name given to the WebSphere JMS Provider implementation supplied as part of the unit test environment. Once startup is complete, an "open for e-business" message should be displayed (Figure 7–9).

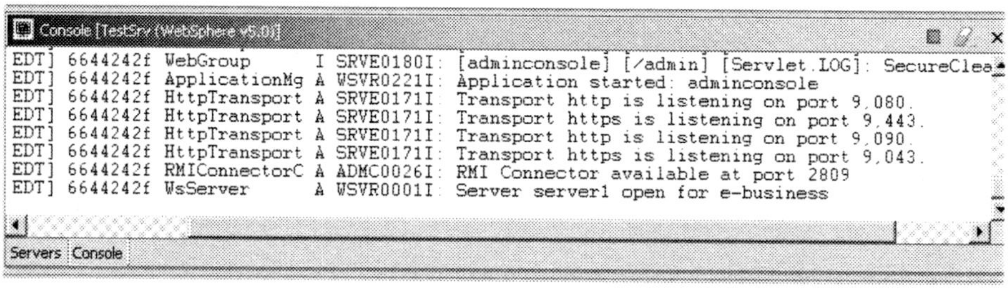

```
Console [TestSrv (WebSphere v5.0)]                                              x
EDT] 6644242f WebGroup        I SRVE0180I: [adminconsole] [/admin] [Servlet.LOG]: SecureClea
EDT] 6644242f ApplicationMg  A WSVR0221I: Application started: adminconsole
EDT] 6644242f HttpTransport  A SRVE0171I: Transport http is listening on port 9,080.
EDT] 6644242f HttpTransport  A SRVE0171I: Transport https is listening on port 9,443.
EDT] 6644242f HttpTransport  A SRVE0171I: Transport http is listening on port 9,090.
EDT] 6644242f HttpTransport  A SRVE0171I: Transport https is listening on port 9,043.
EDT] 6644242f RMIConnectorC  A ADMC0026I: RMI Connector available at port 2809
EDT] 6644242f WsServer       A WSVR0001I: Server server1 open for e-business

Servers Console
```

Figure 7-9 Server Console: Server Started

11. In the Servers panel, switch back to the **Server** tab. Right-click on **TestSrv** and select **Run Administrative Console**.

12. At the administration console's login page, supply a user ID (e.g., admin). Click **OK**.

13. The administration console is now ready for use (Figure 7–10). Note that if you double-click on the Admin Console tab, the administration console's window will be maximized.

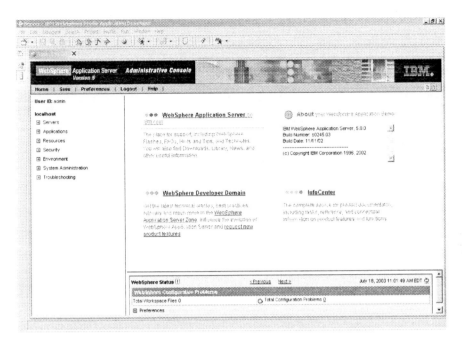

Figure 7-10 Administration Console

Create Administered Objects We need to create a `QueueConnectionFactory` and `Queue` object for the sender session bean that will provide access to the embedded WebSphere JMS Provider, which we are using for testing.

1. In the administration console's menu pane, expand **Resources** and select **WebSphere JMS Provider**. This opens up the provider pane (Figure 7–11).
   1. Click on the **WebSphere Queue Connection Factories** link.
   2. In the resulting page, click **New** to open the definitions form.
   3. In the definitions form (Figure 7–12), specify the following:
      - Name: **jms.sample.SenderQCF**
      - JNDI Name: **jms.sample.SenderQCF**
      - XA Enabled: uncheck the check box
      - Accept all other defaults

Note that the naming of the connection factory is independent of the name specified in the JMS client. This is possible because the WebSphere Application Server, through its use of resource references, allows us to isolate the application from actual object names. This is useful because it allows us to easily change the administered object used without changing the JMS client code. Given that we are using the WebSphere JMS Provider, we have very few properties that we need to define (see Chapter 6, "IBM

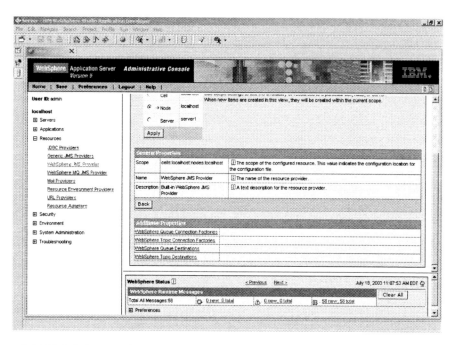

Figure 7-11 WebSphere JMS Provider

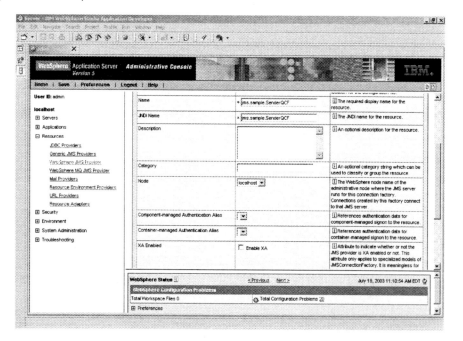

Figure 7-12 WebSphere QueueConnectionFactory

JMS–Administered Objects"). As we are not interested in global transactions here, we uncheck the XA enabled flag.

2. Click **OK** at the end of the form to save the object definition.

3. Return to the WebSphere JMS Provider page and select the **WebSphere Queue Destinations** link.

4. In the resulting page, click **New** to open the definitions form.

5. In the definitions form (Figure 7–13), specify the following:

- Name: **jms.sample.Queue**
- JNDI Name: **jms.sample.Queue**
- Accept all other defaults

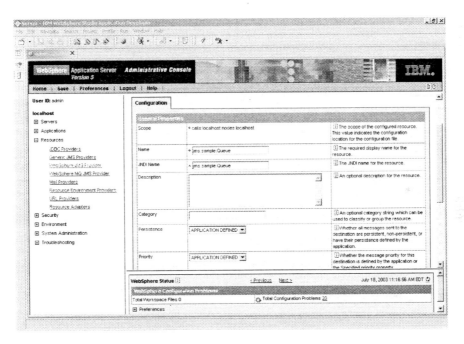

Figure 7-13 WebSphere Queue

We adopt a similar naming convention and accept all other default values. By accepting the defaults, we are allowing the message persistence, priority, and expiry to be defined by the JMS client application. We could, of course, override the client's settings by setting the appropriate properties if we needed to.

6. Click **OK** at the end of the form to save the object definition.

7. In the administration console's menu bar, click **Save** to apply your changes.

8. You can log out from the administration console.

Update the JMS Server Configuration   Recall from our discussions in Chapter 6 that once a WebSphere `Queue` has been defined, it must be added to the JMS server's list of queues. This enables the JMS server to create the underlying queue that this administered object represents. To do this, we modify the server configuration file.

1. Switch to the Server Configuration Panel and double-click on **TestSrv** to open the server configuration file.
2. Return to the **JMS** tab and click **Add** to add the name of the WebSphere queue that we just created (`jms.sample.Queue`) to the list of queue names (Figure 7–14).

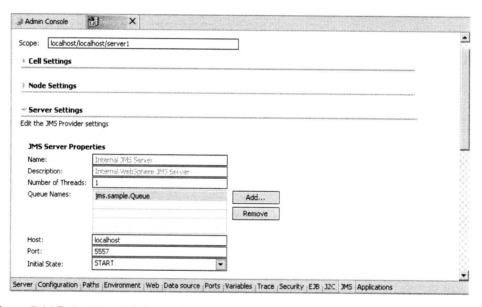

Figure 7-14 Embedded JMS Server Queues

3. Save the configuration file.

Deploy the Sender Enterprise Application

Before deploying `EmpRecordSender`, we create resource references for the sender session bean to link the JNDI names specified in code to the administered objects we have defined. We then generate deploy code and add the enterprise application to the server.

Define Resource References

1. In Application Developer, return to the **J2EE** perspective.

2. In the J2EE Hierarchy Panel, right-click on the EJB Module **EmpRecordSenderEJB** and select **Open With ▸ Deployment Descriptor Editor** (alternatively, double-click on **EmpRecordSenderEJB**). This displays the deployment descriptor for EJBs defined in this module.

3. Click the **References** tab and select our session bean **EmpRecordSender**. We can now add resource references (Figure 7–15).

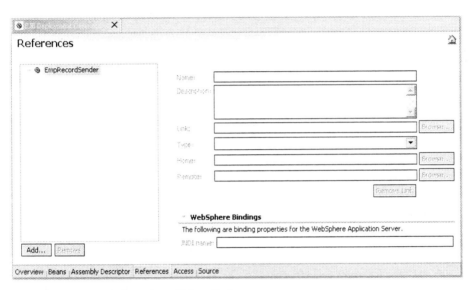

Figure 7-15 Deployment Descriptor Editor: References

4. Click **Add**, and in the resulting wizard select **EJB Resource Reference** as the type of reference to be created. We use this to define the `QueueConnectionFactory`. Click **Next**.

5. On the Resource Definition page specify the name as **jms/SenderQCF**. Select a type of **javax.jms.QueueConnectionFactory** from the dropdown list and set Authentication to **Application** (Figure 7–16). Click **Finish**.

6. **jms/SenderQCF** should now be listed on the references page. Note that the name corresponds to the JNDI name we used in the JMS client.

7. Select **jms/SenderQCF**. In the right-hand pane under WebSphere Bindings, supply the name of the associated administered object in the WebSphere namespace, **jms.sample.SenderQCF** (Figure 7–17). This binds the resource reference to the `QueueConnectionFactory` we defined earlier.

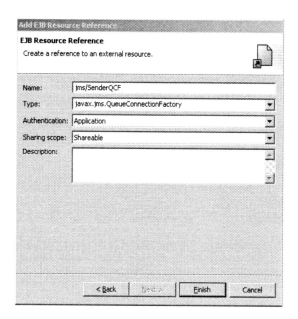

Figure 7-16 EJB Resource Reference

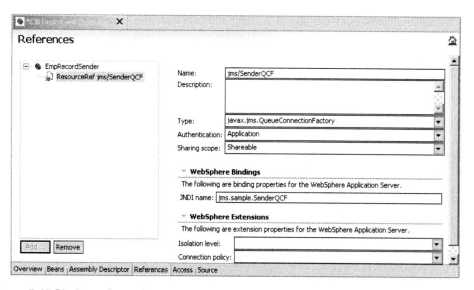

Figure 7-17 Bindings: QueueConnectionFactory Resource Reference

8. Save the Deployment Descriptor, then select **EmpRecordSender** and click **Add**.

9. In the resulting wizard select **Resource Environment Reference**. We use this to define the Queue. Click **Next**.

10. On the Resource Definition page specify the name **jms/SenderQ** and select a type of **javax.jms.Queue** from the dropdown list (Figure 7–18). Click **Finish**.

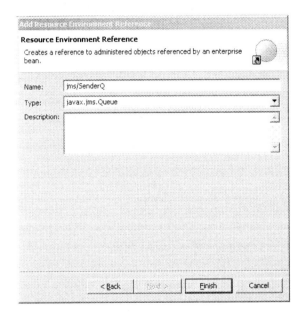

Figure 7-18 Resource Environment Reference

11. javax.jms.Queue should now be listed in the resources panel. We bind the administered object jms.sample.Queue with the resource reference by selecting it and filling in the JNDI name (Figure 7–19).

12. Save the deployment descriptor. We have now defined our resource references.

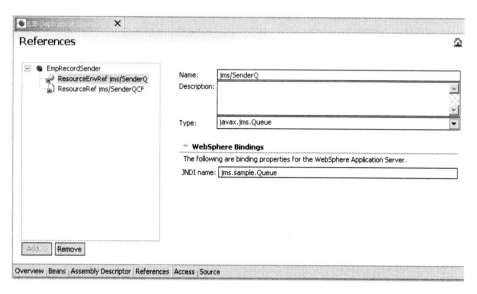

Figure 7-19 Bindings: Queue Resource Reference

Add the Enterprise Application to the Server

1. In the J2EE Hierarchy Panel, right-click on the EJB Module **EmpRecordSenderEJB** and select **Generate ⟶ Deploy and RMIC Code....**
2. In the resulting dialog ensure that **EmpRecordSender** is selected and click **Finish**.
3. Switch to the **Server** perspective. In the Server Configuration panel, right-click on **TestSrv** and select **Add ⟶ EmpRecordSender**.
4. We now need to restart the server, log out from the administration console if it is still active, and then in the Servers panel right-click on **TestSrv** and select **Restart**.
5. Check the console tab and confirm that the server has successfully restarted. You will observe console entries listing the administered objects we defined, as they are bound into the namespace. You will also see an entry signifying that the application **EmpRecordSender** has started.

We have successfully deployed the sender session bean. We now create and deploy the MDB before testing. You may have observed that in terms of implementation effort, coding the JMS client was relatively straightforward. However, there are quite a few tasks associated with configuring and deploying J2EE applications.

Create the Message-Driven Bean

The MDB will retrieve messages from the same destination that the sender session bean sends them to. In keeping with our scenario we implement the MDB as part of a different enterprise application project (representing Application B). We focus on message handling only and simply code the MDB to print out the received message. We define required administered objects and then deploy the MDB. This part of the tutorial assumes that we are now familiar with many of the tasks that we need to undertake, as such repeated steps are not detailed to the same level. You can consult previous instructions should you need too for reference.

Implement the MDB

The MDB will be packaged as part of an enterprise application project that represents Application B.

1. In Application Developer switch to the **J2EE** perspective.
2. Create a J2EE 1.3 Enterprise Application Project, specifying the project name **EmpRecordUpdate**. As before, create only an EJB module.
3. In the J2EE Hierarchy Panel, expand the **EJB Modules** folder, then right-click on **EmpRecordUpdateEJB** and select **New ➡ Enterprise Bean**.
4. In the resulting wizard ensure that **EmpRecordUpdateEJB** is selected as the project for the EJB. Click **Next**.
5. On the next page, select **Message-driven bean** as the EJB type and supply a name **EmpRecordMDB** and package **jms.book.sample.ejb** for the EJB (Figure 7–20). Click **Next**.

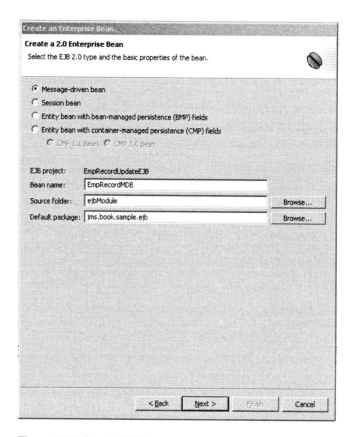

Figure 7-20 Create MDB

6. On the Enterprise Bean Details page, accept the default transaction type of **Container** and select a destination type of **Queue**. Leave Message selector and Listener port name blank (Figure 7–21).

If we required message retrieval to be based on a message selector, we would have specified the selector here. Note that **AcknowledgeMode** is grayed; this is because any transactions will be handled by the container, and messages will be acknowledged at the end of the transaction. If you select Bean-managed transactions, then the options for **AcknowledgeMode**, discussed in Chapter 4, become available for selection.

7. Accept the defaults on the final page and click **Finish**.

8. In the J2EE Hierarchy Panel, expand **EmpRecordMDB** and open **EmpRecordMDB-Bean.java**. This is the implementation bean class for our MDB.

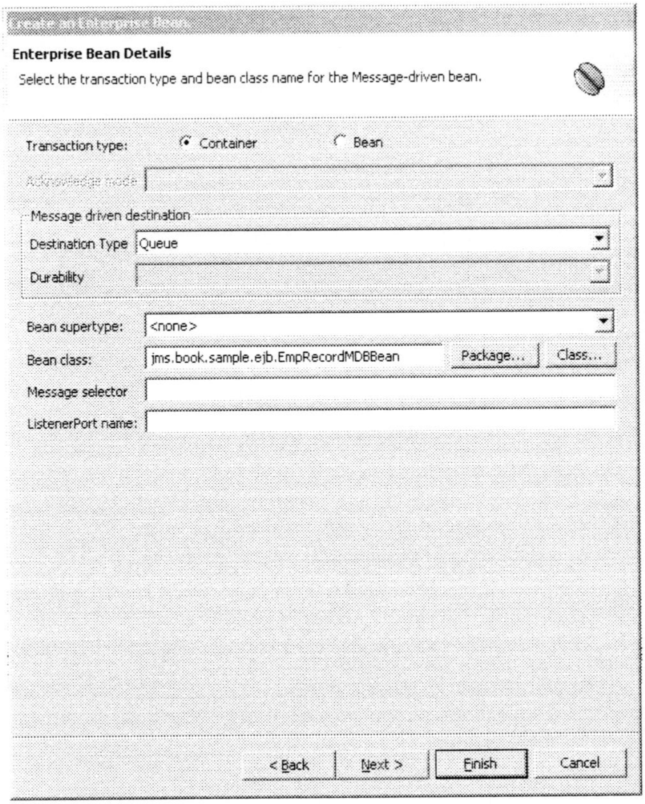

Figure 7-21 Message-Driven Bean Details

9. Add the following import statements for JMS and JNDI packages. We need the JNDI package to look up the home interface for the session bean that the MDB passes retrieved data too:

```
import javax.jms.*; //jms classes
import javax.naming.*;    // JNDI imports
```

10. The only method that we are really interested in is the `onMessage` method. The `onMessage` method is passed the JMS message by the container, and we use it to implement our message handling code. At this stage we insert a simple code block to confirm the message type, unpack the message, and print it to the server console.

```
public void onMessage(javax.jms.Message msg) {
    try{
        if(msg instanceof TextMessage){
            System.out.println("message received");
```

```
            TextMessage tMsg = (TextMessage)msg;
            String message = tMsg.getText();

            System.out.println("message: " + message);

            //parse received message
            //initialize variables
            String employeeID = "";
            String firstName = "";
            String lastName = "";
            String email = "";

        //use java.util.StringTokenizer to parse string
        java.util.StringTokenizer st = new
        java.util.StringTokenizer(message, ";");
            while (st.hasMoreTokens()) {
                employeeID = st.nextToken();
                firstName = st.nextToken();
                lastName = st.nextToken();
                email = st.nextToken();
            }


        }else{
    System.out.println("unexpected message instance received by
    EmpRecordMDB");
    System.out.println("message type received: " +
    msg.getJMSType() +", " + "TextMessage expected");
            }
        }catch(Exception e){
            System.out.println("Exception thrown " + e);
        }
    }
```

We can adopt various approaches to handling unexpected messages or messages with bad data. In this instance we are printing an error message and then discarding the JMS message. If an exception is thrown, however, the message is returned to the queue and could be redelivered. We could start the code block with a check of the `JMSRedelivered` property in the JMS message header to ascertain if the message is being redelivered. We can additionally check the `JMSXDeliveryCount` to see how many times it had been redelivered. As we see shortly, we can also configure the response of the message listener service to messaging exceptions.

11. Save your work and fix any compilation errors.

Define Administered Object and Listener Port

The MDB is associated with a listener port, which specifies the `ConnectionFactory` and `Destination` that will be monitored by the message listener service. We define a new

`QueueConnectionFactory` for the MDB, as its connection is configured differently from the sender session bean. We reuse the existing `Queue` object, and then define the listener port.

Create the QueueConnectionFactory

1. Switch to the **Server** perspective and launch the administration console.
2. Log in and navigate to the WebSphere JMS Provider page (expand **Resources** in the menu pane).
3. Click on the **WebSphere Queue Connection Factories** link, and in the resulting page, click on **New** to open the definitions form.
4. In the definitions form specify the following:
   - Name: **jms.sample.XAReceiverQCF**
   - JNDI Name: **jms.sample.XAReceiverQCF**
   - XA Enabled: ensure the check box is checked.
   - Accept all other defaults
5. Click **OK** at the end of the form to save the object definition.

As we require the retrieval of the message and update to the system of record to be potentially handled as an XA global transaction, we define this `QueueConnectionFactory` as XA enabled.

Define the Listener Port   1.In the administration console's menu pane, expand **Servers** and click on **Application Servers**. This lists the application servers that can be managed from this administration console. You should see a listing for our test server, called **server1** (Figure 7–22).
2. Click on the link **server1**, and in the resulting page scroll down and locate the **Message Listener Service** link. Click **Message Listener Service**.
3. This leads to the Message Listener Service page. Click on the link for **Listener Ports**.
4. In the resulting page, click on **New** to open the definitions form.

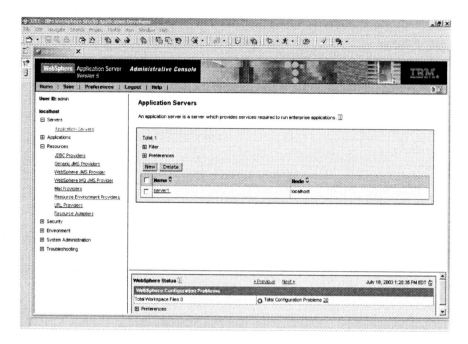

Figure 7-22 Application Servers

5. In the definitions form (Figure 7–23), specify the following:
- Name: **MDBListenerPort**
- Initial State: select **Started**
- Connection Factory JNDI Name: **jms.sample.XAReceiverQCF**
- Destination JNDI Name: **jms.sample.Queue**
- Accept all other defaults

6. Click **OK** at the end of the form to save the object definition.

The listener port specifies our previously defined QueueConnectionFactory and Queue. The destination queue matches the target queue for the sender session bean, ensuring that messages sent there will be retrieved by the message listener service. We specify an initial start state of started, and thus the port will be activated once we restart the server. The other properties listed affect how the listener port performs its duties. Of particular interest is the Maximum Retries property that defaults to zero. At this setting the port will not redeliver a message if message processing fails; instead it will stop. Thus, if EmpRecordMDB throws an exception during message processing, the message will not be redelivered. Rather, the listener port will stop, preventing any other message from being delivered to the EmpRecordMDB. We would then have to manually restart the listener port once the cause of the exception had been resolved.

7. In the administration console's menu bar, click **Save** to apply the changes we have made.

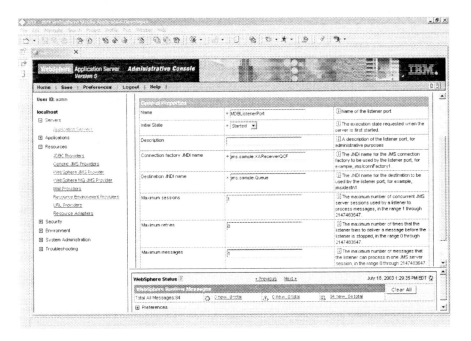

Figure 7-23 Listener Port Definition

8. You can log out from the administration console.

Deploy the Receiver Enterprise Application

Before deploying EmpRecordUpdate, we associate the MDB with the listener port that we just defined. We also specify a Required transaction attribute for the onMessage method, ensuring that message retrieval is done as part of a transaction. Because it is an MDB and can only be interacted with via JMS messages, there is no need to generate deploy and RMIC code.

1. Switch to the **J2EE** perspective and double-click on **EmpRecordUpdateEJB** to open the deployment descriptor.
2. Click the **Bean** tab and select **EmpRecordMDB**, displaying the associated properties.
3. In the Listener Port field specify the name of the listener port associated with this MDB, in this case **MDBListenerPort** (Figure 7–24).

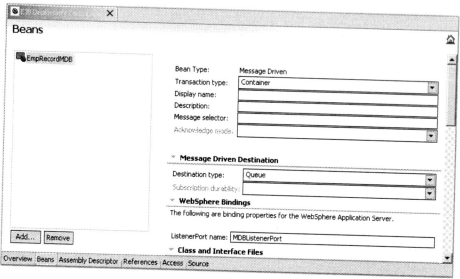

Figure 7-24 Listener Port Definition

4. Click on the **Assembly Descriptor** tab and use the **Add** button under Container Transactions to add the `onMessage` method with a `Required` transaction attribute (Figure 7–25).

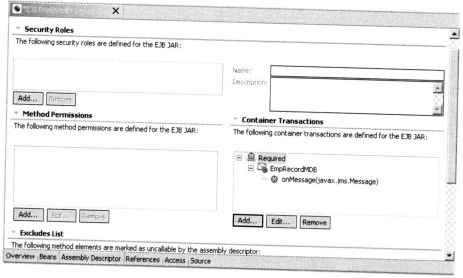

Figure 7-25 MDB Transactional Context

5. Save the deployment descriptor.

6. Switch to the **Server** perspective, and in the Server Configuration panel add **EmpRe-cordUpdate** to **TestSrv**.

7. In the Servers panel, switch to the **Servers** tab. Check the Server State; it should say that the server needs to be restarted and republished.

8. Log out from the administration console if it is still active, then in the Servers panel right-click on **TestSrv** and select **Restart**. This will republish and restart the server.

9. Check the server console; you should find an entry signifying that **EmpRecordUpdate** has started.

Test the Scenario Implementation

To test the message exchange, we use the universal test client supplied as part of Application Developer to invoke EmpRecordSender's submit method. This sends a message to the monitored destination, and we should see an entry in the server console posted by EmpRe-cordMDB when it receives the message.

1. In the Servers panel, switch to the **Servers** tab, right-click **TestSrv**, and select **Run Universal Test Client**. This loads the Universal Test Client (UTC) homepage (Figure 7–26).

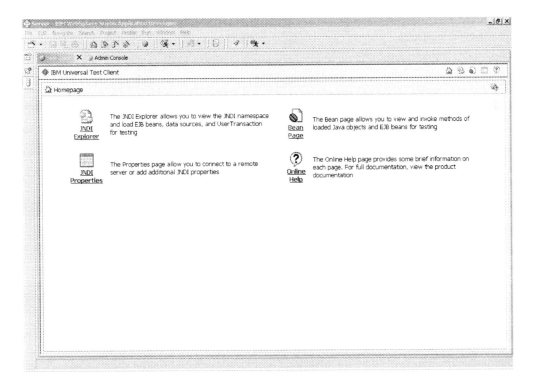

Figure 7-26 Universal Test Client Homepage

2. Select **JNDI Explorer** in the UTC homepage, and expand the **ejb** folder in the resulting page to display **EmpRecordSenderHome** (Figure 7–27).

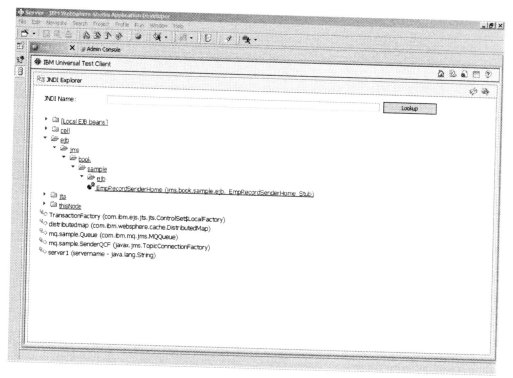

Figure 7-27 EJB Home Interface

3. Select **EmpRecordSenderHome**; this takes you to the Test page.

4. In the References pane, select the **create** method defined by EmpRecordSenderHome.

5. Invoke the **create** method by clicking the **invoke** button in the parameters pane (Figure 7–28).

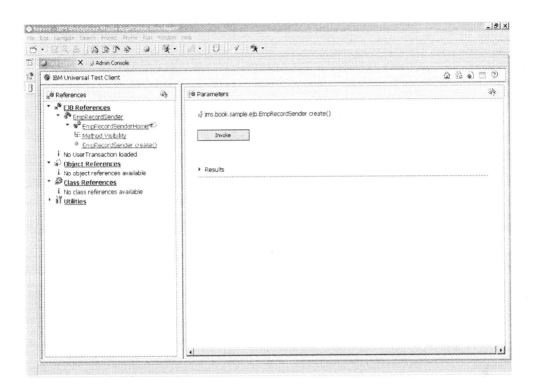

Figure 7-28 Create EJB Instance

6. This creates an instance of `EmpRecordSender`; click **Work with Object** (Figure 7–29).

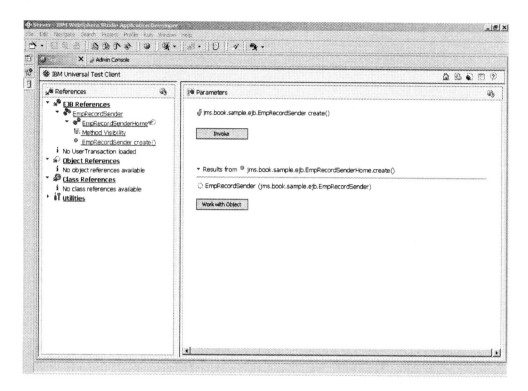

Figure 7-29 Work with EJB Instance

7. In the references pane, expand the **EmpRecordSender** instance and select the **submit** method. This is the method we defined to send employee data. A form is displayed to supply the arguments for the method; however, the argument variable names are not displayed, only their type. Populate the form with an employee ID, first name, last name, and email address. Then invoke the method (Figure 7–30).

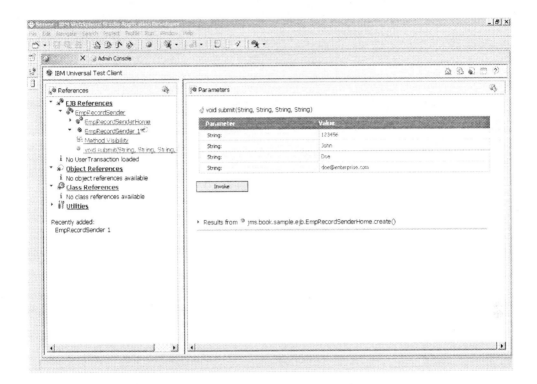

Figure 7-30 Invoke Service Call

8. You should see the message "The method completed successfully" in the results pane (Figure 7–31).

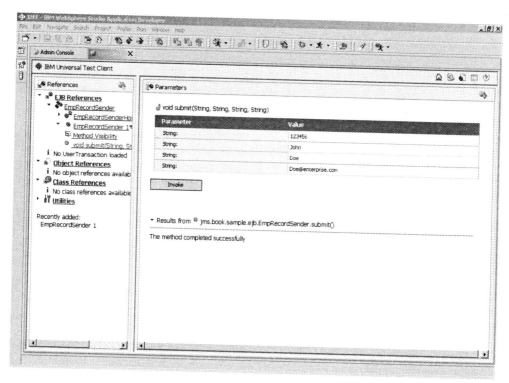

Figure 7-31 Service Call Results

9. Check the server console; you should find an entry signifying that **EmpRecordMDB** successfully retrieved the message we just sent (Figure 7–32).

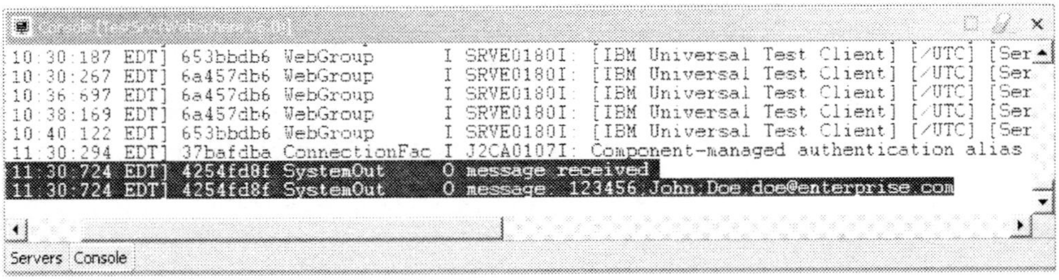

```
10:30:187 EDT] 653bbdb6 WebGroup      I SRVE0180I: [IBM Universal Test Client] [/UTC] [Ser
10:30:267 EDT] 6a457db6 WebGroup      I SRVE0180I: [IBM Universal Test Client] [/UTC] [Ser
10:36:697 EDT] 6a457db6 WebGroup      I SRVE0180I: [IBM Universal Test Client] [/UTC] [Ser
10:38:169 EDT] 6a457db6 WebGroup      I SRVE0180I: [IBM Universal Test Client] [/UTC] [Ser
10:40:122 EDT] 653bbdb6 WebGroup      I SRVE0180I: [IBM Universal Test Client] [/UTC] [Ser
11:30:294 EDT] 37bafdba ConnectionFac I J2CA0107I: Component-managed authentication alias
11:30:724 EDT] 4254fd8f SystemOut     O message received
11:30:724 EDT] 4254fd8f SystemOut     O message 123456;John;Doe;doe@enterprise.com
```

Servers   Console

Figure 7-32 MDB Output

We have now successfully implemented the exchange of messages between a session bean and an MDB. Using an MDB greatly simplified our message consumer implementation, since we did not have to write any connectivity code—that is, create QueueConnection and so on. Instead, it was primarily an exercise in configuration. In keeping with the scenario, our next step is to call a session bean, using code similar to the following:

```
//bind to container namespace
InitialContext context = new InitialContext();
//retrieve home interface
home = (EmpRecordUpdateLocalHome)context.lookup("java:comp/
env/ejb/EmpRecordUpdate");
...
//invoke EmpRecordUpdate
EmpRecordUpdateLocal handler = home.create();
handler.update(employeeID, firstName, lastName, email);
```

Note that we used the session bean's local interface, since the MDB and session bean are running in the same container. This is an optimization offered by EJB 2.0 (J2EE 1.3). The retrieval of the message and the call to onMessage are done as part of a transaction managed by the container; we thus propagate that transaction onto the session bean via the call to its update method. Assuming the resource it invokes is appropriately configured, we then have a global XA transaction, as we are using an XA-enabled WebSphere QueueConnectionFactory. In Appendix B we extend our implementation to include a system of record implemented by a database. We use a session bean and entity bean to access the database, and we see how to configure the interaction such that the retrieval of the message and the update to the database is done as a single global XA transaction.

Scenario 2: Implementing Publish-Subscribe

In our basic scenario we considered the exchange of messages between two known applications. If the scenario is extended to require that employee record updates should be sent to any application that has expressed an interest, then our message distribution pattern shifts into the realm of publish-subscribe.

As shown in Figure 7–33, our solution architecture varies only in that we now have multiple recipients for a single message. We can thus implement the scenario in a similar manner, using a session bean to implement a `Topic` publisher (message producer) and MDBs to implement subscribers (message consumer). Depending upon the usage requirements, the MDBs could be defined as durable or nondurable subscribers, allowing in the case of durable subscribers for the application to continue to receive publications even if it is not running. Transaction considerations discussed earlier also still apply.

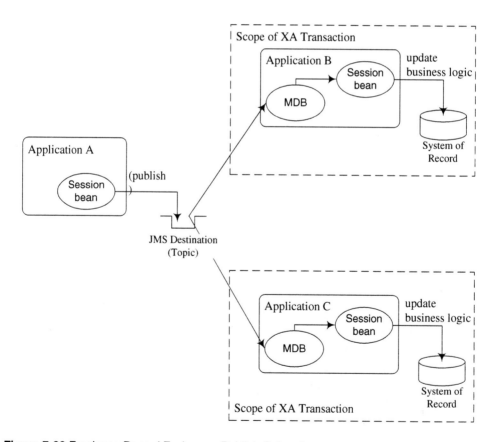

Figure 7-33 Employee Record Exchange: Publish-Subscribe

The design of the Topic name hierarchy that binds publishers and subscribers and the design decisions that go into deciding how information is categorized are probably the most underestimated efforts associated with utilizing publish-subscribe messaging. The design is driven by application need, which is influenced by the degree of granularity required. For instance, is an application interested in every employee record update or just those associated with a specific department? A key question that must also be answered is whether topic names are static (i.e., predefined) or can be dynamic (i.e., made up by the application based on certain parameters). The importance of this is that the answer affects how topic names are represented. Static topic names can be encapsulated and stored in `Topic`-administered object. Dynamic names cannot, since they are not known before hand. To accommodate the use of dynamic topic names, JMS supports the creation of the `Topic` object by the JMS client based on a topic name defined in a URI format (see Chapter 4). The format of the topic name is JMS provider–specific, and in the case of the WebSphere JMS and WebSphere MQ JMS providers takes the form

```
//create Topic using dynamic topic name
String topicName = name + "/" + dept; //based on arguments
Topic topic = session.createTopic("topic://" + topicName);
```

It is important to note that a subscriber that uses dynamic topic names cannot be implemented using an MDB. As we have seen, the MDB is configured using a listener port that specifies a `ConnectionFactory` and `Destination` object; thus the administered object must be predefined.

Publishers and subscribers can of course be implemented by other J2EE entities such as servlets and portlets. In Chapter 4 we extensively discussed considerations associated with using these components to implement JMS clients. It is worth repeating that because both servlets and portlets implement essentially a request-response invocation pattern. Careful thought has to be given to their design if they are used to implement subscribers, as you must decide how to handle waiting for messages to arrive and how that impacts the invocation model.

In applications that are human-facing, such as Web portals, there is the general question of how screen updates are handled, because currently, refreshing a portlet refreshes the entire page. This takes on even greater importance in publish-subscribe scenarios, where messages can arrive regularly, particularly if it is desired that the content of the message be displayed in real time.

For the purposes of this implementation scenario, we implement a publisher using a session bean and subscribers using MDBs. We implement both a durable and nondurable subscriber to explore the differences in their behavior, and for simplicity we use a single-level topic name hierarchy. Testing is done using the WebSphere JMS Provider embedded in Application Developer. Once again, the tutorial assumes you have established some familiarity with the tools based on the last tutorial.

Create the Publisher Session Bean

Following a similar pattern to the first tutorial, we create a session bean, which we use to create the JMS client. We then create administered objects in the WebSphere namespace and deploy the session bean to the application server.

Implement the Publisher Session Bean

The session bean will be packaged as part of an enterprise application project, which represents the publishing application.

1. Launch Application Developer (if it is not already running), and switch to the **J2EE** perspective.
2. Create a J2EE 1.3 Enterprise Application Project, specifying the project name **EmpRecordPublisher**. As before, create only an EJB module.
3. Create a session bean in the EJB module **EmpRecordPublisherEJB**, specifying the name **EmpRecordPublisher** and package **jms.book.sample.ejb**.
4. Open **EmpRecordPublisherBean.java**, the bean implementation class, in the Java editor. We follow exactly the same implementation pattern used for EmpRecordSender.
5. Add the following import statements for JMS and JNDI packages. Because these are packaged by the J2EE environment, you do not need to specify any additional class path settings:

```
import javax.jms.*;              // JMS classes
import javax.naming.*;           // JNDI imports
```

6. Add the following variables to the class definition. We need these in our method implementations:

```
//attributes
private TopicConnectionFactory factory = null;
private TopicConnection conn = null;
private TopicSession session = null;
private Topic topic = null;
private TopicPublisher publisher = null;
```

7. Save your work. You can use the keyboard shortcut Ctrl-s, then right-click in the editor to launch a context menu or the File toolbar.

Modify ejbCreate and ejbRemove

1. Modify the `ejbCreate` method to retrieve a `TopicConnectionFactory` and `Topic`, then establish a `TopicConnection`, `TopicSession`, and finally a `TopicPublisher`:

```
public void ejbCreate() throws javax.ejb.CreateException {
//on create retrieve administered objects, establish session
and publisher
```

```
try{
    //bind to container namespace
    InitialContext context = new InitialContext();

    //lookup factory and topic
factory = (TopicConnectionFactory)context.lookup("java:comp/
env/jms/PubTCF");
topic = (Topic)context.lookup("java:comp/env/jms/PubTopic");

    //create connection, session, and publisher
    conn = factory.createTopicConnection();
session = conn.createTopicSession(false,
Session.AUTO_ACKNOWLEDGE);
    publisher = session.createPublisher(topic);
}catch(NamingException ne){
System.out.println("NamingException thrown in ejbCreate " +
ne);
    throw new javax.ejb.CreateException(ne.getMessage());
}catch(JMSException je){
System.out.println("JMSException thrown in ejbCreate " + je);
    Exception e = je.getLinkedException();
    if(e != null){
       System.out.println("JMS Linked Exception: " + e);
    }
    throw new javax.ejb.CreateException(je.getMessage());    }
}
```

Notice that the code is virtually identical to that implemented in **EmpRecordSender**, with the exception that here we use the publish-subscribe domain. We specified JNDI names java:comp/env/jms/PubTCF and java:comp/env/jms/PubTopic for the TopicConnectionFactory and Topic respectively. As before, we use resource references to bind them to administered objects in the JNDI namespace.

2. Modify ejbRemove, adding code to close the TopicConnection. This has a cascading effect on all other open JMS resources derived from it.

```
public void ejbRemove() {
//clean up resources
try{
      conn.close();
}catch(JMSException je){
System.out.println("JMSException thrown in ejbRemove " + je);
      Exception e = je.getLinkedException();
      if(e != null){
System.out.println("JMS Linked Exception: " + e);
      }
}
}
```

Implement the publish Method   We introduce the `publish` method to handle publication of employee data. It is identical in implementation to the submit method of
EmpRecordSender.

1. Add the implementation for the publish method to **EmpRecordPublisherBean.java**:

```
public void publish(String employeeID, String firstName,
String lastName, String email) throws javax.ejb.EJBException
{
    try {
        TextMessage msg = session.createTextMessage();
        //message created as a delimited text string
msg.setText(employeeID + ";" + firstName + ";" + lastName +
";" + email);
        publisher.publish(msg);
    }catch (JMSException je){
System.out.println("JMSException thrown in submit " + je);
        Exception e = je.getLinkedException();
        if(e != null){
        System.out.println("JMS Linked Exception: " + e);
        }
    throw new javax.ejb.EJBException(je.getMessage());


    }
}
```

2. Add the `publish` method definition to the remote interface defined in **EmpRecord-
Publisher.java**:

```
public void publish(
    String employeeID,
    String firstName,
    String lastName,
    String email)
throws javax.ejb.EJBException,java.rmi.RemoteException;
```

3. Save your work and fix any compilation errors if they occur.

Define Administered Objects

We define the `TopicConnectionFactory` and `Topic` object that is used by the publisher
session bean. They are based on the WebSphere JMS Provider, which we are using for testing.
The following instructions require that you have a configured unit test environment. If you
skipped scenario 1, refer back to the section on setting up a unit test environment.

1. Launch the administration console and ensure your server is started if it is not already running.

2. Navigate to the **WebSphere JMS Provider** page, and click on the **WebSphere Topic Connection Factories** link. In the resulting page click on **New** to open the definitions form.

3. In the definitions form (Figure 7–34), specify the following:
   - Name: **jms.sample.PubTCF**
   - JNDI Name: **jms.sample.PubTCF**
   - Port: select **QUEUED**
   - XA Enabled: uncheck the check box
   - Accept all other defaults

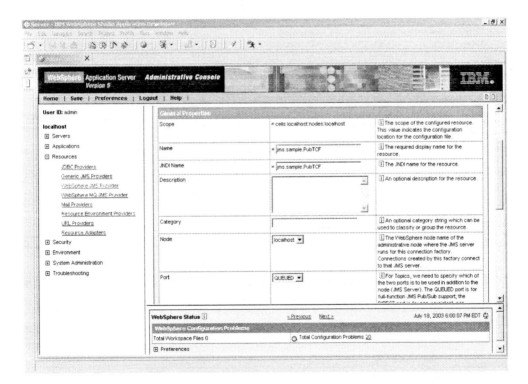

Figure 7-34 WebSphere TopicConnectionFactory

As discussed in Chapter 6, specifying a value QUEUED for port reflects the use of the embedded JMS Server's WebSphere MQ implementation. The other option is DIRECT, which maps to the MQ Real-time Transport.

4. Click **OK** to save the object definition.

5. Click the **WebSphere Topic Destinations** link on the provider page, and then click **New** to open the definitions form.

6. In the definitions form (Figure 7–35), specify the following:

- Name: **jms.sample.Topic**
- JNDI Name: **jms.sample.Topic**
- Topic: **employeeData**
- Accept all other defaults

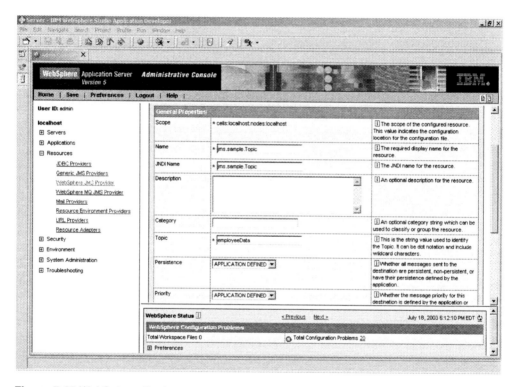

Figure 7-35 WebSphere Topic

We specify a single-level topic name, which defines the topic on which data will be published and subscribed.

7. Click **OK** to save the object definition.

8. In the administration console's menu bar, click **Save** to apply your changes.

9. You can log out from the administration console.

Note that unlike WebSphere Queues, there is no need to add WebSphere Topic names to the JMS Server.

Deploy the Publisher Enterprise Application

The deployment process follows the same steps employed for EmpRecordSender. We create the appropriate resource references for the publisher session bean, generate deploy code, then add the application to the application server.

Define Resource References

1. In Application Developer, return to the **J2EE** perspective and open the deployment descriptor for **EmpRecordPublisherEJB**.

2. Click on the **References** tab and create an EJB Resource Reference for **EmpRecord-Publisher** called **jms/PubTCF**. Remember to specify a type of **javax.jms.TopicConnectionFactory** and authentication value of **Application**.

3. Bind **jms/PubTCF** to **jms.sample.PubTCF**.

4. Similarly, create a Resource Environment Reference called **jms/PubTopic** of type **javax.jms.Topic**. Then bind it to **jms.sample.Topic**.

5. The deployment descriptor should be similar to that shown in Figure 7–36.

Figure 7-36 Publisher Session Bean Deployment Descriptor

6. Save the deployment descriptor.

Add the Enterprise Application to the Server

1. In the J2EE Hierarchy Panel, right-click on the EJB Module **EmpRecordPublish-erEJB**, and select **Generate ▸ Deploy and RMIC Code....**

2. In the resulting dialog box ensure that **EmpRecordPublisher** is selected and click **Finish**.

3. Switch to the **Server** perspective. In the Server Configuration panel, right-click on **TestSrv** and select **Add ▸ EmpRecordPublisher**.

4. Log out from the administration console if it is still active, then in the Servers panel right-click on **TestSrv** and select **Restart**.

5. Check the console tab to that the server has successfully restarted. You will observe console entries listing the administered objects we defined, as they are bound into the namespace. You will also see an entry signifying that the application **EmpRecordPub-lisher** has started.

We have successfully deployed the publisher session bean. We now create and deploy the subscriber MDB before testing. As you have no doubt observed, its implementation is practically identical to that of the sender session bean. The main difference is that we have used the publish-subscribe APIs and defined administered objects associated with the publish-subscribe domain.

Create the Subscriber Message-Driven Beans

We use two MDBs to implement a durable and nondurable subscriber. This allows us to explore the differences in configuration (which are minimal) and behavior. We use the same implementation for the `onMessage` method that we previously defined for EmpRecordMDB, which unpacks and prints out the message received. Both MDBs are associated with listener ports that listen to the `Topic` that the publisher session bean publishes on. We define the listener ports, create any required administration objects, then deploy the solution.

Implement the Subscriber MDBs

For convenience we package both MDBs in the same enterprise application project.

1. Launch Application Developer (if it is not already running), and switch to the **J2EE** perspective.

2. Create a J2EE 1.3 Enterprise Application Project, specifying the project name **EmpRecordSubscribers**. As before, create only an EJB module.

3. Create an MDB in the EJB module **EmpRecordSubscribersEJB**, specifying the name **EmpRecordNonDurMDB** and package **jms.book.sample.ejb**.

4. On the Enterprise Bean Details page, accept the default transaction type of **Container**, select the destination type **Topic**, and specify a durability of **NonDurable**. Leave Message Selector and Listener Port name blank (Figure 7–37).

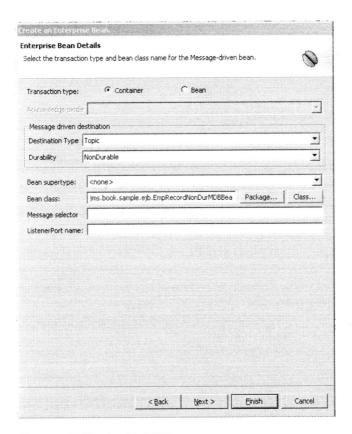

Figure 7-37 Nondurable MDB

5. Similarly, create another MDB called **EmpRecordDurMDB**. This time specify a durability of **Durable** (Figure 7–38).

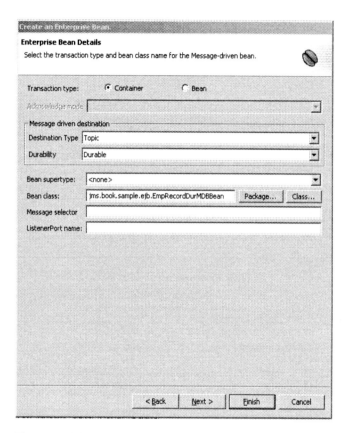

Figure 7-38 Durable MDB

6. Open the implementation bean class for EmpRecordNonDurMDB: **EmpRecordNon-
DurMDBBean.java**.

7. Add import statements for the now familiar JMS and JNDI packages:

```
import javax.jms.*; //jms classes
import javax.naming.*;      // JNDI imports
```

8. Modify the onMessage method to unpack the JMS message and print its contents to
the server console. You can copy the code we implemented in EmpRecordMDB-
Bean.java. Modify the print statements to reflect this MDB so that we can identify its
output in the console (shown in **bold**):

```
public void onMessage(javax.jms.Message msg) {
    try{
        if(msg instanceof TextMessage){
System.out.println("message received by non-durable MDB");

            TextMessage tMsg = (TextMessage)msg;
            String message = tMsg.getText();

            System.out.println("message: " + message);

            //parse received message
            //initialize variables
            String employeeID = "";
            String firstName = "";
            String lastName = "";
            String email = "";

    //use java.util.StringTokenizer to parse string
    java.util.StringTokenizer st = new
    java.util.StringTokenizer(message, ";");
            while (st.hasMoreTokens()) {
                employeeID = st.nextToken();
                firstName = st.nextToken();
                lastName = st.nextToken();
                email = st.nextToken();
            }

        }else{
System.out.println("unexpected message instance received by
EmpRecordNonDurMDB");
System.out.println("message type received: " +
msg.getJMSType() +", " + "TextMessage expected");
        }
    }catch(Exception e){
        System.out.println("Exception thrown " + e);
    }
}
```

9. Repeat steps 7 and 8 for the **EmpRecordDurMDB**, modifying **EmpRecordDurM-DBBean.java**. Remember to update the print statements as shown:

```
System.out.println("message received by durable MDB");
System.out.println("unexpected message instance received by
EmpRecordDurMDB");
```

10. Save your work and fix any compilation errors.

Define Administered Objects and Listener Ports

We define separate listener ports for the durable and nondurable MDB. While this is not strictly necessary as they can share a listener port, it does give each MDB its independence and makes it easy to modify their behavior independently. Also, in reality they would both be part of different applications and thus would use separate listener ports.

We also define a single `TopicConnectionFactory` that will be used by the listener ports. We define it as being XA-enabled, enabling the message to be processed as part of a global transaction. This underscores the point that the message distribution paradigm adopted (point-to-point or publish-subscribe) does not affect how the message is ultimately processed. We reuse the existing `Topic` object.

Create the TopicConnectionFactory

1. Launch the administration console, ensure your server is started if it is not already running.
2. Navigate to the WebSphere JMS Provider page, and click on WebSphere Topic Connection Factories link. In the resulting page click on New to open the definitions form.
3. In the definitions form, specify the following:
   - Name: **jms.sample.XASubTCF**
   - JNDI Name: **jms.sample.XASubTCF**
   - Port: select "**QUEUED**"
   - Client ID: **client01**
   - XA Enabled: ensure the check box is checked
   - Accept all other defaults

You will note that we specify a value for client ID. This is because the TopicConnection-Factory will be used to create a durable subscriber. As you will recall from our earlier discussions, setting the client ID is mandatory if durable subscribers are used. The client ID is used by the provider to associate durable subscriptions with related Connections (see Chapter 6).

Define the Listener Ports

1. In the administration console, navigate to the **Message Listener Service** page (via the **server1** application server link).
2. Click on the link for **Listener Ports**, and then click on **New** to open the definitions form.
3. In the definitions form specify the following:
   - Name: **NonDurMDBListenerPort**
   - Initial State: **Started**
   - Connection Factory JNDI Name: **jms.sample.XASubTCF**
   - Destination JNDI Name: **jms.sample.Topic**
   - Accept all other defaults
4. Click **OK** at the end of the form to save the object definition.

5. Create another listener port definition, specifying the following:
- Name: **DurMDBListenerPort**
- Initial State: **Started**
- Connection Factory JNDI Name: **jms.sample.XASubTCF**
- Destination JNDI Name: **jms.sample.Topic**
- Accept all other defaults

6. In the administration console's menu bar, click **Save** to apply the changes.

7. You can log out from the administration console.

Deploy the Subscribers Enterprise Application

Before deploying EmpRecordSubscribers, we associate the MDBs with the listener ports that we just defined. We similarly define a `Required` transaction attribute for the `onMessage` methods. Remember, however, that there is no need to generate deploy and RMIC code, because MDBs can interact only with JMS messages.

1. Switch to the **J2EE** perspective and double-click on **EmpRecordSubscribersEJB** to open the deployment descriptor.

2. Click the **Bean** tab and select **EmpRecordNonDurMDB**, displaying the associated properties.

3. In the Listener Port field specify the name of the listener port associated with this MDB, in this case **NonDurMDBListenerPort**.

4. Similarly, modify **EmpRecordDurMDB** to specify the listener port **DurMDBListenerPort**. At this stage your deployment descriptor should look similar to that shown in Figure 7–39.

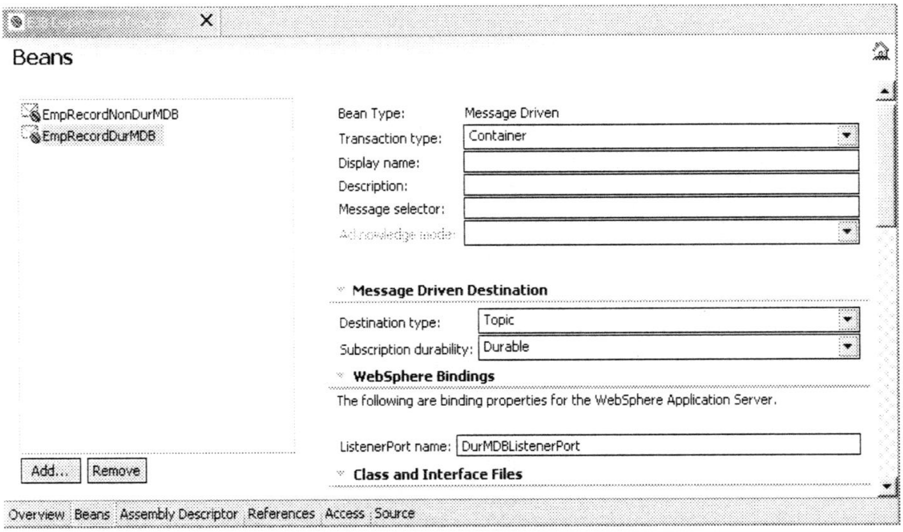

Figure 7-39 Subscriber MDBs Deployment Descriptor

5. Click on the **Assembly Descriptor** tab and use the **Add** button under Container Transactions to add both MDB `onMessage` methods with a transaction attribute of
`Required` (Figure 7–40).

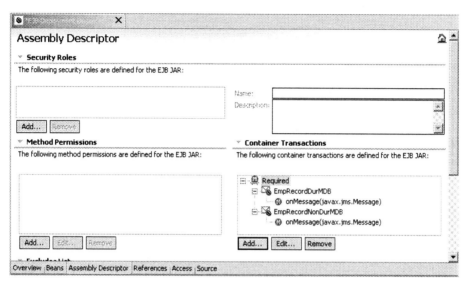

Figure 7-40 Subscriber MDBs Transactional Context

6. Save the deployment descriptor.
7. Switch to the **Server** perspective, and in the Server Configuration panel add
EmpRecordSubscribers to **TestSrv**.
8. Log out from the administration console if it is still active. Then in the Servers panel
right-click on **TestSrv** and select **Restart**. This will republish and restart the server.
9. Check the server console; you should find an entry signifying that **EmpRecordSubscribers** has started.

Test the Scenario Implementation

To test the message exchange, we once again use the universal test client. This time we will
invoke `EmpRecordPublisher`'s `publish` method. This publishes the message on the
defined topic, and we should see both `EmpRecordNonDurMDB` and `EmpRecordDurMDB`
receive the message. To test the behavior of the durable subscriber, we stop the MDB application
EmpRecordSubscribers and then publish a few more messages. When we restart the application,
we should see the durable subscriber MDB receive the messages we published.

1. Right-click **TestSrv** and launch the UTC.

2. Using the JNDI Explorer, create an instance of **EmpRecordPublisher** (Figure 7–41).

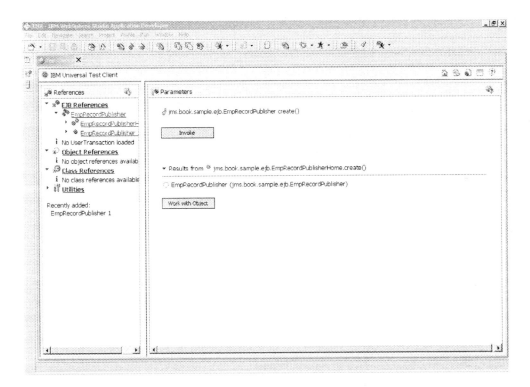

Figure 7-41 Publisher Session Bean Instance

3. Invoke the publish method, supplying test data for employee ID, first name, last name, and email address. You should see a success message in the results pane (Figure 7–42).

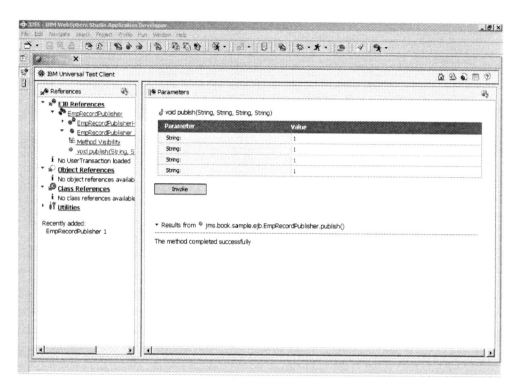

Figure 7-42 Invoke the Publish Method

4. Check the server console. You should find entries from both subscriber MDBs (Figure 7–43).

Figure 7-43 Subscriber MDBs Output

5. Now launch the administration console, expand **Applications**, and select **Enterprise Applications**. Check the checkbox next to **EmpRecordSubscribers** and click **Stop** (Figure 7–44).

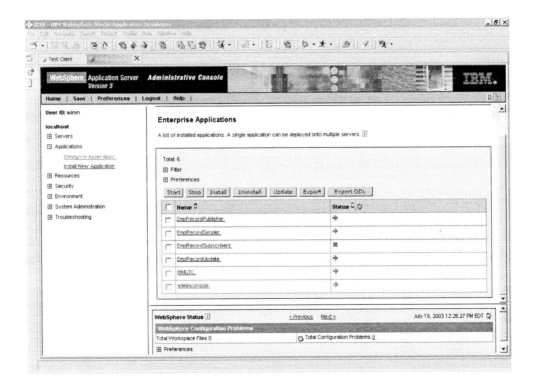

Figure 7-44 Stop Subscribing Application

6. Return to the UTC and invoke the `publish` method again. If you check the server console, there should be no entries from the MDBs, since they are not running.

7. Return to the administration console and start **EmpRecordSubscribers**.

8. In the server console you should find an entry from the durable MDB based on the message we published while the application was stopped (Figure 7–45).

Figure 7-45 Durable Subscriber MDB Output

We have now successfully implemented message exchange utilizing publish-subscribe. Once again, using MDBs as the subscribers (message consumers) simplified our coding requirements. However, given that we did not write the subscriber implementation, the question arises as to how the durable subscriber MDB eventually unsubscribes. Recall from Chapter 4 that this action normally requires the JMS client to invoke the `unsubscribe` method call. In the case of an MDB, removing (undeploying) the application from the WebSphere Application Server causes the application server to deregister the subscription on the MDBs' behalf.

In our implementation we used the WebSphere JMS Provider, as its use greatly simplified our development environment. For enterprise deployments we would use the WebSphere MQ JMS Provider comprising WebSphere Business Integration Event or Message Broker, along with WebSphere MQ. This change does not affect the implementation of the JMS applications, but it does require that the message broker be configured and different administered objects be created. In Appendix C, we modify our implementation to use the WebSphere MQ JMS Provider and detail the required configuration steps.

Scenario 3: Communicating with Non-JMS Clients

Up until this point, our scenarios have strictly focused on the exchange of messages between JMS clients. However, enterprise messaging often occurs between disparate applications that are not written in the same language or run on the same platform. How does this impact our approach to implementation?

Figure 7–46 depicts the messaging solution architecture for the point-to-point messaging scenario, where Application A is still a J2EE application, but Application B is a non-Java application written, for example, in the language C. Notice that in comparison to Figure 7–1, which depicted the solution architecture for two J2EE applications, there is little or no difference between the two solutions. Being non-Java based, Application B does not use JMS nor does it implement MDBs, but the interaction model is identical. To implement this scenario, we require the WebSphere MQ JMS Provider as defined by WebSphere MQ, because it supports both JMS and non-JMS applications and the exchange of messages between them.

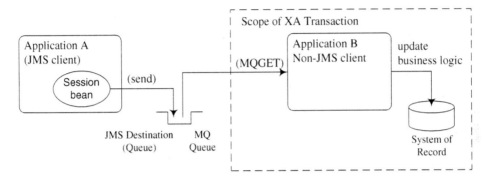

Figure 7-46 Employee Record Exchange: Non-JMS Client

Using WebSphere MQ, implementation simply involves Application A sending a message using JMS to an MQ queue manager, and Application B retrieving it using the MQI, which is WebSphere MQ's native API (see Chapter 5). However, when knowingly communicating between JMS and non-JMS applications, thought must be given to how the WebSphere MQ JMS implementation maps JMS messages to MQ messages and vice versa, and the effect, if any, on the communicating applications.

Recall from our discussions in Chapter 5 that JMS message header properties that have equivalent attributes in the MQMD of the MQ message are simply mapped. Those that do not, particularly application-specific properties, are copied to the RFH2 header. The JMS message body is copied to the MQ message body and placed after the RFH2 header (Figure 7–47).

If we assume that the employee data being exchanged in the message body can be processed by both applications (in our implementation it is in a tagged/delimited format), then the first question we must ask is whether the non-JMS application can parse an RFH2 header. Most MQI applications, unless written to interact using publish-subscribe, don't implement support for the RFH2 header, particularly if they were written before the RFH2 header was introduced by WebSphere MQ. Thus, in this scenario, if the JMS client implemented in the session sender bean sends the message to the non-JMS client, the non-JMS client will fail to process it, as it will not be able to parse the RFH2 header that forms part of the MQ message body. The WebSphere MQ JMS implementation provides an easy solution to this problem. It allows the RFH2 header to be omitted from the MQ message body so that the MQ message comprises only the MQMD and data contained in the JMS message body. This is done via the TARGCLIENT property of the MQQueue and MQTopic administered objects.

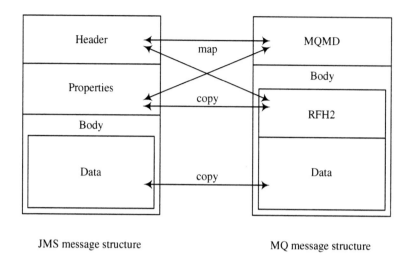

JMS message structure   MQ message structure

Figure 7-47 JMS Message to MQ Message Mapping

In the reverse case, where the non-JMS client sends a message to the JMS client, the JMS client can successfully receive the message because it is not dependent on the presence of the RFH2 header. This is true up to a point. If you inspect the JMS message object retrieved by the JMS client, you will notice that certain header properties, specifically JMSDestination, JMSExpiration, and JMSType, are not set. These properties are all carried in the JMS folder in the RFH2 header, and in its absence cannot be populated. From a message processing perspective, they are hardly critical. However, if a JMS application is dependent on application-specific properties, used as part of a message selector, for instance, then some difficulty does arise. Application-specific properties are JMS-specific and have no meaning outside of a JMS context. They are similarly carried in the JMS folder of the RFH2 header, and a typical non-JMS application would be unable to set these values. Hence, if the JMS client is dependent on application-specific properties, it can only communicate directly with other JMS applications.

WebSphere MQ provides a number of message headers that are utilized to convey instructions to certain system applications. Two popular examples are the CICS bridge header (MQCIH) and the IMS information header (MQIIH), which are used by the target system (i.e., CICS or IMS) to trigger transactions based on the receipt of an MQ message. Let's assume that our employee data is to be sent via WebSphere MQ to one of these target applications. Our first question is easily answered: neither the CICS bridge nor the IMS bridge support the RFH2 header, and thus we would need to suppress its inclusion via administered object settings. However, we do have a new consideration: How does the JMS client build a JMS message that translates into the required MQ message, which must now include the appropriate command header at the correct position in the message?

As we discussed in Chapter 5, an MQ message comprises an MQMD and a message body, which can contain a number of headers, followed by the actual message data. In this particular scenario we require an MQ message that comprises an MQMD followed by an MQCIH or MQIIH and then the message data. Our approach to solving this is relatively straightforward. From Figure 7–47 we know that the JMS header values map to the MQMD and the RFH2 header (which we will suppress), while the JMS message body maps to the MQ message body. Therefore, to include an MQCIH or MQIIH at the start of the MQ message body, we must insert into the JMS message body, a data structure that corresponds to the MQCIH or MQIIH, followed by the actual data we wish to send.

This approach is applicable to a number of scenarios, and as you would expect, the structure of MQ headers is extensively detailed in the WebSphere MQ user guides. Thus, building the data structure in Java is a simple matter of programming, and populating the message body is an exercise in applying the right method calls in the right sequence (see Chapter 3). Note that because of the nature of the data structures, you must use a JMS `BytesMessage`. However, there is one more twist. Because an MQ message can contain any given header, the format field in the MQMD must contain the name of the header that succeeds it. Typically, we are not concerned with the value of the MQMD format field, as we rely on the JMS implementation to map an appropriate value based on the configuration of the JMS message. But in this instance we must specify an explicit value. WebSphere MQ provides access to the MQMD format field via a provider-specific property called `JMS_IBM_Format`, used as follows:

```
//MQIIH header follows MQMD
bOutMsg.setStringProperty("JMS_IBM_Format", ("MQIMS    ");
```

An alternative approach to dealing with issues pertaining to communicating between different applications in general is to introduce a message broker. WebSphere Business Integration Message Broker handles, among other things, the transformation of messages between applications. Using Message Broker, we could send out the message in some convenient format and with no consideration to whether or not the receiver is a JMS client. Message Broker would then handle the transformation of the message into a format suitable for the target application. This could include the removal or inclusion of required headers. Use of a message broker helps us keep the messaging applications simple. It also allows us to isolate the applications from the details of the message formats associated with applications they might interact with. Thus, in addressing our scenario in which the JMS client is sending a message to CICS, IMS, or some other non-JMS client, we could use Message Broker as shown in Figure 7–48.

To implement our JMS client to non-JMS client scenario, we first modify the configuration of the sender session bean (`EmpRecordSender`) to use the WebSphere MQ JMS Provider, and then we explore the effects of changing administered object settings on the message formats generated.

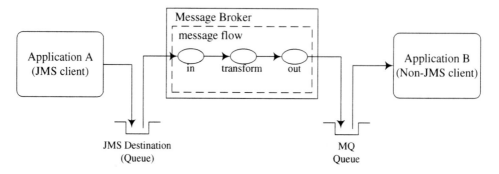

Figure 7-48 Employee Record Exchange: Using a Message Broker

Using the WebSphere MQ JMS Provider

First, we use the administration console to define the administered objects used by
EmpRecordSender to access WebSphere MQ. Then, we ensure that any referenced Web-
Sphere MQ resources actually exist. Finally, we modify the resource references used by
EmpRecordSender to reference the MQ JMS–administered objects that we defined. Note
that at no point do we need to modify the JMS client code, which underscores the portability of
our JMS client implementation.

Create Administered Objects

We will create a QueueConnectionFactory and Queue object for the sender session
bean, which provides access to an MQ queue manager and queue.

1. In Application Developer, ensure that **TestSrv** is running, and launch the administration console.
2. In the administration console's menu pane, expand **Resources** and select **WebSphere
   MQ JMS Provider**. This opens up the provider pane (Figure 7–49).
   Observe that the provider has a class path and library path setting, defined by the variable MQJMS_LIB_ROOT. MQJMS_LIB_ROOT points to the installation directory for
   the WebSphere MQ JMS classes, and its definition can be found by expanding **Environment** and selecting **Manage WebSphere Variables** in the menu pane. The classes
   are installed as part of the application server runtime structure, so for MQ JMS applications running in the WebSphere Application Server, the JMS implementation classes
   are already installed. They are, of course, also installed as part of WebSphere MQ, and
   if you wish to ensure that you use a single set of classes in your solution, you can either
   modify the variable to point at your WebSphere MQ installation or alternatively copy
   the classes over from the WebSphere MQ installation directory.

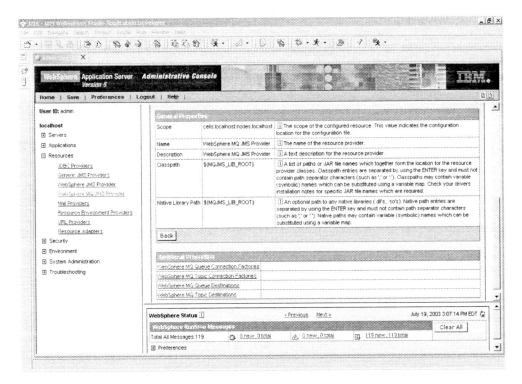

Figure 7-49 WebSphere MQ JMS Provider

3. Click on the **WebSphere MQ Queue Connection Factories** link.

4. In the resulting page, click **New** to open the definitions form.

5. In the definitions form (Figure 7–50), specify the following:

- Name: **mq.sample.SenderQCF**
- JNDI Name: **mq.sample.SenderQCF**
- Queue Manager: **JMSSVR**
- Transport Type: select **BINDINGS**
- XA Enabled: uncheck the check box
- Accept all other defaults

Our definition results in the creation of an MQQueueConnectionFactory. The Transport Type setting reflects that the JMS client is running on the same machine as the queue manager **JMSSVR** and thus can establish a local connection.

6. Click **OK** at the end of the form to save the object definition.

7. Return to the WebSphere MQ JMS Provider page, and select the **WebSphere MQ Queue Destinations** link.

8. In the resulting page, click **New** to open the definitions form.

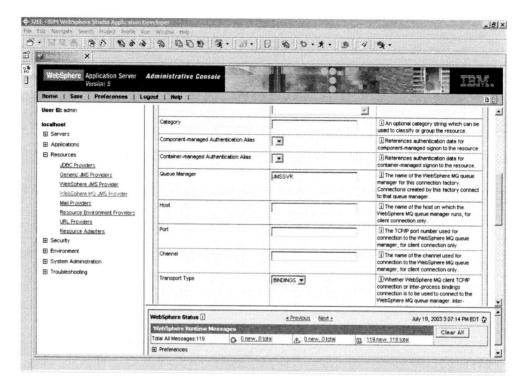

Figure 7-50 MQQueueConnectionFactory

9. In the definitions form (Figure 7–51), specify the following:

- Name: **mq.sample.Queue**
- JNDI Name: **mq.sample.Queue**
- Base Queue Name: **UPDATEQ**
- Accept all other defaults

The key attribute is the name of the MQ queue to which the message will be sent. Its value, **UPDATEQ**, must map to an actual MQ queue on the target queue manager **JMSSVR**. By accepting all other defaults, we are once again allowing the message persistence, priority, and expiry to be defined by the JMS client application. We could, of course, override the client's settings by setting the appropriate properties.

10. Click **OK** at the end of the form to save the object definition.

11. In the administration console's menu bar, click **Save** to apply your changes.

12. You can log out and close the administration console.

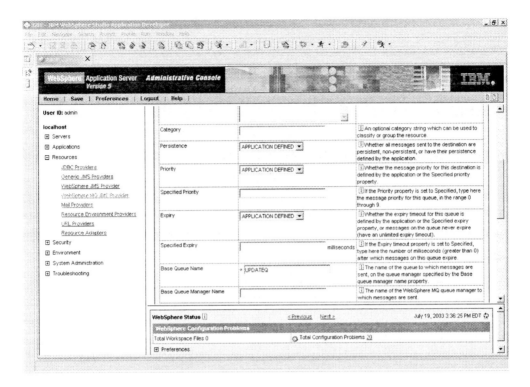

Figure 7-51 MQQueue

Define WebSphere MQ Resources

Before we can test the JMS client, we need to ensure that the referenced MQ resources exist. From our administered object definitions, we require a queue manager called **JMSSVR** with a queue **UPDATEQ** (names are case sensitive).

If you are familiar with WebSphere MQ, you should ensure that these resources have been created. The following instructions detail how to create a queue manager using the WebSphere MQ Explorer.

1. Launch the WebSphere MQ Explorer from the Windows Start menu.

2. In the WebSphere MQ Explorer, right-click on the **Queue Managers** folder and select **New → Queue Manager**.

3. In the resulting wizard specify the name of the queue manager **JMSSVR** and optionally check the checkbox marked "Make this the default queue manager." Also specify **SYSTEM.DEAD.LETTER.QUEUE** for the dead letter queue (Figure 7–52). Click **Next**.

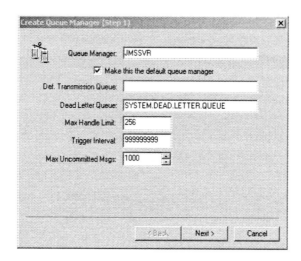

Figure 7-52 Create MQ Queue Manager

The dead letter queue is used by the queue manager to place messages that can't be delivered. It is a good practice to ensure that one is always defined. The specified queue, SYSTEM.DEAD.LETTER.QUEUE, is a standard queue automatically created by all queue managers.

4. Accept the defaults on the following pages and click **Finish**. The defaults additionally specify that a listener on port 1414 be created.

5. The queue manager is created and started. An entry is placed in the **Queue Managers** folder.

6. Expand **JMSSVR** and right-click on the **Queue** folder. Select **New ➠ Local Queue**.

7. In the resulting dialog box, specify the name of the queue **UPDATEQ** (Figure 7–53). Accept all other defaults and click **OK**.

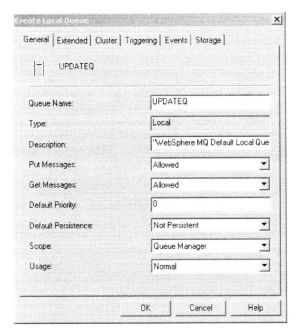

Figure 7-53 Create MQ Queue

We have successfully defined the queue and queue manager.

Modify and Deploy the Sender Enterprise Application

Before redeploying EmpRecordSender, we modify the resource references associated with the sender session bean so that they point at the WebSphere MQ JMS–administered objects. Then we restart the server.

1. In Application Developer, return to the **J2EE** perspective.
2. Double-click on **EmpRecordSenderEJB** to open the deployment descriptor, and click the **References** tab.
3. Bind **jms/SenderQCF** to **mq.sample.SenderQCF**.
4. Similarly, bind **jms/SenderQ** to **mq.sample.Queue**.
5. Save the deployment descriptor.
6. Switch to the server perspective and restart **TestSrv**.

Testing the Scenario Implementation

To test the scenario, we use the UTC to invoke EmpRecordSender's submit method, and we use the WebSphere MQ Explorer to examine the messages placed on the queue UPDATEQ.

1. Use the UTC to send a message using the `submit` method of **EmpRecordSender**.

2. To view the message sent, go to the WebSphere MQ Explorer and double-click on the queue **UPDATEQ**. This will display a message browser dialog box. You should see a single message displayed. Double-click the listed message to view its properties dialog. Switch to the **Data** tab. You will find the details you inserted (Figure 7–54).

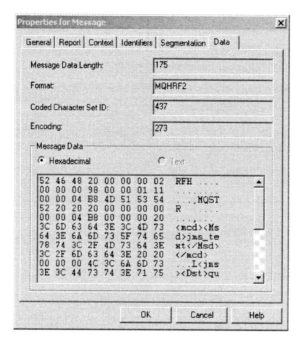

Figure 7-54 MQ JMS Message with RFH2 header

Note that the format of the MQ message is defined as MQHRF2, signifying the inclusion of the RFH2 header at the start of the MQ message body. If you inspect the message data box, you will spot the entry `MQSTR`. This is the value of the format field in the RFH2 header and signifies that the data following the header (the JMS message body) is a character string. Recall that we used a JMS `TextMessage` object, so this is consistent with our message format.

Now we edit the `Queue`-administered object retrieved by `EmpRecordSender` to suppress the use of the RFH2 header. We do this by setting the Target Client (`TARG-CLIENT`) property to the value `MQ`.

3. Use the administration console to access the administered object **mq.sample.Queue**. Modify the **Target Client** property to the value **MQ**.

4. Because we designed **EmpRecordSender** to create its QueueSender in the ejb-Create method, the easiest way to flush our current bean instance is to restart the server.

5. Send another test message, using the UTC and **EmpRecordSender**, and inspect the second message on **UPDATEQ** (Figure 7–55).

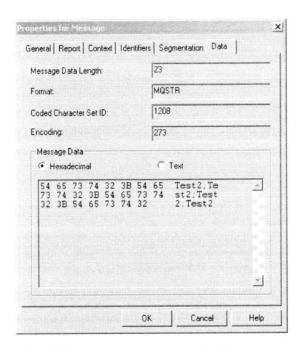

Figure 7-55 MQ JMS Message without RFH2 header

The format of the MQ message has changed to MQSTR, signifying that a character string is contained in the MQ message body. Inspection of the message data box shows only the test data, with no RFH2 header. This version of the message would be successfully parsed by the non-JMS client in our scenario. If the second message does not change as expected, confirm that you applied the specified fixpak (FP1) to the unit test environment.

Scenario 4: Securing JMS Communications

In our scenarios we have exchanged messages containing employee data, which by definition is typically confidential in nature, as it can include details such as current salary, performance ratings, and other personal information. As our applications move toward enterprise deployment, the question soon arises as to how this exchange is secured. Security is always a far-reaching concern and can be approached in a myriad of ways. However, from the perspective of the JMS client, there are two main areas of interest: access control and authentication.

Access control ensures that the connecting JMS client has authority to access the underlying JMS provider's resources, while authentication addresses the question of whether the JMS client is truly who it claims to be and not an impersonating rogue application. The concept further extends to how data is exchanged between authentic parties (in this case the JMS client and the JMS provider) in such a way that it is secured from tampering and subsequent modification. From the perspective of our enterprise-level WebSphere MQ JMS Provider, we can address this in a number of ways.

In WebSphere MQ access control is based on operating system user names and the groups to which they belong. If the JMS client is using a local connection (i.e., running on the same machine as the queue manager), then its user name is typically the user name under which the hosting JVM process is running. This user name must have appropriate authority to allow the JMS client to connect to the queue manager and access queues. On development systems, the user name is often defined as a member of the mqm group, which gives the JMS client administrative rights and thus full access to WebSphere MQ resources. In production environments where such authority is typically not appropriate, the WebSphere MQ setmq-auth command can be used to give the user name the required authority.

If the JMS client is using a client connection (i.e., running on a machine that is remote from that of the queue manager's), then the user name it adopts is based on its channel definition. The server connection channel (SVRCONN) on which the client connection is based has an attribute called MCAUSER (MCA user ID), which contains a user name. By default, this user name is used for the JMS client access control checks. The default server connection channel, SYSTEM.DEF.SVRCONN, defined by the MQQueueConnectionFactory and MQTopicConnectionFactory, has a blank MCAUSER attribute. This results in the JMS client being assigned the default MQ administrator identifier, MUSR_MQADMIN, which gives it full access to the queue manager and associated queues. In practice, with security in mind, the WebSphere MQ administrator could define a server connection channel for use by a particular JMS client application (or set of applications) and set its MCAUSER attribute to a user name that has been given restricted authority based on application needs.

WebSphere MQ supports authentication by enabling server and client channels to be optionally secured via the Secure Socket Layer (SSL) protocol. Prior to the introduction of SSL, the authentication of parties communicating over MQ channels required you to implement a security exit. In the case of the JMS client, the exit was implemented at the queue manager and optionally at the JMS client, and allowed you to intercept the connection request and authenticate using some appropriate approach. If you wished to secure the actual data exchanged, you implemented send and receive exits, which intercept data before it is sent over the channel and after it is received respectively. Clearly, implementation of custom exits was not the most favored approach, and thus the introduction of SSL provided a popular open-standards based approach to securing the communications between the JMS client and its underlying provider, the MQ queue manager. It is useful to note that communication over the WebSphere MQ Real-time Transport to the Message Broker can also be optionally secured using SSL.

In our implementation, we focus on updating the configuration of the sender session bean (EmpRecordSender) to use a client connection, which is secured using SSL to communicate with the queue manager. We make no changes to our JMS client implementation code, but focus on configuring administered objects and the required SSL infrastructure. This is important, as it reinforces the JMS concepts of portable JMS code, with provider-specific configuration encapsulated in administered objects. Thus, we can significantly change the behavior of our JMS client by simple reconfiguration of the administered object it retrieves. Before we delve into the resource configuration required to implement the scenario, we review some basic SSL concepts and understand how they are supported by WebSphere MQ.

SSL Concepts

The SSL protocol utilizes the concepts of secret key and public key encryption, digital signatures, and digital certificates to establish a secure connection between parties, facilitating the transmission of secure data over an insecure network. To understand these concepts, it is useful to review the problems they are aimed at solving: eavesdropping, tampering, and impersonation.

Eavesdropping

Eavesdropping occurs when unknown parties secretly listen to and understand the data passed between communicating parties. Clearly, this is a particularly sensitive issue if the data being passed is confidential in nature. To protect against eavesdropping, an application encrypts the data prior to sending it. The process of encryption converts the data from plain text to unreadable cipher text, the form in which it is then transmitted. The receiving application decrypts the data, converting from cipher text back to plain text, and can subsequently processes the data. The theory is that any potential eavesdropper will not know how to decrypt the message. Encryption and decryption are collectively called cryptography and rely upon the use of mathematical algorithms.

Encryption algorithms encrypt or decrypt messages by performing a sequence of mathematical operations on the message, transforming its appearance but not its content. The algorithm is called a stream or block cipher depending on whether the algorithm transforms the message one byte at a time or a block (8 bytes) at a time. The encryption algorithm is created specific to the particular use case based on a key fed into the algorithm. The key is typically a random sequence of bits; its size categorizes the strength of the encryption algorithm.

The encryption algorithm uses keys in one of two ways:

- A symmetric algorithm requires that both the sender and receiver of the message use the same secret key; this is often called secret key cryptography.
- An asymmetric algorithm uses a different key for encrypting or decrypting the message; one of the keys must be kept secret, and the other key is usually made public.

In this case, a sender might encrypt the message using the receiver's public key, but only the receiver has the secret key that is used to decrypt the message. This approach involving private and public key pairs is also called public key cryptography.

Symmetric algorithms have faster performance than asymmetric algorithms, but passing the secret key securely between participants poses a distribution problem. First, how do you pass the key secretly, and second, how do you scale the approach to many sender/receiver pairs? With private and public key pairs, the distribution problem is alleviated because the receiver publishes a public key for all senders to use to encrypt information, and it uses a private (secret) key to decrypt all information received. The public key cannot be reverse-engineered to get the private key, and the private key is known only to the receiver. This, however, comes at the expense of increased performance overhead.

Tampering

Tampering occurs when a message is modified by an unknown party during the transmission of the message between communicating parties. Tampering is detected through the use of a message digest, which is a fixed-size numeric representation of the contents of a message. The message digest (also called the message authentication code) is computed using a hash function. This is one-way only, which means that it is not possible to reverse the function and find the message corresponding to the digest. It is also implemented in such a way that it is computationally unfeasible to find two different messages that hash to the same digest. Once computed, the digest is transmitted along with the message. The receiver then invokes the same hash function on the received message and compares the generated digest to the one received. If the digests are the same, then the message was not tampered with en route. Utilization of this approach requires that the communicating parties agree on the hash function that will be used before transmission begins.

Impersonation

Impersonation occurs when the message is sent by an entity other than the actual specified sender. To address this problem, we must verify that the message was actually sent by the sender and authenticate the partner with whom the messages are exchanged.

Digital signatures are used to verify that the message was actually sent by the sender. They are based on the use of message digests and public key cryptography. The process involves the sender generating the message digest, then encrypting the digest using its private key, which creates the digital signature. The receiver then decrypts the message digest using the sender's public key, confirming that the message was indeed sent by the sender. Comparing the digest with the one the receiver generates further confirms that the message has not been tampered with since it was signed. However, the question still arises as to how the receiver knows that the public key can be trusted. Often referred to as the "man-in-the-middle" attack, this problem occurs when an unknown third party intercepts the sender's public key and swaps it for its own. The rogue agent then impersonates the original sender and signs intercepted messages. Because the receiver is able to decrypt the sent messages, the receiver does not know that it is interacting with a rogue user. To limit this risk, the partner with whom messages are being exchanged must be authenticated. Digital certificates address this problem by certifying that a public key belongs to a named entity. The digital certificate is typically issued by a trusted third party called a certification authority (CA). For a fee, the CA will generate a digital certificate that contains:

- The owner's public key
- The owner's distinguished name
- The distinguished name of the CA that issues the certificate
- The date from which the certificate is valid
- The expiry date of the certificate
- A version number
- A serial number

Before issuing a certificate, CA runs appropriate background checks on the requestor to verify that the requestor is who he or she claims to be. All certificates issued by a CA are digitally signed by the CA and can be verified using the CA's certificate (which contains the CA's public key). The exchange between the sender and receiver now takes on an additional verification step. Instead of simply sending its public key to the receiver, the sender sends its digital certificate issued by a CA. The receiver uses the CA's certificate to verify the sender's certificate, ascertaining that the public key contained in the certificate truly belongs to the owner. During the lifetime of a digital certificate, the issuing CA might determine that the certificate is no longer to be trusted. Such certificates are published to a certificate revocation list against which both the sender and receiver can choose to check the received certificates.

SSL Handshake

SSL defines a protocol that utilizes cryptography, digital certificates, and digital signatures to establish a secure communication link between participants. The protocol refers to the participants as the *SSL client*, who initiates the SSL connection, and the *SSL server*, which is the responding application. In the context of our scenario, the JMS client is the SSL client, and the queue manager is the SSL server. The interaction between the SSL client and SSL server required to establish a secure link is called the SSL handshake. It involves the following:

1. The SSL client initiates the conversation and sends information such as the SSL version along with the encryption algorithms and hash functions it supports.
2. The SSL server responds with the encryption algorithm and hash function to be used. This is selected from the list provided by the client. It also sends a session ID, a random byte string, and its digital certificate. The server can optionally include a request for the client's digital certificate.
3. The SSL client authenticates the SSL server by verifying the digital signature on the supplied digital certificate and the digital certificate itself, using the issuing CA's certif-

icate. The server's certificate might be optionally checked against a certificate revocation list.

4. If satisfied, the SSL client sends the secret key that will be used to encrypt further exchanges. The secret key is itself encrypted using the SSL server's public key obtained from the server's digital certificate. In addition, the client might send its digital certificate if requested by the server.

5. The SSL server decrypts and stores the secret key, using its private key. It optionally authenticates the client, similarly using the issuing CA's certificate and potentially associated certificate revocation lists. This step occurs only if the server requested the client's certificate in step 2.

6. The SSL client sends a message encrypted with the secret key, indicating that the client part of the SSL handshake is complete.

7. The SSL server responds with a message similarly encrypted with the secret key, indicating that the server part of the handshake is complete.

8. A secure connection is now established, and communication for the rest of the session is encrypted using the secret key.

To facilitate the specification of the encryption algorithms and hash functions that are used during an SSL session, the algorithms are grouped into CipherSuites. A CipherSuite defines the key exchange and authentication algorithm used during the SSL handshake as well as the associated CipherSpec. The CipherSpec further defines the encryption algorithm used to secure data and the hash function used to generate the message digest.

WebSphere MQ 5.3 supports only the RSA key exchange and authentication algorithms. Details of some of the supported CipherSpecs are listed in Table 7–1.

Table 7–1 WebSphere MQ 5.3: Supported CipherSpecs

CipherSpec	Hash Algorithm	Encryption Algorithm	Encryption Bits
NULL_MD5	MD5	None	0
NULL_SHA	SHA	None	0
RC4_MD5_EXPORT	MD5	RC4 (stream cipher)	40
RC4_MD5_US	MD5	RC4	128
RC4_SHA_US	SHA	RC4	128
RC2_MD5_EXPORT	MD5	RC2 (block cipher)	40
DES_SHA_EXPORT	SHA	DES (block cipher)	56
RC4_56_SHA_EXPORT1024	SHA	RC4	56
DES_SHA_EXPORT1024	SHA	DES	56
TRIPLE_DES_SHA_US3	SHA	3DES (block cipher)	168

- RC2 is a block cipher algorithm. It encrypts the data by blocks (8 bytes long) and supports key lengths of 40 bits, 64 bits, and 128 bits. RC4 is a stream cipher algorithm operating on each byte of data; like the RC2, it supports key lengths of 40 bits, 64 bits, and 128 bits. Both RC2 and RC4 are produced by RSA Data Security, Inc.
- DES, the United States Data Encryption Standard, is a block cipher algorithm with 8-byte blocks and a key length of 56 bits. Triple DES is a variation of DES, with a key length of 168 bits.
- In terms of performance, from fastest to slowest, they are RC4, DES, RC2, and TripleDES.
- SHA stands for Secure Hash Algorithm and MD5 stands for Message Digest Version 5. Choosing between MD5 and SHA-1 is a tradeoff between security and performance. The SHA algorithm is more secure, producing a 160-bit output compared to the MD5 algorithm's 128-bit output. However, the MD5 algorithm is much faster in calculating the message digest.

The CipherSuite name is a combination of the key exchange and authentication and the CipherSpec name. Thus, for WebSphere MQ, which supports only the RSA key exchange and authentication algorithm, a valid CipherSuite would be SSL_RSA_WITH RC4_SHA_US.

Configuring WebSphere MQ SSL

Configuring the MQ queue manager and the JMS client to enable SSL communication involves obtaining and exchanging certificates for both the queue manager and the JMS client, then configuring the queue manager's server connection channel and the JMS client's `Connection-Factory` object to support SSL. Note that the JMS client certificate is only required if the client will be additionally authenticated by the queue manager (see the section on the SSL handshake). We thus implement the scenario by undertaking the following steps:

1. Obtain and exchange digital certificates for the queue manager and JMS client.
2. Configure MQ resources and JMS administered objects.
3. Test the configuration.

Note that the MQ queue manager used was created in the previous implementation scenario on communicating with non-JMS clients. If you skipped scenario 3, refer back to the section on creating WebSphere MQ Resources.

Obtaining Digital Certificates

A digital certificate can be obtained in one of two ways: you can either request a digital certificate from a certification authority or use platform-specific tools to generate a self-signed certificate. With a self-signed certificate, you act as you own certification authority, and thus self-signed certificates can be useful for test environments because you can generate them locally and you do not have to pay fees to a certification authority. However, many certification authorities offer a demo facility that lets you generate demo (test) certificates at no charge; for example, DigitalSignatureTrust *(http://www.digsigtrust.com/prod_serv/index.html)* offers such a facility.

In our implementation we use the OpenSSL Toolkit *(www.openssl.org)* to generate a self-signed certificate for the queue manager, and we use the Java keytool utility to generate a self-signed certificate for the JMS Client application. Certificates are stored in repositories that vary based on the operating system and the tools used to access them. On the Windows platform, certificates are stored in Microsoft Certificate Stores, and you can view and manipulate them using Internet Explorer. In a Java environment, certificates are stored in key stores, which resolve to a flat file in a directory structure. The key stores are manipulated using keytool, a utility that ships as part of the Java SSL support infrastructure. On UNIX, you use the iKeyman key management tool to handle digital certificates. Thus, handling digital certificates is environment-specific, and you need to be familiar with the digital certificate infrastructure support provided by or supplied for the operating environment in question. Since our development environment is based on the Windows platform, we focus on the tools it and Java provide. However, the process of handling and exchanging certificates is fairly generic, the main difference being the commands that are used.

Generate the MQ Queue Manager's Certificate   We create a self-signed certificate for the queue manager using the OpenSSL toolkit. Then, we import it into the queue manager's certificate store and assign it to the queue manager.

1. Open a command prompt and navigate the directory in which **OpenSSL** is installed. Under Cygwin this should default to **cygwin\bin**.
2. Enter the command

```
openssl genrsa -out jmssvr.key 1024
```

This generates an RSA private key. We specified that the key should be 1024 bits and stored in the file **jmssvr.key**. I based the filename on the name of the queue manager (Figure 7–56).

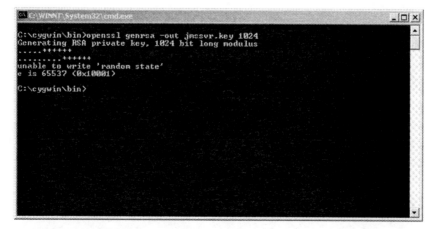

Figure 7-56 OpenSSL: Generate Private Key

3. Enter the command

```
openssl req -x509 -new -out jmssvr.pem -key jmssvr.key -days 365
```

This generates a self-signed certificate using the private key we just created, `jmssvr.key`. We specified that the certificate be written to the file `jmssvr.pam` and that it should be valid for 365 days. You will be prompted to enter a number of values. Of particular importance is the value you specify for **Common Name**, which is used to identify the certificate. We use the name of the queue manager, **JMSSVR** (Figure 7–57).

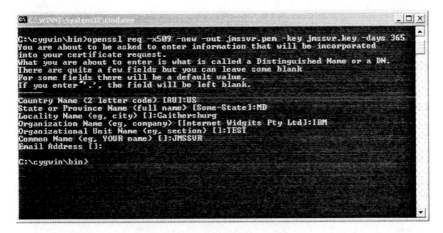

Figure 7-57 OpenSSL: Generate Private Certificate

4. We convert the generated certificate to the PKCS12 format, which is a format used by Windows applications such as Internet Explorer. Enter the command

```
openssl pkcs12 -export -in jmssvr.pem -out jmssvr.pfx -inkey
jmssvr.key -name "JMSSVR Certificate"
```

You will be prompted for an export password; we use **passw0rd** (Figure 7–58).

5. We also need to generate a public certificate based on the private certificate; the public certificate will be shared with the JMS client. To generate the public certificate, enter the command

```
openssl x509 -in jmssvr.pem -out jmssvr.crt
```

This generates the public certificate using the X.509 format (Figure 7–59).

6. We can now assign the private certificate to the queue manager. Launch the WebSphere MQ Explorer from the Start menu (if it is not already open).

Figure 7-58 OpenSSL: Convert Private Certificate to PKCS12 Format

Figure 7-59 OpenSSL: Generate Public Certificate

7. Right-click on the queue manager **JMSSVR** and select **Properties**. In the resulting Properties dialog box, select the **SSL** tab, then click **Manage SSL Certificates** (Figure 7–60).

8. The resulting dialog box lists the certificates currently located in the queue manager's certificate store. We add the private certificate that we generated. Click **Add** (Figure 7–61).

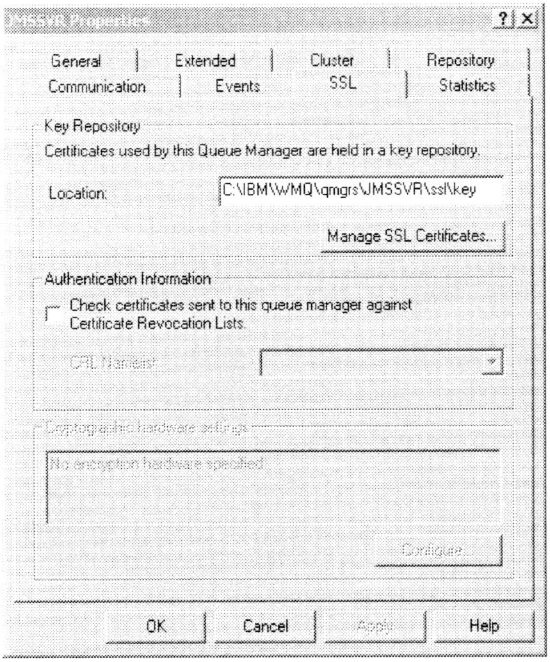

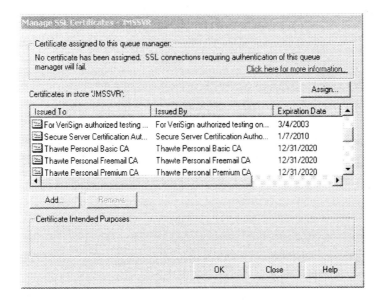

Figure 7-60 MQ Queue Manager Properties

Figure 7-61 MQ Queue Manager Certificate Store

9. Select the **Import from File** radio button, specify the location of **jmssvr.pfx** (it should be in cygwin\bin), and the export password, **passw0rd**. Click **Add** (Figure 7–62).

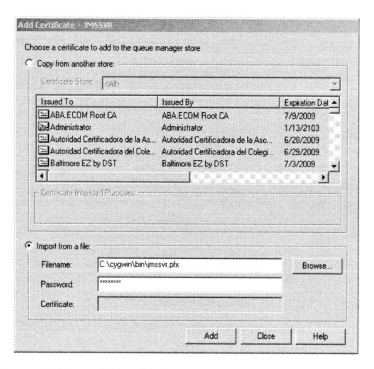

Figure 7-62 Import Private Certificate

10. The certificate JMSSVR should now be listed in the queue manager's certificate store (Figure 7–63). To assign it to the queue manager, click **Assign**.

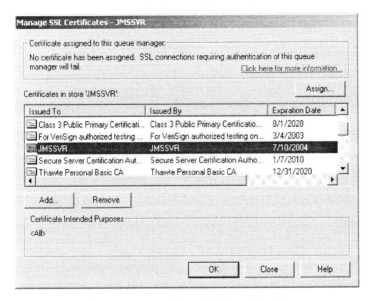

Figure 7-63 Updated MQ Queue Manager Certificate Store

11. Select the certificate **JMSSVR** and click **Assign** (Figure 7–64).

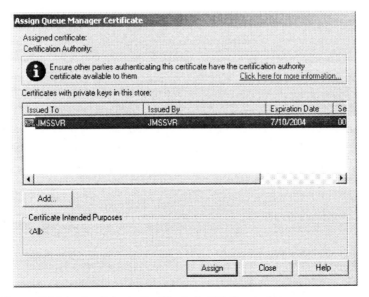

Figure 7-64 Assign Private Certificate to MQ Queue Manager

12. The queue manager has now been assigned a private certificate with which it can be authenticated (Figure 7–65). Click **OK** to close the open dialog boxes.

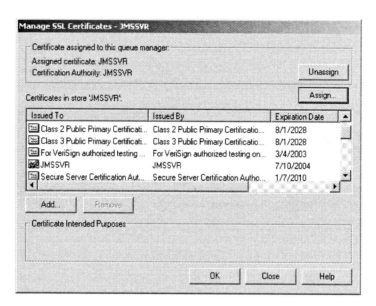

Figure 7-65 Private Certificate Successfully Assigned

Generate the JMS Client's Certificate We generate a private certificate for the JMS client using the keytool utility and store it in a key store, which will be accessed by the JMS client. Keytool is part of the Java runtime and infrastructure support for SSL, which is encapsulated in JSSE (Java Secure Socket Extension). The WebSphere Application Server bundles IBM JRE 1.3.1 and the IBM JSSE 1.0.3 package, providing a preconfigured SSL environment. However, it is important to note that extended functions such as certificate revocation lists are not supported at the 1.3.1 level as the extended functions are defined as part of the CertAPI, which ships with JRE 1.4. Thus, for a full-featured SSL environment, JRE 1.4 is required.

The JRE used by Application Developer to run the unit test environment is located at `<installation_directory>\runtimes\base_v5\java\jre\bin`. We run keytool and create our key stores at this location. It is important to note that the key store should be created in the location from which it will be used. It should not be copied to another location once created.

1. Open a command prompt and navigate to Application Developer's runtime environment, **<installation_directory>\runtimes\base_v5\java\jre\bin**.
2. At the command prompt enter

```
keytool -genkey -keystore jmskeystore -storepass passw0rd -
keypass passw0rd -alias jmsclient -keyalg RSA -keysize 1024
```

This generates a 1024 private key based on RSA and creates a self-signed certificate located in the key store **jmskeystore**. You will be prompted to enter a number of values. Of particular importance is the value you specify for Common Name, which is used to identify the certificate. We use the name **JMSClient** (Figure 7–66).

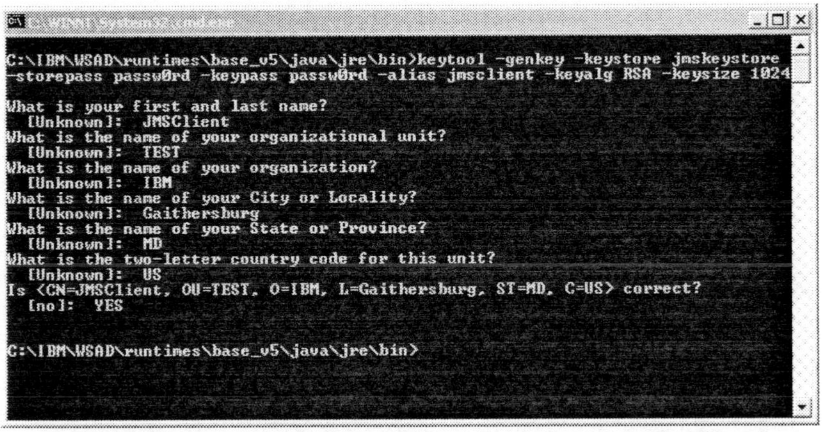

Figure 7-66 Keytool: Generate Private Certificate

3. We similarly need to generate a public certificate to be shared with the queue manager. Enter the command

```
keytool -export -keystore jmskeystore -storepass passw0rd -
alias jmsclient -file jmsclient.crt.
```

The public certificate is stored in the file `jmsclient.crt` (Figure 7–67).

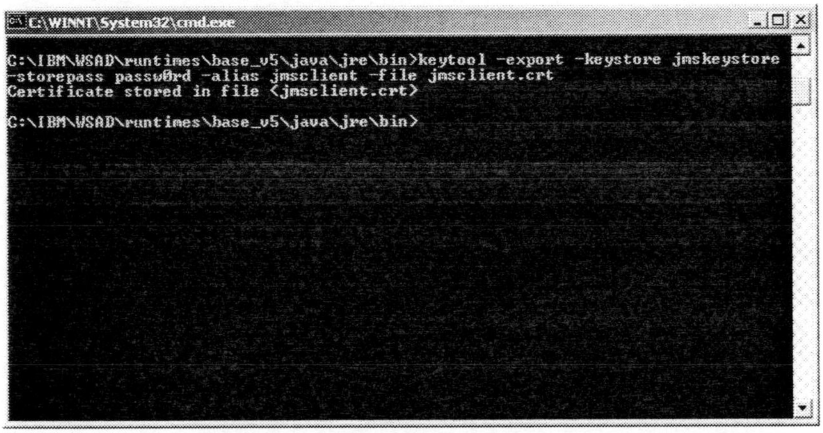

Figure 7-67 Keytool: Generate Public Certificate

Exchange Public Certificates   Our final step is to import the public certificates into the appropriate certificate stores; that is, the queue manager's public certificate is imported into a Java key store, and the JMS client's public certificate is imported by the queue manager.

1. Using the WebSphere MQ Explorer, access queue manager **JMSSVR** certificate store. As before, click **Add** to add a certificate and import the file **jmsclient.crt**. No password is needed, as this is a public certificate (Figure 7–68).

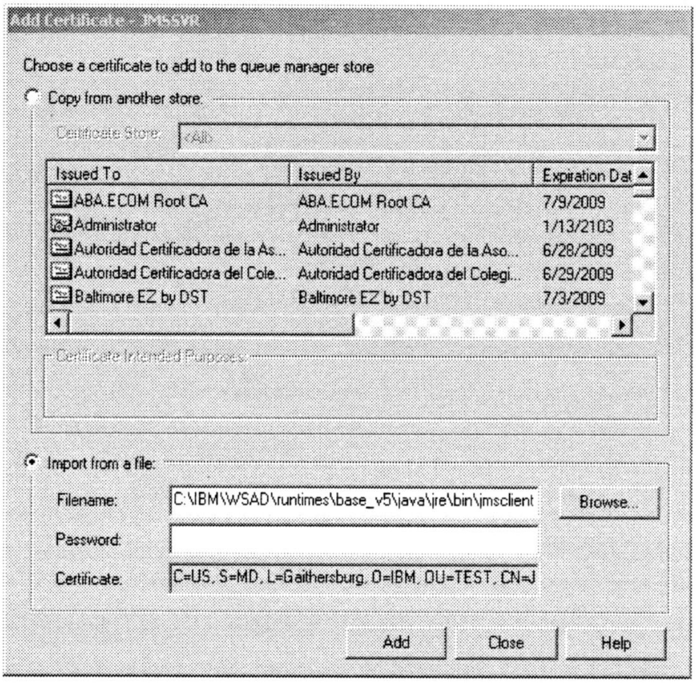

Figure 7-68 Import JMS Client Public Certificate

2. Similarly, from the command prompt, enter the following command to import **jmssvr.crt** into a key store:

```
keytool -import -file c:\cygwin\bin\jmssvr.crt -keystore
truststore -storepass passw0rd -alias JMSSVR
```

You will be asked if this certificate can be trusted. Type **Y** and press **Enter**. The certificate is now added (Figure 7–69).

Figure 7-69 Import Queue Manager Public Certificate

Note that there is a default key store called cacerts for public certificates. It is located at the `<install dir>\runtimes\base_v5\java\jre\lib\security` directory and has a default password of *changeit*. However, we adopted the approach of storing public certificates in our own key store. We have now successfully configured private certificates for both the queue manager and JMS client, and have exchanged their public certificates with each other. We can now configure the required resources.

Configuring Resources

We begin by configuring the MQ server connection channel that used by the JMS client for SSL secured communication. Then, we will an `MQQueueConnectionFactory` with the SSL attributes configured. We are, however, faced with a slight problem. At the time of writing, the WebSphere MQ JMS Provider in the WebSphere administration console does not expose the SSL properties for the `MQQueueConnectionFactory`. Consequently, we must define the `MQQueueConnectionFactory` in a file system–based namespace using JMSAdmin. Using the administration console, we define a generic JMS provider so that we can access the external namespace. We then update the properties of the application server's JVM and complete our configuration by updating the resource references associated with our session bean to reference the newly defined administered objects.

Configure the Server Connection Channel   The server connection channel is used by the JMS client to communicate with the queue manager. We could update the properties of SYSTEM.DEF.SVRCONN, which is the default specified by the WebSphere MQ `ConnectionFactory` objects, but we simply create a new channel instead.

1. In the WebSphere MQ Explorer, select the queue manager **JMSSVR**, and expand its **Advanced** folder.

2. Select the **Channels** folder, right-click and select **New ➡ Server Connection Channel**.

3. In the resulting dialog, on the **General** tab, specify the name **JMS.SSL.SVRCONN** for the channel name (Figure 7–70).

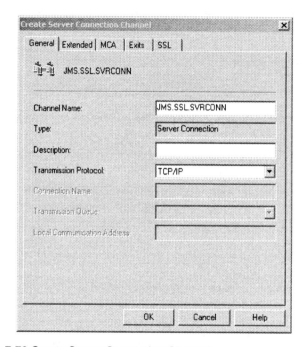

Figure 7-70 Create Server Connection Channel

4. Click the **SSL** tab, and select the **CipherSpec** that the queue manager will support with this channel. We use **RC4_MD5_US**. Make sure the checkbox specifying that the client should be authenticated is checked (Figure 7–71). Click **OK**. The server connection channel is created.

The CipherSpec that we specify here defines the encryption algorithm and hash function that the queue manager will support for SSL communication. As we will see shortly, the JMS client must specify the same CipherSpec for communication to be successfully established.

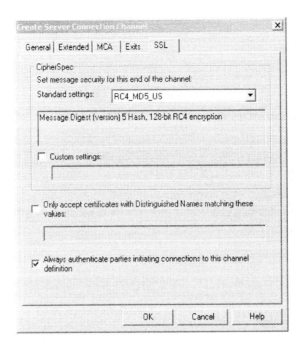

Figure 7-71 Specify Server Connection Channel CipherSpec

Create JMS-Administered Objects   As we discussed in Chapter 6, JMSAdmin is a command-line tool for creating WebSphere MQ–administered objects. To configure it to use a file system–based namespace, ensure that the following options are set in its configuration file **jmsadmin.config**, with all other options commented out:

```
//excerpt from JMSAdmin.config
INITIAL_CONTEXT_FACTORY=com.sun.jndi.fscontext.RefFSContextFac
tory
PROVIDER_URL=file:/C:/JNDINamespace
SECURITY_AUTHENTICATION=none
```

This sets up a namespace located at C:\JNDINamespace. Ensure that the directory specified exists.

1. Open a command prompt and run JMSAdmin (it should be in **<mq install dir>\java\bin**).

2. At the prompt enter the following command (Figure 7–72):

```
DEF QCF(SSLQCF) QMANAGER(JMSSVR) TRANSPORT(CLIENT) HOST-
NAME(localhost) PORT(1414) CHANNEL(JMS.SSL.SVRCONN) SSLCIPHER-
SUITE(SSL_RSA_WITH_RC4_128_MD5)
```

Figure 7-72 SSL enabled MQQueueConnectionFactory

This creates an `MQQueueConnectionFactory` with a JNDI name of **SSLQCF**. It
defines a client connection to the queue manager via port **1414**. It additionally specifies
a value for the `SSLCIPHERSUITE` attribute, which enables an SSL connection to be
initiated. The `SSLCIPHERSUITE` value is a valid CipherSuite implemented by the
JSSE implementation. As we discussed earlier, the value specified must match that
defined for the server connection channel. However, WebSphere MQ components specify a CipherSpec, as only SSL_RSA is supported. Consequently, you must specify a
CipherSuite that is functionally equivalent to WebSphere MQ's SSL support
(SSL_RSA) and the CipherSpec defined for the channel. Table 7–2 is taken from
Appendix H in the *WebSphere MQ 5.3 Using Java* user guide, which details the JSSE
CipherSuite and associated WebSphere MQ CipherSpec. Note that the names differ
slightly between both environments.

Table 7–2 WebSphere MQ 5.3 CipherSpecs and JSSE CipherSuites Association

MQ CipherSpec	JSSE CipherSuite
NULL_MD5	SSL_RSA_WITH_ NULL_MD5
NULL_SHA	SSL_RSA_WITH_ NULL_SHA
RC4_MD5_EXPORT	SSL_RSA_EXPORT_WITH_ RC4_40_MD5
RC4_MD5_US	SSL_RSA_WITH_ RC4_128_MD5
RC4_SHA_US	SSL_RSA_WITH_ RC4_128_SHA
RC2_MD5_EXPORT	SSL_RSA_EXPORT_WITH_ RC2_CBC_40_MD5
DES_SHA_EXPORT	SSL_RSA_WITH_ DES_CBC_SHA
RC4_56_SHA_EXPORT1024	SSL_RSA_EXPORT1024_WITH_ RC4_56_SHA
DES_SHA_EXPORT1024	SSL_RSA_EXPORT1024_WITH_ DES_CBC_SHA
TRIPLE_DES_SHA_US3	SSL_RSA_WITH_ 3DES_EDE_CBC_SHA

3. We also define an `MQQueue` object that provides access to the MQ queue **UPDATEQ**. Enter the following command (Figure 7–73):

```
DEF Q(SENDERQ) QUEUE(UPDATEQ)
```

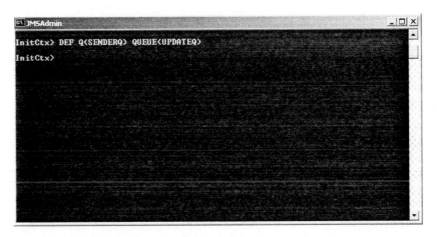

Figure 7-73 MQQueue Definition

This defines an `MQQueue` with a JNDI name **SENDERQ**; it similarly points to the MQ queue **UPDATEQ**.

4. We have now defined an `MQQueueConnectionFactory` and `MQQueue` in our file system–based JNDI namespace. Terminate the JMSAdmin session by typing **END** at the prompt.

Creating a Generic JMS Provider   Because we have defined our administered objects in an external JNDI namespace, we use the administration console to define a generic JMS provider that references the external namespace. This enables the application server to access the external namespace on the sender session bean's behalf.

1. Switch to Application Developer and start **TestSrv** if it is not still running.
2. Launch the administration console and click on **Generic JMS Provider**.
3. We create a new provider definition. Click **New** to open the definition form.
4. The form requires a name for the provider, its class path and library path settings, as well as the service class and location for the JNDI namespace. For my WebSphere MQ installation I specified the following (Figure 7–74):
    - Name: **WMQ53**
    - Class path:
      C:\ibm\wmq\Java\lib\providerutil.jar;C:\ibm\wmq\Java\lib\com.ibm .mqjms.jar;C:\ibm\wmq\Java\lib\ldap.jar;C:\ibm\wmq\Java\lib\jta.j

ar;C:\ibm\wmq\Java\lib\jndi.jar;C:\ibm\wmq\Java\lib\jms.jar;C:\ib
m\wmq\Java\lib\connector.jar;C:\ibm\wmq\Java\lib\fscon-
text.jar;C:\ibm\wmq\Java\lib\com.ibm.mq.jar;
C:\ibm\wmq\Java\lib\rmm.jar;C:\ibm\wmq\Java\lib\

- Native Library path: **C:\ibm\wmq\Java\lib**
- External Initial Context Factory:
  com.sun.jndi.fscontext.RefFSContextFactory
- External Provider URL: **file:/C:/JNDINamespace**

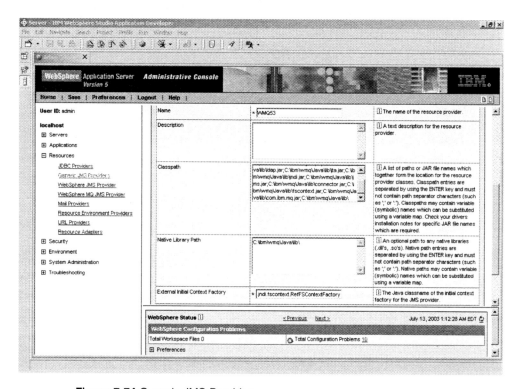

Figure 7-74 Generic JMS Provider

This defines WebSphere MQ as a generic JMS provider and references the file system–
based namespace that we populated using JMSAdmin. We can now create in the
generic JMS provider administered object references that point to the administered
objects we defined externally.

5. Click **Apply** to save the provider definition, then scroll down the definition form and
locate the link **Generic JMS Destinations**. Click on the link.

6. In the resulting page, click **New** to open the definitions form.

7. Specify the following (Figure 7–75), then click **OK**:

- Name: **mqssl.sample.Queue**
- Type: **QUEUE**
- JNDI Name: **mqssl.sample.Queue**
- External JNDI Name: **SENDERQ**

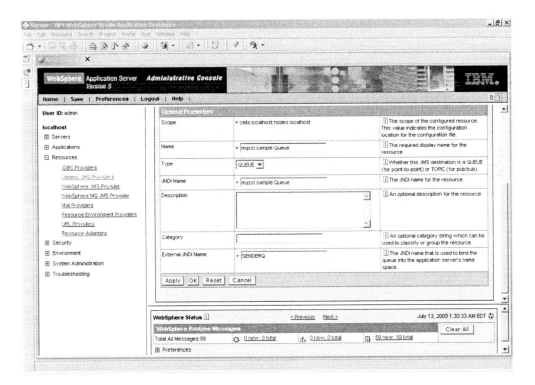

Figure 7-75 Generic JMS Destination

This creates a local alias in the WebSphere namespace to the object SENDERQ, which we defined in the file system–based namespace. We repeat the process to create a reference to the MQQueueConnectionFactory.

8. Return to the **Generic JMS Provider** page and click **JMS Connection Factories** and then **New**.

9. Fill in the definitions page, specifying the following (Figure 7–76), and then click **OK**:
   - Name: **mqssl.sample.SenderQCF**
   - Type: **QUEUE**
   - JNDI Name: **mqssl.sample.SenderQCF**
   - External JNDI Name: **SSLQCF**

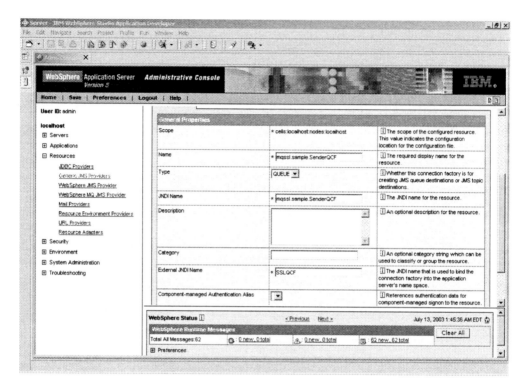

Figure 7-76 Generic JMS Connection Factory

10. Save the configuration.

Set JVM Properties In order to enable the JMS client to use SSL, we must pass a number of parameters to the application server's JVM. The parameters identify the key stores where certificates can be found.

1. In the administration console expand **Servers** in the menu pane, click **Application Servers,** and then click **server1**.
2. Scroll down the resulting page and locate the link **Process Definition**. Click it.
3. On the resulting page locate the link **Java Virtual Machine**, and then click it to open up the settings page.
4. In the field **Generic JVM Arguments** add the following, separating each entry with a space (Figure 7–77):
    - -Djavax.net.ssl.keyStore= C:\IBM\WSAD\runtimes\base_v5\java\jre\bin \jmskeystore
    - -Djavax.net.ssl.keyStorePassword=passw0rd

- -Djavax.net.ssl.trustStore=   C:\IBM\WSAD\runtimes\base_v5\java\jre\ bin\truststore
- -Djavax.net.ssl.trustStorePassword=passw0rd
- -Djavax.net.debug=true

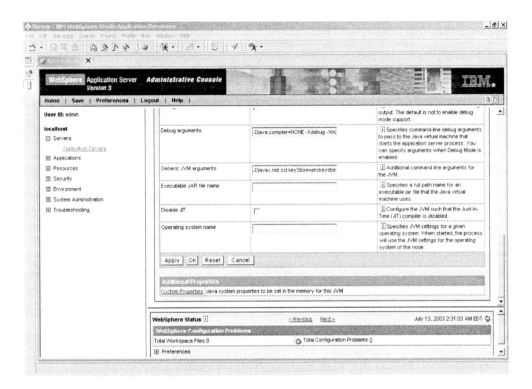

Figure 7-77 Application Server JVM Settings

We specify the location of the key store, which contains the JMS client's private certificate, and the trust store, which contains the queue manager's public certificate. Note that you must specify the full path for the key stores. We run the SSL session in debug mode so that we can confirm that an SSL session is actually established.

5. Click **OK** to save the settings, then save the configuration.

Modify the Sender Session Bean's Resource References To complete the configuration, we must update the resource references for the sender session bean to reference the SSL-enabled `MQQueueConnectionFactory` defined in the generic JMS provider. This results in the JMS client retrieving the new objects the next time it is run.

1. Switch to the **J2EE** perspective, and open the EJB deployment descriptor for **EmpRecordSenderEJB**.
2. Click the **References** tab and update the bindings for **jms/SenderQCF** and **jms/SenderQ** to reference the definitions we created in the generic JMS provider: **mqssl.sample.SenderQCF** and **mqssl.sample.Queue** respectively.
3. Save the deployment descriptor.

Testing the Scenario Implementation

We use the UTC to invoke the sender session bean as before.

1. Switch the **Server** perspective, and in the Servers panel select **TestSrv** and restart it.
2. Once the server is running, launch the **UTC** and use it to invoke EmpRecord-Sender's submit method.
3. The method should return successfully, and inspection of the console should show SSL trace entries output, since we set the debug option to true (Figure 7–78).

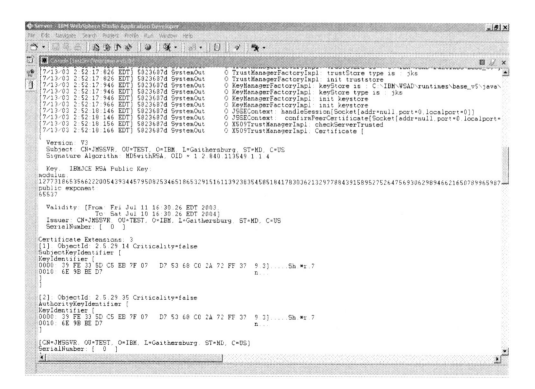

Figure 7-78 SSL Trace Entries

We have now successfully tested the configuration, demonstrating how communication between the JMS client and the underlying queue manager can be secured using SSL. It is important to remember that we achieved this without modifying a single line of code.

Summary

The objective of this chapter was to provide guidance on implementing solutions to common JMS usage scenarios through discussion and hands-on instructions. To this end we detailed the implementation of four scenarios, covering basic messaging and advanced configuration options.

Scenario 1 was concerned with the exchange of messages between two J2EE applications. We used a session bean and MDB to implement this interaction, discussing best practices in terms of application design and code implementation. We extended the scenario in scenario 2 to the realm of publish-subscribe and used MDBs to implement both durable and nondurable subscribers. We explored the behavior of both subscriber types and contrasted our implementation of the publishing session bean to the sending session bean created earlier.

Scenario 3 delved into the considerations around exchanging messages with non-JMS clients, and we reviewed and tested the facilities WebSphere MQ provides to support this interaction. Because we used the unit test WebSphere JMS Provider up until this point, scenario 3 had the additional benefit of requiring us to change JMS providers. We thus gained first-hand experience on how the use of administered objects makes JMS client implementations portable.

Scenario 4 introduced the use of WebSphere MQ SSL support for authenticating JMS clients as part of a wider discussion on securing communications. We reviewed various options and then modified our JMS client configuration to use SSL.

We have so far focused on the development of JMS applications, and in the next chapter we discuss a number of considerations associated with how JMS applications might be deployed.

CHAPTER 8

Enterprise Deployment

T he ultimate objective of any JMS application development effort is that the application is deployed in the enterprise, fulfilling the purpose for which it was designed. To conclude our examination of enterprise messaging using JMS and IBM WebSphere, we review a number of considerations associated with deploying JMS applications within the enterprise. We focus on the operating environment for the JMS client, as provided by WebSphere Application Server, and its enterprise-level JMS provider implemented by WebSphere MQ and WebSphere Business Integration Message Broker.

We begin by examining where the JMS provider might be physically located in relation to the JMS client. We then review a number of clustering topologies, and then close our discussion with the considerations around selecting a JNDI namespace provider.

JMS Provider Location

When planning the deployment of JMS applications, one of the first questions that must be addressed is, What is the location of the JMS provider in relation to the JMS application? In the context of our discussions, the question can be rephrased: Where is the WebSphere MQ queue manager and/or Message Broker located in relation to the JMS application?

Let us revisit scenario 1: the basic point-to-point messaging scenario that we implemented in Chapter 7, "JMS Implementation Scenarios." It defined the exchange of messages between two J2EE applications implemented by a session bean and an MDB, which were linked by a common destination (queue) to which messages are sent and from which they are retrieved. As shown in Figure 8–1, this interaction can be implemented using WebSphere MQ in a number of ways.

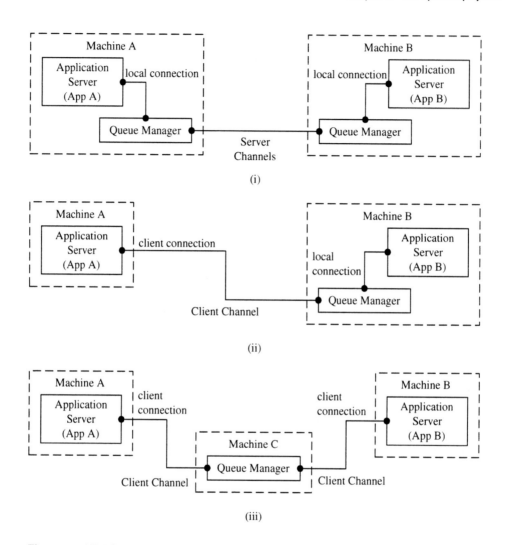

Figure 8-1 WebSphere MQ Topologies

Each application can be collocated with a local queue manager to which it establishes a local connection. The queue managers are then linked together using server channels, and they exchange messages on behalf of the applications (i). Alternatively, a single queue manager could be collocated with application B, and application A (which runs on a different machine) establishes a client connection to the remote queue manager (ii). The third variation has the queue manager placed on a separate machine, and both applications use client connections to connect to it (iii). There is, of course, potentially a fourth configuration in which both applications and queue manager are collocated on a single physical machine. In general, the choice of topology is primarily driven by performance requirements, application design, and administrative considerations.

By virtue of their communication mechanism, local connections are faster than client connections, as they use interprocess memory to exchange commands with the queue manager. They provide the shortest path between the application and the queue manager, and remove any network connectivity considerations from the realm of the application. In addition, the server channels used to connect the queue managers can move data over the network more efficiently than can client connections. Server channels have tuning parameters that allow messages to be sent in suitable batch sizes or at appropriate batch intervals. Server channels are also more tolerant of network outages in unreliable networks, as they have built-in retry capabilities.

Client connections utilize a synchronous protocol exchange, comprising an API request followed by a results reply, to communicate with the queue manager. Clearly, this introduces additional overhead (in comparison to local connections), and we should ascertain that such overhead is acceptable given the application's performance requirements. When using client connections, unstable network performance can result in an "in-doubt state" in which the client does not know whether or not its API request was honored by the queue manager, as the connection was broken before a response was received. This concern particularly applies to the sending case, where the message was sent to the queue manager, who acknowledges its receipt, but the application never receives the acknowledgment. Does the application send the message again? Can the receiving application tolerate duplicate messages? These are all questions that must be addressed when using client connections. Based on the nature of the application, the answers can sometimes be very simple. Application handling of in-doubt states can be mitigated through the use of XA transactions, as then responsibility for the in-doubt transaction is handled by the transaction manager: the WebSphere Application Server. Of course, invoking transactions attracts its own performance penalties, and their use should be married to the business requirements.

XA support over a client connection is a relatively new feature available as purchasable option for WebSphere MQ 5.3. Prior to its availability, XA transactions were only supported by local connections, implying that the application and queue manager had to be collocated if the interaction involved XA transactions.

In the event of network outages, a local queue manager provides the sending application with a store-and-forward capability. The application can continue to operate and pass messages to the queue manager. The messages are then sent by the queue manager when the network becomes available. If the application is connecting to a remote queue manager, then a network outage implies that messages cannot be sent. Hence, the decision must be made as to whether the application is allowed to continue to operate. If it is, temporary storage for the data may have to be designed.

Collocating the queue manager with the application, in our case hosted by the application server, can increase the administrative overhead. From an administrative viewpoint, it might be impossible, impractical, or simply undesirable to place a queue manager on every machine running the application. This could be due to physical numbers, administrative controls, configuration requirements, application isolation, licensing costs, and so forth. In such cases the client connection provides a viable alternative. As we see in the next section, the location of the queue manager also impacts the choice and configuration of clustering topology options.

In publish-subscribe scenarios the centralized nature of Message Broker, which services a varying number of publishing and subscribing applications, suggests that it is typically located remote from the applications it supports. As shown in Figure 8–2, the broker is itself hosted by a queue manager, and JMS clients may use either the WebSphere MQ Transport or the Real-time Transport to communicate with it. In the case where WebSphere MQ is used, the applications can either use a client connection to connect directly to the broker's queue manager or access the broker's queue manager via a local queue manager to which they have a local connection.

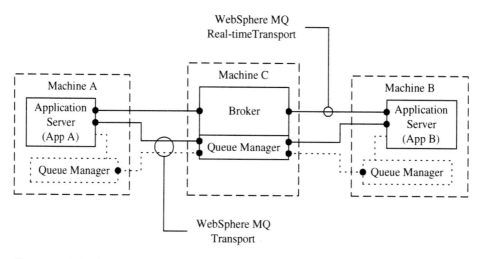

Figure 8-2 WebSphere MQ Topologies Including Message Broker

From the JMS client's perspective, the most important thing to remember is that the JMS provider location need have no explicit effect on the JMS client's implementation. As discussed in Chapter 6, "IBM JMS–Administered Objects," and demonstrated in Chapter 7, the transport choice and connection type are all defined by the connection factory objects, which insolates the JMS client from deployment specifics.

Clustering Topologies

For reasons ranging from workload balancing to fault tolerance and high availability (HA), we can expect to consider clustering solutions as we plan for the enterprise deployment of JMS applications. High-availability and workload management clusters typically define the type of cluster under consideration, and we examine them in the context of WebSphere Application

Server, WebSphere MQ, and WebSphere Business Integration Message Broker. We also examine clustering topologies specifically enabled by Message Broker in support of its publish-subscribe function. Useful references that document how to implement the software configurations we discuss are listed in Appendix D.

High-Availability Clusters

High availability is concerned with ensuring that application services are always available and minimizing unavailability due to outages. High-availability clusters are generally implemented using a combination of redundant hardware and platform-specific clustering software. The basic premise is that if a given machine or the applications it runs fails, work is transferred to a different machine with the capability to provide the same service. Referred to as *failover*, clustering packages differentiate themselves by the platforms they support, the time taken to fail over, and the physical distance that can exist between backup machines. Common examples of clustering software include HACMP, Veritas Clusters, Sun Clusters, MC/Service Guard, and Microsoft Clusters.

Figure 8–3 depicts a high-availability topology based on the application server and the queue manager residing on the same physical machine.

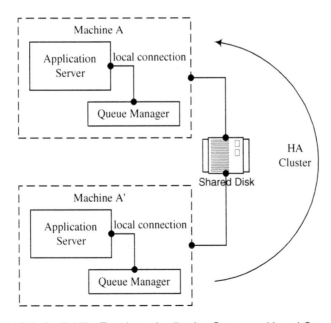

Figure 8-3 High-Availability Topology: Application Server and Local Queue Manager

In this case there are a number of failure scenarios to consider:

1. The application server instance fails.
2. The queue manager fails.
3. The machine fails.

While distinct, each of the three scenarios results in a denial of application service. In the first instance the JMS client is not available to process messages. In the second the JMS provider is unavailable to the JMS client, and of course in the third the machine itself is unavailable. In a collocated configuration it is best to consider the application server and queue manager as a service node, and the failure of either is considered a failure of both. Thus, a failure of any component (or the machine) results in all work being transferred to the backup machine. Since the application server and queue manager are separate entities running totally different processes, achieving this means that they must be grouped together and defined as a failure unit by the clustering package. It is important to remember that both the queue manager and application server have data repositories in the form of configuration files and logs. In high-availability clusters these data files need to be accessible to both the primary and backup machine. Consequently, the use of high-availability clusters requires a shared storage solution that is accessible to both machines. In Figure 8–4 the queue manager and application server are placed on separate boxes.

The queue manager is placed in a high-availability cluster, ensuring that it remains available, and the application server can be similarly clustered. However, we do have the option, as shown, to simplify the application server configuration by using its workload management services. The workload management services provide a level of availability by sharing the work-

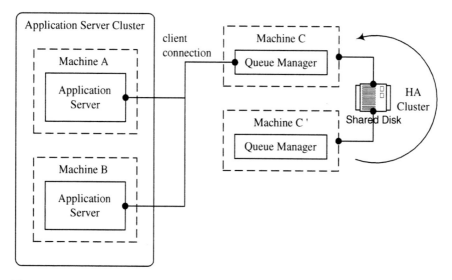

Figure 8-4 High-Availability Topology: Application Server and Remote Queue Manager

load among a number of cloned application servers. This ensures that the service provided by the JMS client is always available: if one application server fails, work is simply spread among those that are available. This approach is particularly suitable if the applications are stateless; however, if the applications are executing XA transactions, when an application server fails, a number of in-flight transactions may have to be recovered. To recover these transactions, we need to start an application server instance that can access the existing transaction logs. This, of course, is a service that a high-availability cluster would provide.

Brokers are hosted by queue managers and can be similarly configured as part of a high-availability cluster. In this case the broker is grouped with the queue manager as a single failure unit. Each broker requires access to a database to persist its state. If the database is located on the same machine as the broker, it must also be defined as part of the failure unit. It may, however, exist on a separate machine, in which case its availability is treated separately.

Implementing high-availability clusters can prove expensive, and sometimes the applications require some redundancy but not to the level of robustness that high-availability clusters provide. Figure 8–5 shows what I have termed a *soft cluster configuration* involving an application server and remote queue manager.

The sending JMS client is programmed such that if it loses its connection to the primary queue manager, it retrieves a connection factory that connects it to the secondary queue manager. The receiving application uses two MDBs to monitor both potential destinations, ensuring that messages sent are retrieved and processed. However, if a queue manager fails before the MDB has finished processing all the messages on its queue, the messages will be unavailable to any application until the hosting queue manager is restarted. This is only true if the messages are persistent; nonpersistent messages are discarded, as they are only held in memory and not

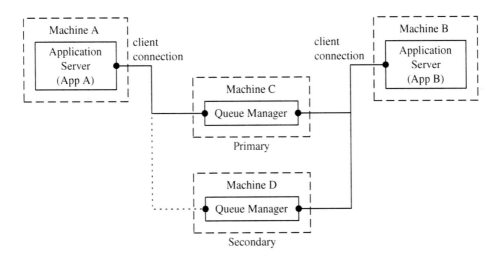

Figure 8-5 Soft Cluster: Application Server and Remote Queue Manager

backed up to the queue manager's logs. On the zOS platform the issue of stranded messages can be avoided if they are held in a shared queue. Shared queues are a shared resource (held in a coupling facility) that can be accessed by multiple queue managers. In this case the messages are retrieved via the secondary queue manager.

As you can imagine, you could design topologies that are variations of these themes. For instance, you could have a local queue manager with the application server, and if only the queue manager process fails, have the JMS client connect to a backup remote queue manager. Irrespective of the approach taken to addressing availability, the overall objective remains to avoid a single point of failure and provide some level of redundancy for application services.

Workload Management Clusters

Workload management clusters are designed to facilitate the scalability of a solution and provide some level of fault tolerance. We have already mentioned that the WebSphere Application Server provides workload management services that enable work to be distributed among a cluster of available application servers. WebSphere MQ provides similar functionality, and Figure 8–6 shows how these can be combined in a single topology.

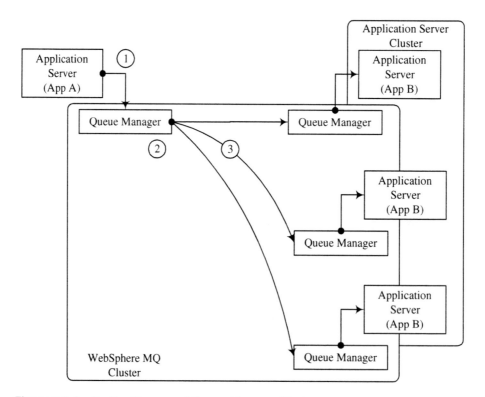

Figure 8-6 Application Server and Queue Manager Clusters

WebSphere MQ clusters allow messages to be load-balanced among a number of receiving (target) queue managers. The load balancing works in the following way:

1. The sending JMS client connects to a queue manager (using either a local or client connection) and sends a message specifying a target destination queue. This queue manager is the gateway to the cluster, and it must not host the queue specified.
2. Being part of the cluster, the gateway queue manager can determine which queue managers in the cluster host the specified queue. The gateway queue manager then picks one of the eligible queue managers and passes it the message.
3. By default, the gateway queue manager loops among the eligible queue managers for each subsequent send by the JMS client, passing the next message in turn. WebSphere MQ allows the default algorithm for distributing messages among eligible recipients to be modified to suit the needs of the business.

The WebSphere MQ cluster is fault-tolerant, and if any of the target queue managers become unavailable, it is no longer sent any messages. However, we still have the potential for messages to be stranded at the failed queue manager until it is restarted. Consequently, a high-availability cluster might be introduced to fail over the failed queue manager and provide access to the stranded messages.

With reference to Figure 8–6, it should be remembered that from the perspective of a given JMS client, WebSphere MQ clusters do not address the redundancy of its queue manager. Rather, alongside WebSphere Application Server clusters, WebSphere MQ clusters enable us to distribute work among a number of redundant nodes. This point is of particular relevance to the sending JMS client, since its access to the WebSphere MQ cluster is via a gateway queue manager. If the gateway queue manager becomes unavailable, there must be an alternative queue manager for it or other JMS client instances to access the WebSphere MQ cluster.

As with high-availability clusters, workload management clusters do not necessarily have any explicit effect on how the JMS client is implemented. In application server clusters, multiple JMS client instances (e.g., session beans or MDBs) can access the same WebSphere MQ resources, allowing processing to be shared. In publish-subscribe scenarios, if you're using a durable subscriber MDB and want publications to be load-balanced among a number of MDB clones, set the clone support (CLONESUPP) attribute of the MQTopicConnectionFactory to enabled. This results in only a single subscription being registered, and the resulting publication is sent to only one of the MDB clones. With nondurable subscriber MDBs, cloning creates a replication effect, as each MDB will register a subscription, and thus there will be as many publications as there are clones.

For JMS clients sending messages via a gateway queue manager to a WebSphere MQ cluster, it is important that the queue manager (QMANAGER) property of the MQQueue object is blank. This is its default setting, and it allows the gateway queue manager to select from the list of eligible queue managers. If a queue manager name is specified, then the load balancing algorithm is skipped, and the message is sent directly to that queue manager.

Message Broker Collectives and Clones

WebSphere Business Integration Message Broker supports the definition of broker networks that enable publications to be efficiently distributed among dispersed publishers and subscribers. As shown in Figure 8–7, broker networks involve linked brokers that can be grouped in collectives.

Brokers that are linked, either explicitly or by virtue of being in a collective, share their subscriptions. This allows publishers and subscribers to be connected to different brokers and still exchange publications. Thus, rather than publishing and subscribing JMS clients having to connect to the same broker, they can connect to their nearest broker, improving their performance. Using collectives helps optimize the flow of publications through the network, particularly when publishers and subscribers are geographically dispersed. Collectives also enable the broker's workload to be shared, as connecting clients can be partitioned among a number of brokers in a collective.

When a subscriber registers with a broker, the subscription is held at that broker, though the broker may register a proxy subscription on behalf of the subscriber with other brokers in its network. If the broker fails, the subscriber stops receiving publications because no other broker in the network holds its actual subscription. While this can be addressed using high-availability clusters, Message Broker provides an alternative by enabling brokers to be cloned.

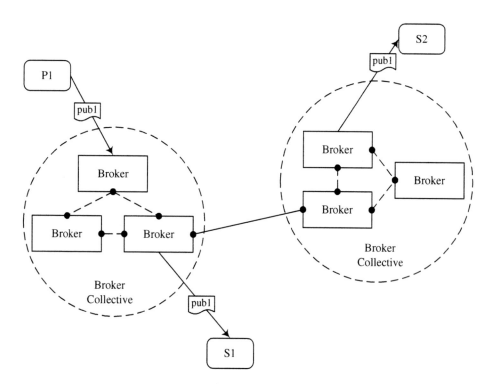

Figure 8-7 Broker Collectives

As shown in Figure 8–8, a cloned broker dynamically replicates its subscription table to all of its clones. This allows the clones to maintain the current state of registered subscribers and their topics of interest. If the cloned broker fails, the replicated subscriptions in its clone become active, and the clone can take over the publication of messages to the subscriber.

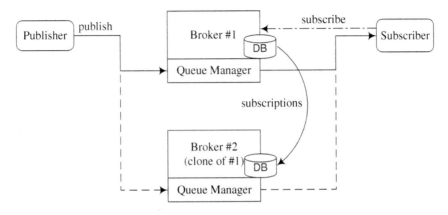

Figure 8-8 Broker Clone

JNDI Namespace Provider

The question of which JNDI namespace should be used to store JMS-administered objects is one that often comes up during discussions as deployments are planned. While the choice is often predetermined, we briefly review our options and their associated considerations.

For the most part we have focused on J2EE-based JMS clients, and thus the natural location for JMS-administered objects is the WebSphere namespace implemented by the WebSphere Application Server. The WebSphere namespace is federated and can thus be shared among a number of application server instances, enabling object definitions to be created once and accessed throughout an application server cluster if required. As we saw in Chapter 7, we can populate the namespace with JMS-administered objects using the administration console (or scripting tool).

LDAP servers can be used to store JMS-administered objects, and their use is most often dictated by architectural standards adopted within the enterprise. With LDAP servers, we use JMSAdmin to populate the namespace, and in my experience, the greatest challenge here can be the appropriate configuration of the LDAP server to store JMS-administered objects (essentially Java objects). Depending upon the version or make of the LDAP server, it might not come pre-configured with the appropriate schema, which then has to be created. The product manual "WebSphere MQ Using Java" documents the schema required, but this is clearly an additional task that must be correctly executed.

A file system–based namespace is relatively easy to set up and is essentially rendered as a flat file in a directory. Its simplicity makes it a particularly attractive choice when deploying standalone JMS client applications. However, because it is a simple file, it has to be replicated to all the locations where the application runs. In large deployments, distributing and synchronizing the file can be a challenge.

If you have to use an external namespace with JMS clients running in the WebSphere Application Server, then as we saw in Chapter 7, you should define a generic JMS provider that references the external namespace. Using the generic JMS provider, you then create aliases in the WebSphere namespace for the administered objects defined externally. The JMS client references the aliases in the WebSphere namespace, and the application server then accesses the external namespace where the real objects are stored on the JMS client's behalf. The need to use an external namespace might arise because use of an LDAP server has been mandated or because you need to access administered object properties that are not currently exposed by the administration console. If you are using a file system–based namespace in this role, it is useful to note that the file synchronization service supplied as part of WebSphere Application Server Network Deployment can be used to distribute the file among the various application servers in the cluster.

Summary

Enterprise deployment represents the successful conclusion of a JMS application development, and we detailed a number of considerations associated with this process. We reviewed our options for locating the queue manager and broker in relation to the JMS client, contrasting the implications of collocation and remote placement on performance, application behavior, and administration.

We discussed various approaches to implementing both high-availability and workload management clusters, and saw how broker networks can be used to provide an efficient and fault-tolerant publish-subscribe infrastructure.

Finally, we considered the alternatives available to implement the JNDI namespace accessed by the JMS client, highlighting known issues and potential workarounds.

JMS Specification Excerpts

I n the course of our discussions about JMS messages and the JMS API, we reviewed the use of message selectors and examined JMS exceptions. As discussed in Chapter 3, JMS enables fairly sophisticated patterns to be defined for message selectors, and the rules regarding selector syntax defined by JMS are extensive. In Chapter 4 we saw that JMS defines a number of exceptions that standardize the reporting of basic error conditions.

The rules that define message selector syntax and govern the throwing of specific exceptions are reproduced here for your convenience from JMS Specification version 1.1, April 12, 2002.

Message Selector Syntax

A message selector is a `String` whose syntax is based on a subset of the SQL92* conditional expression syntax. If the value of a message selector is an empty string, the value is treated as a null and indicates that there is no message selector for the message consumer.

The order of evaluation of a message selector is from left to right within precedence level. Parentheses can be used to change this order. Predefined selector literals and operator names are written here in upper case; however, they are case insensitive.

A selector can contain the following elements:

Literals
- A string literal is enclosed in single quotes, with an included single quote or an apostrophe represented by a doubled single quote; for example, `'literal'` and `'literal''s'`. Like Java `String` literals, these use the Unicode character encoding.

- An exact numeric literal is a numeric value without a decimal point, such as 57, -957, +62; numbers in the range of Java `long` are supported. Exact numeric literals use the Java integer literal syntax.
- An approximate numeric literal is a numeric value in scientific notation, such as 7E3 and -57.9E2, or a numeric value with a decimal, such as 7., -95.7, and +6.2; numbers in the range of Java `double` are supported. Approximate literals use the Java floating-point literal syntax.
- The boolean literals TRUE and FALSE.

Identifiers

- An identifier is an unlimited-length character sequence that must begin with a Java identifier start character; all following characters must be Java identifier part characters. An identifier start character is any character for which the method `Character.isJavaIdentifierStart` returns true. This includes '_' and '$'. An identifier part character is any character for which the method `Character.isJavaIdentifierPart` returns true.
- Identifiers cannot be the names NULL, TRUE, or FALSE.
- Identifiers cannot be NOT, AND, OR, BETWEEN, LIKE, IN, IS, or ESCAPE.
- Identifiers are either header field references or property references. The type of a property value in a message selector corresponds to the type used to set the property. If a property that does not exist in a message is referenced, its value is NULL. The semantics of evaluating NULL values in a selector are described in the JMS Specification version 1.1, Section 3.8.1.2, "Null Values."
- The conversions that apply to the get methods for properties do not apply when a property is used in a message selector expression. For example, suppose you set a property as a string value, as in the following: `myMessage.setStringProperty("NumberOfOrders", "2")`. The following expression in a message selector would evaluate to false, because a string cannot be used in an arithmetic expression: `"NumberOfOrders > 1"`
- Identifiers are case sensitive.
- Message header field references are restricted to JMSDeliveryMode, JMSPriority, JMSMessageID, JMSTimestamp, JMSCorrelationID, and JMSType. JMSMessageID, JMSCorrelationID, and JMSType values may be null, and if so are treated as a NULL value.
- Any name beginning with JMSX is a JMS-defined property name.
- Any name beginning with JMS_ is a provider-specific property name.
- Any name that does not begin with JMS is an application-specific property name.

Whitespace

- Whitespace is the same as that defined for Java: space, horizontal tab, form feed, and line terminator.

Expressions

- A selector is a conditional expression; a selector that evaluates to true matches; a selector that evaluates to false or unknown does not match.
- Arithmetic expressions are composed of themselves, arithmetic operations, identifiers with numeric values, and numeric literals.
- Conditional expressions are composed of themselves, comparison operations, logical operations, identifiers with Boolean values, and Boolean literals.

Standard bracketing

- Standard bracketing, ( ), for ordering expression evaluation is supported.

Logical operators

- Logical operators in precedence order: NOT, AND, OR.

Comparison operators: =, >, >=, <, <=, <> (not equal)

- Only like type values can be compared. One exception is that it is valid to compare exact numeric values and approximate numeric values (the type conversion required is defined by the rules of Java numeric promotion). If the comparison of non-like type values is attempted, the value of the operation is false. If either of the type values evaluates to NULL, the value of the expression is unknown.
- *String* and *Boolean* comparison is restricted to = and <>. Two strings are equal if and only if they contain the same sequence of characters.

Arithmetic operators in precedence order

- +, - (unary)
- *, / (multiplication and division)
- +, - (addition and subtraction)
- Arithmetic operations must use Java numeric promotion.

arithmetic-expr1 [NOT] BETWEEN arithmetic-expr2 and arithmetic-expr3 (comparison operator)

- "age BETWEEN 15 AND 19" is equivalent to "age >= 15 AND age <= 19".
- "age NOT BETWEEN 15 AND 19" is equivalent to "age < 15 OR age >19".

identifier [NOT] IN (string-literal1, string-literal2,...) (comparison operator where identifier has a String or NULL value)

- "Country IN (' UK', 'US', 'France')" is true for 'UK' and false for 'Peru'; it is equivalent to the expression "(Country = ' UK') OR (Country = ' US') OR (Country = ' France')".

- "Country NOT IN (' UK', 'US', 'France')" is false for 'UK' and true for 'Peru'; it is equivalent to the expression "NOT ((Country = ' UK') OR (Country = ' US') OR (Country = ' France'))".
- If *identifier* of an IN or NOT IN operation is NULL, the value of the operation is unknown.

identifier [NOT] LIKE pattern-value [ESCAPE escape-character] (comparison operator, where identifier has a String value; pattern-value is a string literal where '_' stands for any single character; '%' stands for any sequence of characters, including the empty sequence, and all other characters stand for themselves. The optional escape-character is a single-character string literal whose character is used to escape the special meaning of the '_' and '%' in pattern-value.)

- "phone LIKE '12%3'" is true for '123' or '12993' and false for '1234'.
- "word LIKE 'l_se'" is true for 'lose' and false for 'loose'.
- "underscored LIKE '_%' ESCAPE '\'" is true for '_foo' and false for 'bar'.
- "phone NOT LIKE '12%3'" is false for '123' and '12993' and true for '1234'.
- If *identifier* of a LIKE or NOT LIKE operation is NULL, the value of the operation is unknown.

identifier IS NULL (comparison operator that tests for a null header field value or a missing property value)

- "prop_name IS NULL"

identifier IS NOT NULL (comparison operator that tests for the existence of a non-null header field value or property value)

- "prop_name IS NOT NULL"

JMS providers are required to verify the syntactic correctness of a message selector at the time it is presented. A method providing a syntactically incorrect selector must result in a JMS InvalidSelectorException. JMS providers may also optionally provide some semantic checking at the time the selector is presented. Not all semantic checking can be performed at the time a message selector is presented, because property types are not known.

The following message selector selects messages with a message type of car and color of blue and weight greater than 2500 lbs:

```
"JMSType = 'car' AND color = 'blue' AND weight > 2500"
```

JMS Standard Exceptions

In addition to JMSException, JMS defines several additional exceptions that standardize the reporting of basic error conditions. There are only a few cases where JMS mandates that a specific JMS exception must be thrown. These cases are indicated by the words **must be** in the exception description. **These cases are the only ones on which client logic should depend on a specific problem resulting in a specific JMS exception being thrown.** In the remainder of cases, it is strongly suggested that JMS providers use one of the standard exceptions where possible. JMS providers may also derive provider-specific exceptions from these if needed.

JMS defines the following standard exceptions:

- **IllegalStateException:** This exception is thrown when a method is invoked at an illegal or inappropriate time or if the provider is not in an appropriate state for the requested operation. For example, this exception **must be** thrown if `Session.commit()` is called on a nontransacted session. This exception also **must be** called when a domain-inappropriate method is called, such as calling `TopicSession.CreateQueueBrowser()`.
- **JMSSecurityException:** This exception **must be** thrown when a provider rejects a user name/password submitted by a client. It may also be thrown for any case where a security restriction prevents a method from completing.
- **InvalidClientIDException:** This exception **must be** thrown when a client attempts to set a connection's client identifier to a value that is rejected by a provider.
- **InvalidDestinationException:** This exception **must be** thrown when a destination is either not understood by a provider or is no longer valid.
- **InvalidSelectorException:** This exception **must be** thrown when a JMS client attempts to give a provider a message selector with invalid syntax.
- **MessageEOFException:** This exception **must be** thrown when an unexpected end of stream has been reached when a `StreamMessage` or `BytesMessage` is being read.
- **MessageFormatException:** This exception **must be** thrown when a JMS client attempts to use a data type not supported by a message or attempts to read data in a message as the wrong type. It must also be thrown when equivalent type errors are made with message property values. For example, this exception **must be** thrown if `StreamMessage.writeObject()` is given an unsupported class or if `StreamMessage.readShort()` is used to read a Boolean value. This exception also **must be** thrown if a provider is given a type of message it cannot accept. Note that the special case of a failure caused by attempting to read improperly formatted `String` data as numeric values must throw the `java.lang.NumberFormatException`.
- **MessageNotReadableException:** This exception **must be** thrown when a JMS client attempts to read a write-only message.
- **MessageNotWriteableException:** This exception **must be** thrown when a JMS client attempts to write to a read-only message.

- **ResourceAllocationException:** This exception is thrown when a provider is unable to allocate the resources required by a method. For example, this exception should be thrown when a call to `createTopicConnection` fails due to lack of JMS provider resources.

- **TransactionInProgressException:** This exception is thrown when an operation is invalid because a transaction is in progress. For instance, attempting to call `Session.commit()` when a session is part of a distributed transaction should throw a `TransactionInProgressException`.

- **TransactionRolledBackException:** This exception **must be** thrown when a call to `Session.commit` results in a rollback of the current transaction.

Implementing XA
Global Transactions

In Chapter 7, scenario 1, we implemented a sender session bean and receiver MDB. The employee data retrieved by the MDB was destined for a system of record; however, since our implementation was focused on the messaging aspects, we simply printed the received data to the server console. In this appendix we extend our implementation to include a system of record implemented by a database. We use a session bean and entity bean to access the database, and configure the interaction such that the retrieval of the message and the update to the database is done as a single global XA transaction.

Development Environment

In order to execute this tutorial, we need to add a database server to our development environment. You can use any database server supported by WebSphere Application Server 5.0. In this tutorial I use DB2, specifically, DB2 Enterprise Server 8.1 + FP1. Note that the choice of DB2 edition and version is driven primarily by prerequisites for WebSphere Business Integration Message Broker 5.0, which we use in Appendix C.

Using XA Global Transactions

As shown in the solution architecture (Figure B–1), on receipt of a message the MDB invokes a session bean, which in turn uses an entity bean to update the database. The entire interaction is bound by a single global transaction.

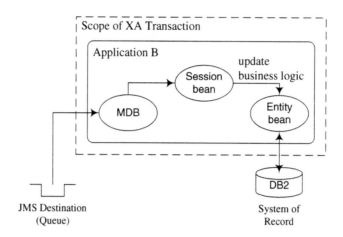

Figure B-1 EJB Interaction

We begin by creating the entity bean and configuring its access to the database. We then create the session bean that accesses the entity bean, and finally we modify our existing MDB to invoke the session bean. We then are ready to retest the scenario implementation. This time we should observe that the data retrieved by the MDB appears as a row in the target database table.

Create the Entity Bean

We use an entity bean to access the employee data database table. We adopt a top-down approach using Application Developer to generate the entity bean and then, based on its definition, generate scripts that create the table in DB2. Application Developer also supports a bottom-up approach (generate entity bean based on existing database table) or a meet-in-the-middle approach (map existing entity bean to existing database table). I have adopted a top-down approach for simplicity, as it minimizes the database configuration required.

Create Employee Record Entity Bean

We create a Container-Managed Persistence (CMP) entity bean, which means that we do not need to explicitly implement any database access code.

1. Launch Application Developer and switch to the **J2EE** perspective.
2. We add this bean to the existing EJB module, **EmpRecordUpdateEJB**, which currently contains the MDB **EmpRecordMDB**.
3. Right-click on **EmpRecordUpdateEJB** and select **New → Enterprise Bean**.
4. This time select **Entity bean with CMP fields** and **CMP 2.0 bean** to define the type. Specify the name **EmpRecord** (Figure B–2). Click **Next**.

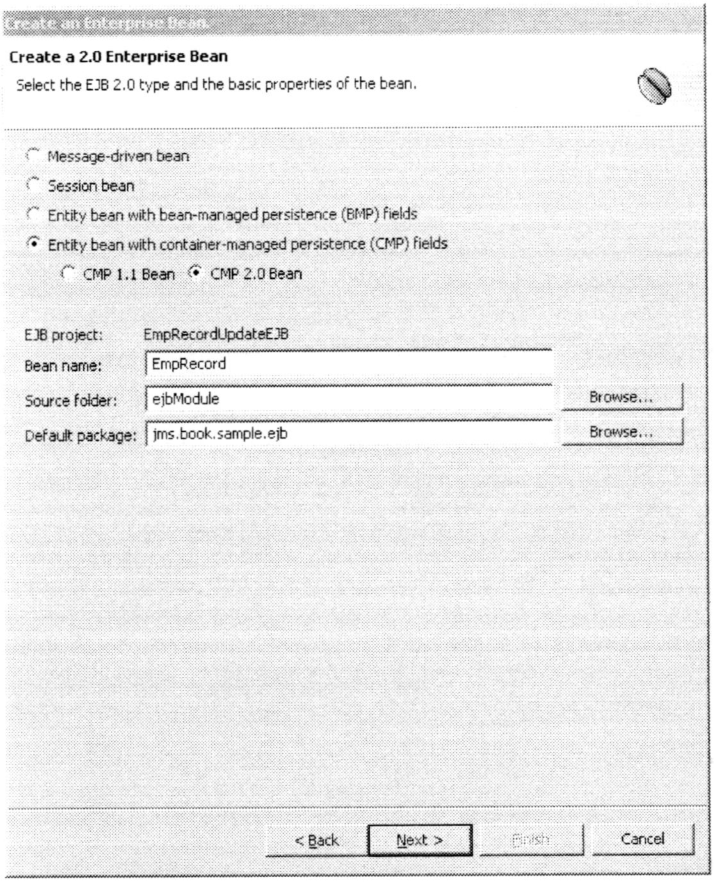

Figure B-2 Create Entity Bean

5. As **EmpRecord** will only be accessed by a local session bean running in the same container, we define only a local interface (Figure B–3).

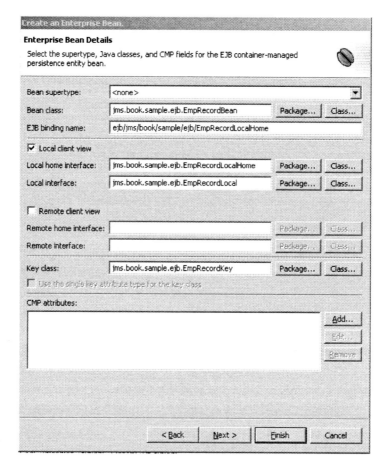

Figure B-3 Enterprise Bean Details

6. We create four CMP fields corresponding to the data that is retrieved by the MDB from the message. Click **Add** next to the CMP attributes list box to launch the **Create CMP Attribute** dialog.

7. For the first attribute, specify the name **employeeID** and type **java.lang.String**. Select the **key field** attribute (Figure B–4). Click **Apply**.

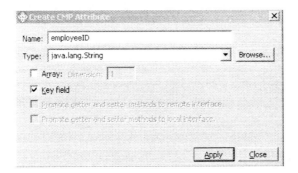

Figure B-4 Define Key Attribute

8. Define the next attribute specifying the name **firstName** and type **java.lang.String**. Accept all other defaults (Figure B–5). Click **Apply**.

Figure B-5 Define Attribute

9. Repeat step 8 to create the attributes **lastName** and **email**, both of type **java.lang.String**.

10. Click **Close**. You should now have four attributes defined (Figure B–6). Click **Next**.

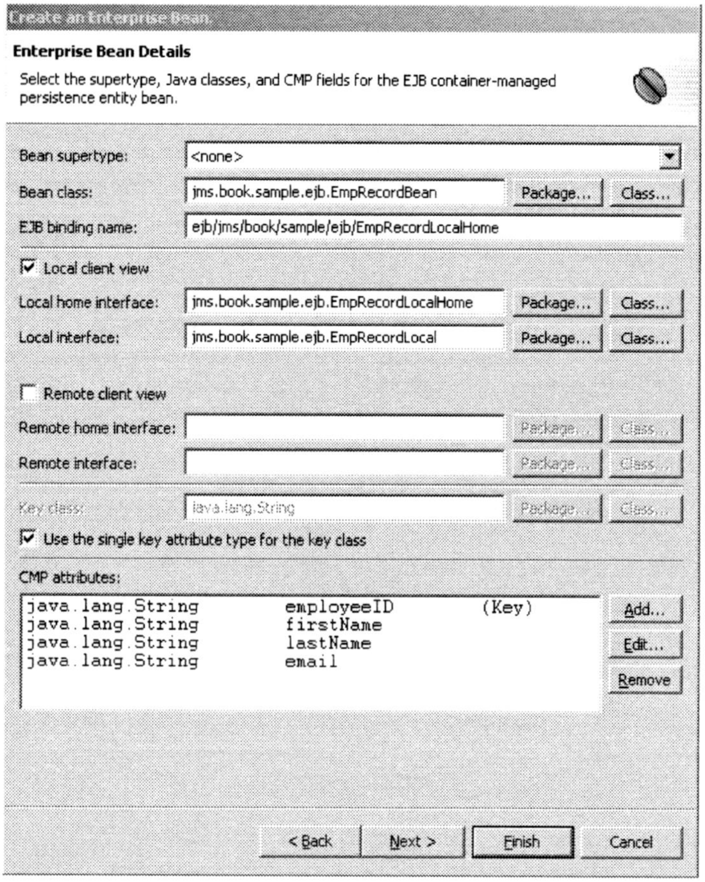

Figure B-6 Entity Bean CMP Attributes

11. Accept the defaults on the following page and click **Finish** to create the entity bean.

Add an ejbCreate method By default the `ejbCreate` method created by the wizard accepts only the key field, `employeeID`. To set any other attributes, we would have to subsequently call their respective setter methods. To allow us to create a fully populated entity bean using `ejbCreate`, we define an overloaded `ejbCreate` that will accept all four attributes. We also need to define a corresponding `ejbPostCreate` and promote `ejbCreate` to the local home interface.

1. Open **EmpRecordBean.java** in the Java editor.

2. Define an `ejbCreate` method that accepts all four attributes as shown:

```
public java.lang.String ejbCreate(String employeeID, String
firstName, String lastName, String email)
        throws javax.ejb.CreateException {
        setEmployeeID(employeeID);
        setFirstName(firstName);
        setLastName(lastName);
        setEmail(email);
        return null;
}
```

3. Define a corresponding `ejbPostCreate` method:

```
public void ejbPostCreate(String employeeID, String firstName,
String lastName, String email)
        throws javax.ejb.CreateException {
}
```

4. Save **EmpRecordBean.java**, then in the outline pane right-click on **ejbCreate(String, String, String, String)** and select **Enterprise Bean → Promote to Local Home Interface**. This adds a definition for the new `ejbCreate` to the interface.

Generate Table Script and Mapping

Having defined the entity bean, we now use it as the basis for generating scripts to create the associated database table.

1. In the J2EE Hierarchy Panel right-click on **EmpRecordUpdateEJB** and select **Generate → EJB to RDB Mapping....**
2. In the resulting dialog accept the default to create a new backend folder and click **Next**.
3. For mapping type, select **Top Down** and click **Next**.
4. In the Top Down mapping options dialog specify
   • Target Database: Select the appropriate Database Server. I use **DB2 Universal Database v8.1**.
   • Database Name: **EMPLOYEE**
   • Schema name: Specify an appropriate identifier. I use **ADMIN**

5. Ensure that the **Generate DDL** checkbox is checked (Figure B–7), and click **Finish**.

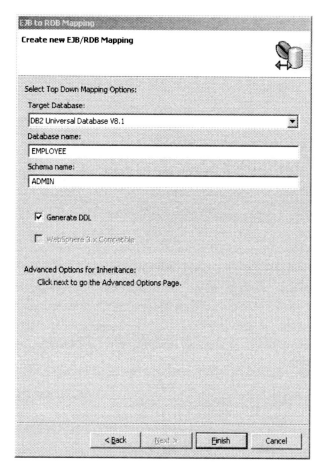

Figure B-7 Configure Top-Down Mapping

6. This opens the generated map **Map.mapxmi**, which maps the attributes of **EmpRecord** to a table in database **EMPLOYEE** called **EMPRECORD**. In the J2EE Navigator panel you will notice a file **Table.ddl** listed beneath Map.mapxmi, which contains the script required to generate the table EMPRECORD in the database (Figure B–8).

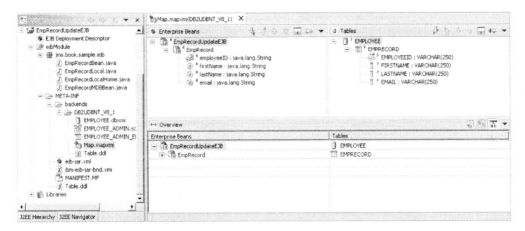

Figure B-8 Generated Map and Script

Configure DB2 Resources

We create a DB2 database called EMPLOYEE, and then use the generated script Table.ddl to create the required table EMPRECORD.

1. Export **Table.ddl** to a temporary directory on your machine. Simply right-click on **Table.ddl** and select **Export**.

2. Select **File System** as the export destination, and in the resulting dialog specify the directory of choice and click **Finish** (Figure B–9).

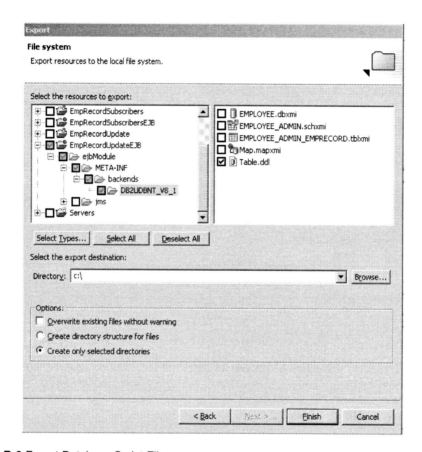

Figure B-9 Export Database Script File

3. Using the Start menu, launch a DB2 Command Window.

4. In the Command Window change to the directory in which you stored Table.ddl.

5. To create the database EMPLOYEE and table EMPRECORD, type the following commands (Figure B–10):

```
db2 create db EMPLOYEE
db2 connect to EMPLOYEE
db2 -tvf Table.ddl
```

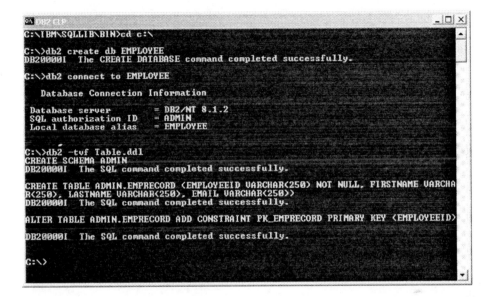

Figure B-10 Create Database Resources

6. We have now defined the database and table that will be accessed by **EmpRecord**. Type **exit** at the prompt to close the DB2 Command Window.

Configure the Entity Bean

We need to associate the bean with a JDBC data source, which will provide it with access to the database, and then generate deploy code.

Define an XA JDBC Data Source   The entity bean utilizes a JDBC data source to access the underlying database server. This is analogous to the JMS client, which uses a ConnectionFactory to access the JMS provider. As with the ConnectionFactory, the Data Source must be configured to support XA global transactions if we desire to have the message retrieved and database updated within the same transaction.

1. In Application Developer, switch to the **Server** perspective.

2. In the Server Configuration Panel, double-click on **TestSrv** to open the server configuration file. Select the **Data Source** tab (Figure B–11).

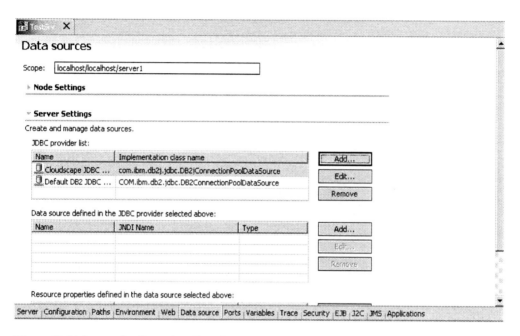

Figure B-11 Server Configuration: Data Source

3. A number of default JDBC providers are defined, including one for DB2. However, the default DB2 provider does not use the XA-enabled drivers; thus we define an XA-enabled JDBC provider for DB2.

4. Next to the JDBC Provider list, click **Add**. In the resulting dialog select the Database type, **DB2**, and the JDBC provider type, **DB2 JDBC Provider (XA)** (Figure B–12). Click **Next**.

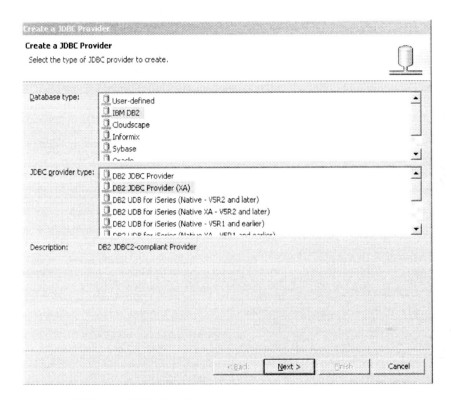

Figure B-12 Create JDBC Provider

5. On the next page specify a name for the JDBC provider: **DB2 XA JDBC Provider** (Figure B–13).

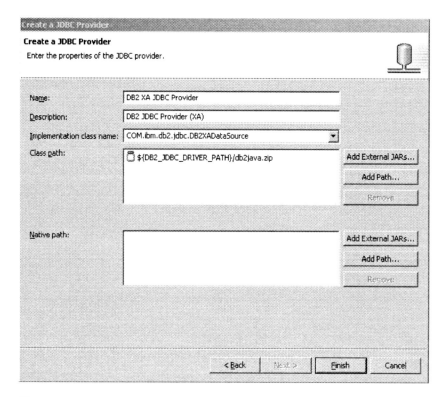

Figure B-13 JDBC Provider Properties

6. Notice that a class path variable, DB2_JDBC_DRIVER_PATH, is used to specify the location of the required jar file. As part of our configuration, we check to ensure that its value corresponds to the appropriate directory for our installation.

7. To create the Data Source, highlight our newly created **DB2 XA JDBC Provider** and click **Add** next to the Data Source list.

8. In the resulting dialog, ensure that a provider type of **DB2 JDBC Provider (XA)** is selected and a **Version 5.0 data source** is defined (Figure B–14). Click **Next**.

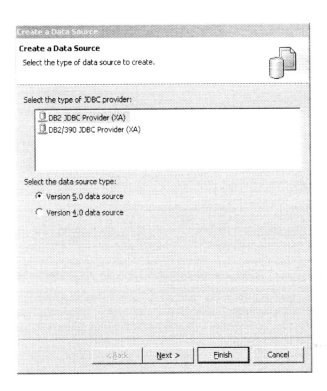

Figure B-14 Create Data Source

9. On the following page specify a data source name and JNDI name of **EMPLOYEE** and **jdbc/db2/XA/Employee** respectively (Figure B–15). Click **Next**.

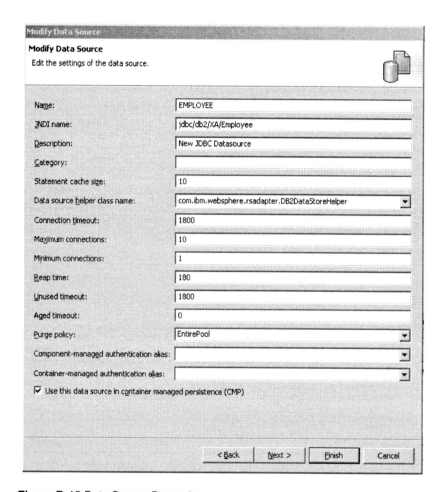

Figure B-15 Data Source Properties

10. On the following page specify the name of the database that we will connect to: **EMPLOYEE** (Figure B–16). Click **Finish**.

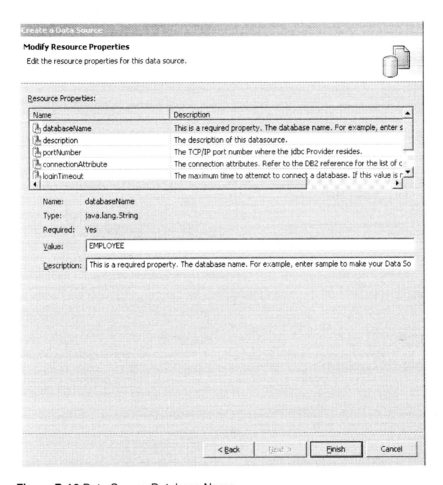

Figure B-16 Data Source Database Name

11. You should now have a data source defined as shown in Figure B–17. Note that as we have not specified any specific user IDs, the application server will use the user under which it runs to access the database.

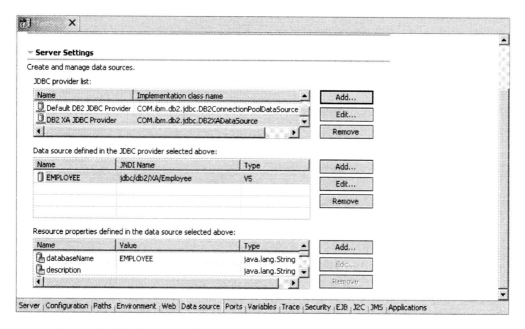

Figure B-17 Defined Data Sources

12. To check the assigned value of DB2_JDBC_DRIVER_PATH, click the **Variables** tab. Under Node Settings you will find a list of defined variables. If your value for DB2_JDBC_DRIVER_PATH is blank, then edit it to point at the location of db2java.zip on your machine (Figure B–18).

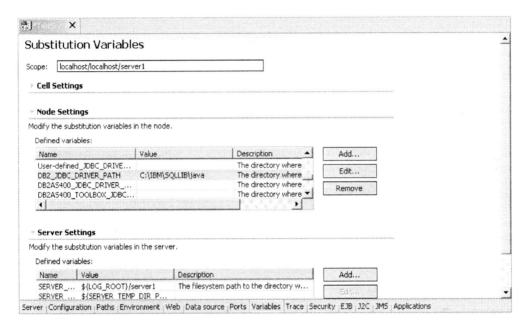

Figure B-18 Variable Values

13. Save the server configuration file.

Update Deployment Descriptor and Generate Deploy Code   We now modify the EJB module deployment descriptor to reference the defined data source.

1. Switch to the **J2EE** Perspective and double-click on **EmpRecordUpdateEJB** to open the deployment descriptor.
2. On the Overview tab, scroll down to the WebSphere Bindings section and enter the JNDI name for the data source: **jdbc/db2/XA/Employee**. If you are configured for multiple databases, ensure that the correct type is selected for **Backend ID** (Figure B–19).

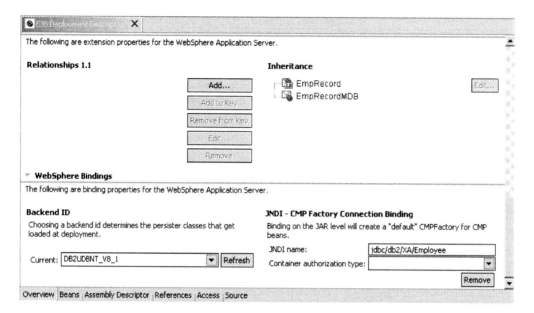

Figure B-19 Reference Data Source

3. Save the deployment descriptor.
4. Right-click on **EmpRecordUpdateEJB** and select **Generate → Deploy and RMIC Code…**.
5. In the resulting dialog, select **EmpRecord** only and click **Finish**.

We have completed configuration of the entity bean. We now create the session bean that will be used to access it.

Create the Session Bean

The session bean provides a façade for the entity bean, supplying the only means by which client applications can access the entity bean. In our case the MDB uses the session bean to pass the retrieved data to the entity bean. We have created a couple of session beans during the course of these tutorials, and thus this part of the tutorial should be relatively familiar to you.

Implement the Session Bean

The session bean is packaged in the same enterprise application project as the MDB and entity bean. It uses the entity beans local home interface to access it, and in a similar vein exposes a local home interface for use by the MDB.

1. As before. create a new session bean in the EJB module **EmpRecordUpdateEJB**, specifying the name **EmpRecordUpdate**. It should specify a local interface only.
2. Open **EmpRecordUpdateBean.java**, the bean implementation class in the Java Editor.
3. Add in an import statement for the JNDI package; we need it in order to retrieve the home interface for the entity bean from the namespace:

```
import javax.naming.*;                    // JNDI imports
```

4. Add a variable definition to hold the local home interface retrieved:

```
private EmpRecordLocalHome home = null;
```

5. Save your work.

We now modify the `ejbCreate` method to retrieve the home interface for the entity bean and introduce a new `update` method to invoke the entity bean with the appropriate data.

Modify ejbCreate

1. Modify **ejbCreate** to retrieve the home interface for **EmpRecord** as shown:

```
public void ejbCreate() throws javax.ejb.CreateException {
    //initialize home
    try{
      //bind to container namespace
      InitialContext context = new InitialContext();

      //retrieve home interface
home = (EmpRecordLocalHome)context.lookup("java:comp/env/ejb/
EmpRecord");
    }catch(NamingException ne){
System.out.println("NamingException thrown in ejbCreate " + ne);
throw new javax.ejb.CreateException(ne.getMessage());
    }
}
```

This is no different from how we retrieved JMS-administered objects. Here we specify a JNDI name, **java:comp/env/ejb/EmpRecord**, that will map to **EmpRecordLocalHome**. We similarly create a resource reference that defines the association.

Define the Update Method   Next, we define the `update` method. It is called by the MDB and passed the retrieved data. It then either creates a new entity bean (database record) or updates an existing one based on the value of the key field `employeeID`.

1. Define the `update` method as shown. Notice that I have inserted a few print statements so that the logic can be easily traced during testing:

```
public void update(String employeeID, String firstName, String
lastName, String email) throws javax.ejb.CreateException
```

```
{
     try{
        //check if record exists
        System.out.println("key = " + employeeID);
        System.out.println("check if exists....");
EmpRecordLocal record = home.findByPrimaryKey(employeeID);

        //if exists then update
          System.out.println("exists so update....");
          record.setFirstName(firstName);
          record.setLastName(lastName);
          record.setEmail(email);
System.out.println("record updated");
     }catch(javax.ejb.FinderException fe){
        //didn't exist create new
        try{
System.out.println("didn't exist create....");
EmpRecordLocal record = home.create(employeeID,
firstName,lastName,email);
System.out.println("record created");
        }catch(javax.ejb.CreateException ce){
System.out.println("CreateException thrown in update " + ce);
        throw ce;
        }
     }
}
```

2. Save your work and then promote the newly defined `update` method to the local home interface by right-clicking on it in the Outline pane and selecting **Enterprise Bean → Promote to Local Home Interface**.

Configure the Session Bean

We define a resource reference to link the specified JNDI name to the actual entity bean home interface. We then generate the deploy code.

1. Double-click on **EmpRecordUpdateEJB** to open the deployment descriptor.
2. Click the **References** tab and select **EmpRecordUpdate**.
3. Click **Add**, and in the resulting wizard select a reference type of **EJB Local Reference**. Click **Next**.

4. In the definitions page specify the name **ejb/EmpRecord** and link it to the entity bean **EmpRecord** (Figure B–20). Click **Finish**.

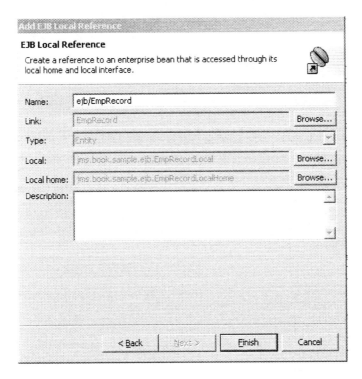

Figure B-20 EJB Local Reference

5. This creates a resource reference, as shown in Figure B–21. Save the deployment descriptor.

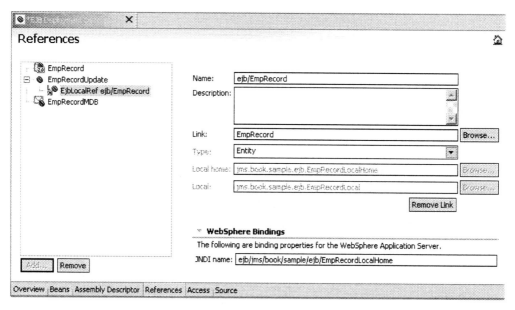

Figure B-21 Resource Reference Session Bean

6. Right-click on **EmpRecordUpdateEJB** and select **Generate → Deploy and RMIC Code...**.

7. Ensure that only **EmpRecordUpdate** is selected and click **Finish**.

Modify the MDB

To enable the MDB to pass data to the session bean and ultimately to the entity bean, we modify our implementation of the onMessage method to invoke EmpRecordUpdate's update method. This requires that we similarly update ejbCreate to retrieve the appropriate local home interface and that we define the associated resource reference.

1. Open **EmpRecordMDBBean.java** in the Java Editor.

2. Add a variable definition to hold the local home interface for **EmpRecordUpdate**:

```
private EmpRecordUpdateLocalHome home = null;
```

3. Modify ejbCreate to retrieve the home interface for **EmpRecordUpdate** as shown:

```
public void ejbCreate() {
    //initialize home
```

```
    try{
      //bind to container namespace
      InitialContext context = new InitialContext();

      //retrieve home interface
home = (EmpRecordUpdateLocalHome)context.lookup("java:comp/env/
ejb/EmpRecordUpdate");
      }catch(NamingException ne){
System.out.println("NamingException thrown in ejbCreate " + ne);

    }
}
```

We similarly specify a JNDI name, which resolves to the appropriate home
interface based on the resource reference.

4. Modify onMessage to invoke EmpRecordUpdate's update method, with data
parsed from the message (shown in **bold**):

```
...
//use java.util.StringTokenizer to parse string
java.util.StringTokenizer st = new
java.util.StringTokenizer(message, ";");
    while (st.hasMoreTokens()) {
        employeeID = st.nextToken();
        firstName = st.nextToken();
        lastName = st.nextToken();
        email = st.nextToken();
    }

//invoke EmpRecordUpdate
EmpRecordUpdateLocal handler = home.create();
handler.update(employeeID, firstName, lastName, email);
...
```

5. Save your work.

6. Open the deployment descriptor for **EmpRecordUpdateEJB**, and define an EJB Local
Reference for **EmpRecordMDB** that links the JNDI name **ejb/EmpRecordUpdate** to
the bean **EmpRecordUpdate** (Figure B–22).

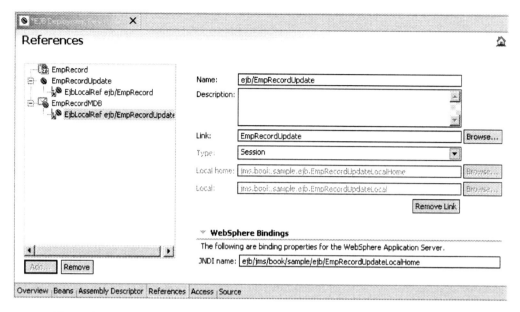

Figure B-22 Resource Reference MDB

7. Save the deployment descriptor.
8. Open the deployment descriptor for **EmpRecordSenderEJB** and ensure that the resource references for **EmpRecordSender** are defined as follows:
   • Bind **jms/SenderQCF** to **jms.sample.SenderQCF**
   • Bind **jms/SenderQ** to **jms.sample.Queue**

   This check is required because, as you will recall from Chapter 7, we use the WebSphere JMS Provider to test this scenario. However, if you completed scenario 3 or scenario 4 prior to this tutorial, then `EmpRecordSender`'s resource references currently reference WebSphere MQ JMS Provider resources.

9. Start or restart **TestSrv** to deploy all of our updates to the application server

Test the Scenario Implementation

As demonstrated in Chapter 7, we use the Universal Test Client (UTC) to test our implementation. As you will recall, EmpRecordMDB specifies a transaction attribute of `Required` for the `onMessage` method. Consequently, the message is retrieved as part of a transaction, since by default the transaction attribute for methods defined by EmpRecordUpdate and EmpRecord is `Required`" The transaction is now propagated to the session and entity bean, and the database is enlisted in the transaction. This is possible because we configured both the `QueueConnectionFactory` used by the MDB and the JDBC provider employed by the entity bean as XA-enabled.

1. To test the implementation, launch the UTC and use it to invoke the send method defined by **EmpRecordSender**.
2. You should find entries logged by **EmpRecordMDB** and **EmpRecordUpdate** in the server console (Figure B–23)

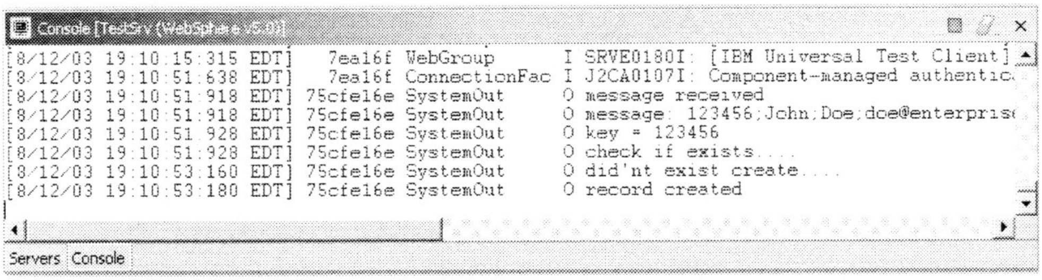

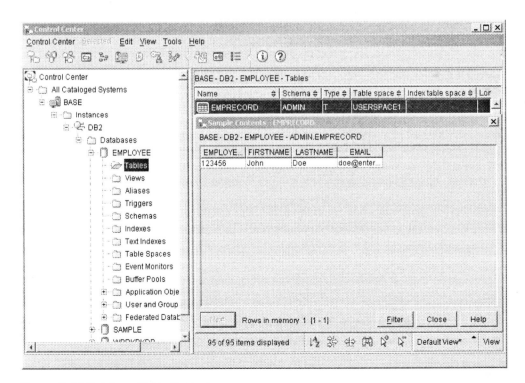

Figure B-23 Successful Transaction

3. You can also inspect the target database table. Figure B–24 shows the contents of the table **EMPRECORD** as displayed by the DB2 Control Center.

Figure B-24 Database Table Contents

We have successfully configured the interaction between the MDB and entity bean such that the update of associated resources is done as part of an XA global transaction. An easy way to verify that the XA global transaction is really working as we expect is to drop the database table that the entity bean is persisted to while the application server is running.

4. Launch a DB2 command window and type the following commands to connect to the database and drop the table:

```
db2 connect to EMPLOYEE
db2 drop table EMPRECORD
```

5. Return to the UTC and send another message. You should see a `PersistanceManagerException` in the server console (Figure B–25).

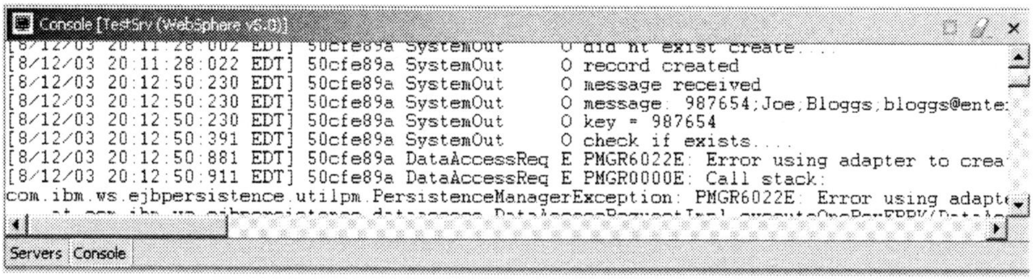

Figure B-25 Failed Transaction

6. Note that `MDBListenerPort` will not try to redeliver the message, as it is configured to stop once it rolls back a message.

7. In the DB2 command window change to the directory where you stored Table.ddl and recreate the table by typing:

```
db2 -tvf Table.ddl
```

8. Restart the listener port using the administration console. You should see the original message retrieved from the queue and successfully reprocessed (Figure B–26).

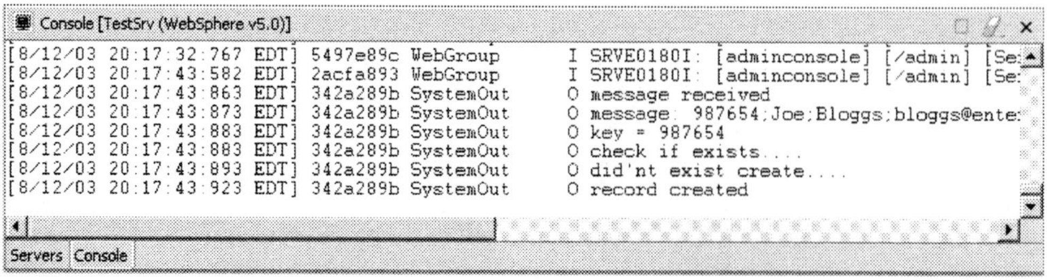

Figure B-26 Recovered Transaction

We have now successfully tested both the commit and rollback logic executed by the container. We did this by configuring an entity bean, which accessed the database, and provided a session bean façade, which the MDB used to ultimately pass data to the database.

Implementing Publish-Subscribe II

In Chapter 7 we implemented the publish-subscribe scenario using the WebSphere JMS Provider. It greatly simplified our development environment; however, for enterprise deployments we would typically use WebSphere Business Integration Event/Message Broker as the publish-subscribe broker. Thus, in this appendix we modify our implementation to use the Message Broker. This change does not affect our current implementation of the JMS clients, the publisher session bean and subscribing MDBs. It does require, however, that Message Broker be configured and that a different set of administered objects are defined.

Development Environment

In order to execute this tutorial, we need to update our development environment as follows:

- WebSphere Business Integration Event Broker (or Message Broker) 5.0 + CSD1
- DB2 Enterprise Server 8.1 + FP1

As we are only interested in using the broker for publish-subscribe, you can install either Message Broker or Event Broker (which is a subset of Message Broker functionality). The instructions are the same regardless which package you use. I used Message Broker while building this tutorial. Note that the choice of DB2 edition and version is driven primarily by prerequisites for the brokers. As before, please note the service levels and ensure that you acquire appropriately licensed software.

The tutorial assumes that you have installed the identified software, and it commences with configuration of required resources, such as the creation of the broker. Installation steps are documented in associated product documentation, and for the most part, are wizard-driven. Links to these documents are included in Appendix D.

Using Message Broker

We begin by configuring Message Broker to support publish-subscribe. Then we use the Web-Sphere administration console to define the required administered objects. Finally, we update resource references to point to these new objects, then redeploy and test the implementation. Note that the MQ queue manager required to host the message broker was created in Chapter 7 in scenario 3. If you skipped scenario 3, refer back to the section on creating WebSphere MQ Resources.

Broker Configuration

In order to configure the broker for publish-subscribe, we create a broker instance, and then create and deploy the message flow required to support publishing applications.

Create the Broker

We use the Getting Started wizard to create a default configuration for the broker. The configuration comprises the broker, its configuration manager, and their supporting databases.

Default Broker Configuration

1. Launch the **Message Brokers Toolkit** from the Start menu.
2. Before running the Getting Started wizard, ensure that the following system groups are defined on your machine: **mqm, mqbrkrs, mqbrasgn, mqbrdevt, mqbrops, mqbrtpic**. If they do not exist, create them.
3. Ensure that the user ID under which you are running is a member of all the identified groups.
4. Open a command prompt and type the command (Figure C–1).

```
mqsisetcapacity -c 4
```

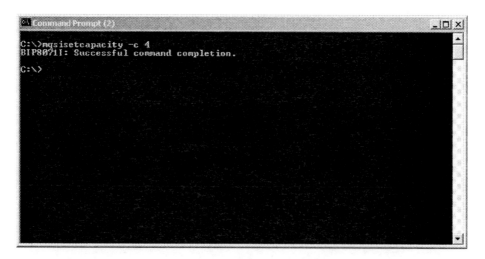

Figure C-1 License Manager

This command sets up the runtime license and must be run before we use the default configuration wizard; otherwise, the configuration wizard will fail to start the broker.

5. To launch the Getting Started wizard, you can either click on the **create default configuration** link under the topic **Getting Started** in the Welcome window, or you can select **File → New → Other**, and in the resulting dialog select **Quick Start Components**, then **Getting Started Wizard** (Figure C–2).

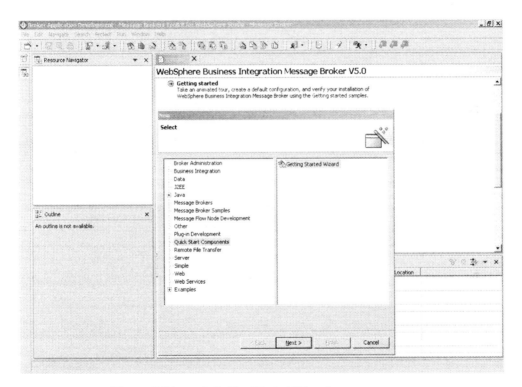

Figure C-2 Launch Getting Started Wizard

6. The wizard displays a welcome page identifying the components that will be created (Figure C–3). Click **Next**.

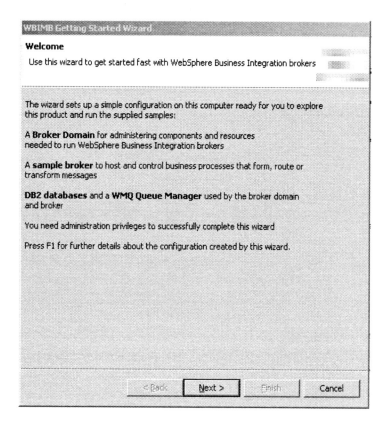

Figure C-3 Welcome Page

7. Specify a user account setting. We use an existing account with administrator capabilities (Figure C–4). Click **Next**.

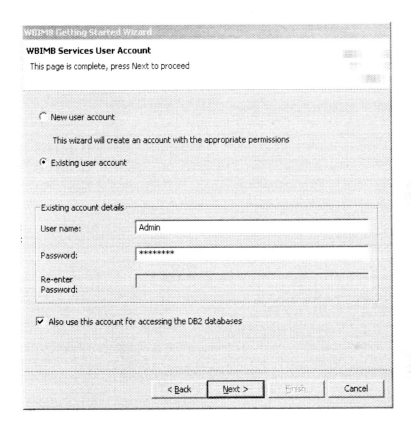

Figure C-4 User Account Settings

8. Specify a Queue Manager name, **JMSSVR**, and port **1414**. Accept all other defaults (Figure C–5). This corresponds to our existing queue manager, which we use to host the message broker. Click **Next**.

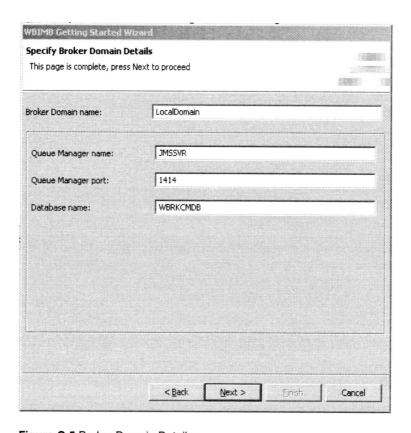

Figure C-5 Broker Domain Details

9. Specify a name for the broker: **JMSBRK**. Accept all other defaults (Figure C–6). Click **Next**.

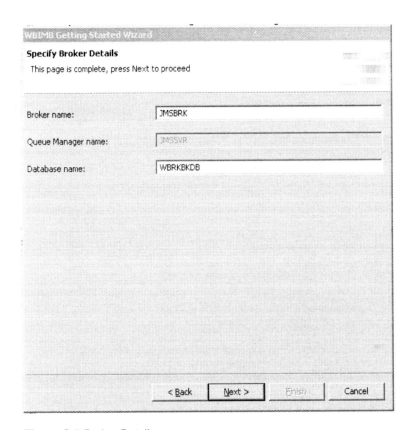

Figure C-6 Broker Details

10. Accept the defaults on the following page, click **Next**, then click **Finish** to create the configuration.

11. Once all tasks are complete, you will be asked to deploy the configuration to the broker. Click **Complete** (Figure C–7).

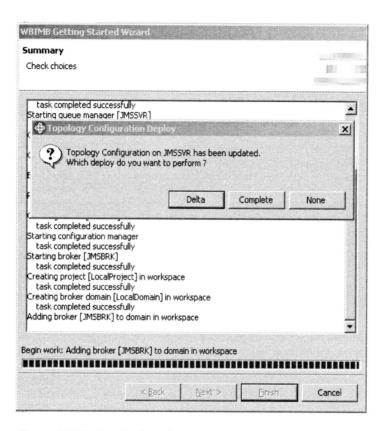

Figure C-7 Deploy Configuration

12. You should see a dialog popup confirming successful deployment (Figure C–8). Click **OK**. Your default configuration is now complete.

Figure C-8 Deployment Status

Configure the Hosting MQ Queue Manager   The WebSphere MQ JMS implementation requires that a number of MQ queues are created on the broker's queue manager.

1. Open a command prompt and navigate to the directory where WebSphere MQ is installed.
2. Locate and inspect the following location: **<installation_directory>\java\bin**. You will find a file, **MQJMS_PSQ.mqsc**, containing the script that creates the required queues.
3. To run the script, we use a command line–based administration tool for WebSphere MQ. Open a command prompt and type the command

```
runmqsc JMSSVR < MQJMS_PSQ.mqsc
```

This runs the script against our existing queue manager, **JMSSVR**, and creates the required queues (Figure C–9).

```
C:\IBM\WMQ\Java\bin>runmqsc JMSSVR < MQJMS_PSQ.mqsc
5724-B41 (C) Copyright IBM Corp. 1994, 2002.  ALL RIGHTS RESERVED.
Starting MQSC for queue manager JMSSVR.


   : ***********************************************************************/
   : * IBM Websphere MQ Support for Java Message Service                 */
   :                                    */
   : * Sample MQSC source defining JMS Publish/Subscribe queues.         */
   : * Installation Verification Test - Setup script                     */
   : *                                                                    */
   : * Licensed Materials - Property of IBM                              */
   : *                                                                    */
   : * 5648-C60 5724-B4 5655-F10                                         */
   : *                                                                    */
   : * (c) Copyright IBM Corp. 1999. All Rights Reserved.               */
   : *                                                                    */
   : * US Government Users Restricted Rights - Use, duplication or       */
   : * disclosure restricted by GSA ADP Schedule Contract with IBM Corp.*/
   : ***********************************************************************/


   : ***********************************************************************/
   : *                                                                    */
   : *     JMS Publish/Subscribe Administration Queue                    */
```

Figure C-9 Create Administration Queues

We also create the queue to which the publisher session bean will send the JMS publications. In Chapter 7 we used the WebSphere MQ Explorer for this task. To illustrate an alternative approach, we use the command-line tool runmqsc.

4. In a command prompt, type the command

```
runmqsc JMSSVR
```

5. At the resulting prompt, type the command

```
DEF QLOCAL(JMSPUBQ)
```

This creates a local queue with default settings called **JMSPUBQ** on queue manager **JMSSVR** (Figure C–10).

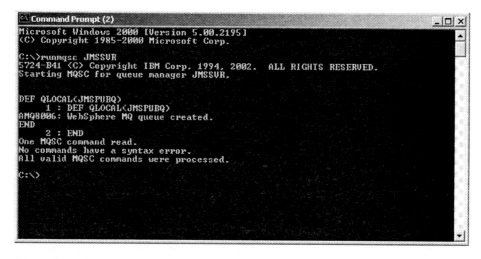

Figure C-10 Create Publish Queue

6. Exit runmqsc by typing **END** at the prompt (Figure C–10).

Define Publish Message Flow

Recall from our discussions in Chapter 5 that a simple publish message flow contains an input node for the transport that is being published on and the Publication node. We thus build a message flow that contains an MQInput node and a Publication node. The MQInput node will be configured to retrieve messages from the queue JMSPUBQ, which is the target destination for the publisher session bean. Once retrieved, the message is passed to the Publication node, which sends the message to interested subscribers.

Create Message Flow   We create a Message Flow project in which we define the publish message flow.

1. In the Message Brokers Toolkit switch to the **Broker Application Development** perspective. This should already be open; if it isn't, access it using the **Window → Open Perspective** menu item.
2. We create a message flow project to hold our message flow. Select **File → New → Message Flow project**.
3. In the resulting dialog supply a project name of **Publishers** (Figure C–11). Click **Finish**.

Figure C-11 Create Message Flow Project

4. In the Resource Navigator pane right-click on the project **Publishers** and select **New** →
Message Flow.

5. In the resulting dialog supply a message flow name of **JMSPublisher** (Figure C–12).
Click **Finish**.

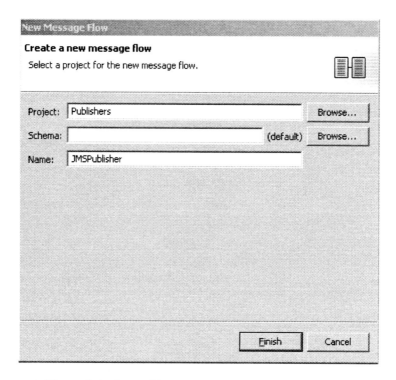

Figure C-12 Create Message Flow

6. This launches the message flow editor. Ensure that the **Selection** cursor is highlighted, and then place an **MQInput** node and a **Publication** node onto the canvas by selecting the node and then clicking on the canvas (Figure C-13).

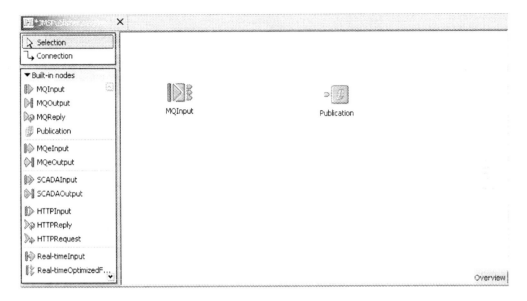

Figure C-13 Select Processing Nodes

7. Highlight the **Connection** cursor and connect the output terminal of **MQInput** node to the input terminal of **Publication** node (Figure C–14).

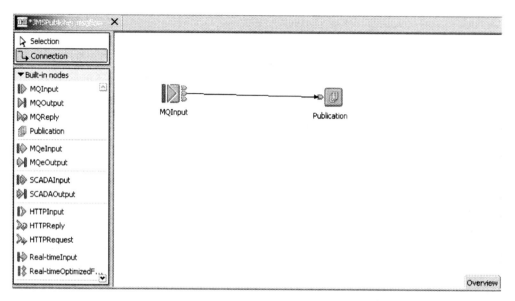

Figure C-14 Connect Processing Nodes

8. Highlight the **Selection** cursor once again and right-click on the **MQInput** node. Select **Properties** to launch its property editor.

9. In the property editor, on the Basic properties page, supply the name of the queue that the node will monitor: **JMSPUBQ** (Figure C–15). Click **OK**.

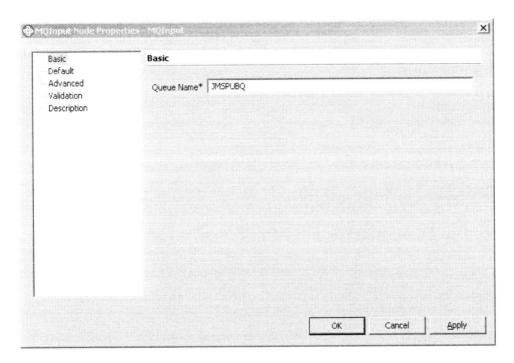

Figure C-15 MQInput Node Properties

10. Save the message flow.

Deploy Message Flow   We package the message flow into a message broker archive, which we then deploy to the broker.

1. In the Message Broker Toolkit, select **Window → Open Perspective → Broker Administration**.

2. In the Broker Administration Navigator pane, expand the **Broker Archives** folder and right-click on the default server project **Local Project**. Select **New → Message Broker Archive**.

3. In the resulting dialog supply the archive name **Publishflows** (Figure C–16). Click **Finish**.

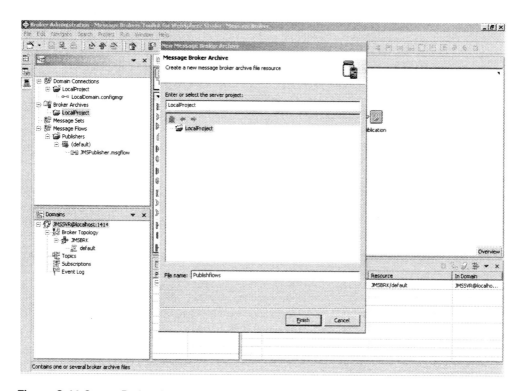

Figure C-16 Create Broker Archive

4. This opens the broker archive editor. Click on the **Add** icon to add **JMSPublisher.msg-flow** to the archive. Select the checkbox to add the message flow source (Figure C–17). Click **OK**.

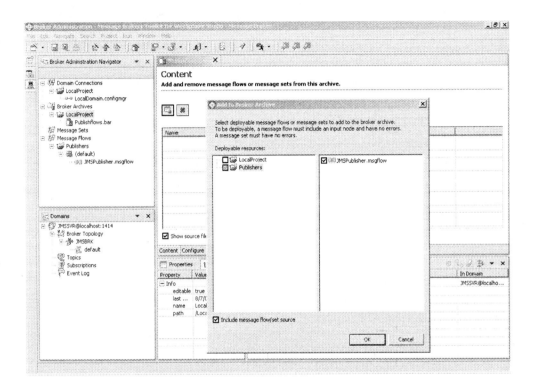

Figure C-17 Edit Broker Archive

5. Save the broker archive. It should now contain **JMSPublisher** in its compiled form
(`*.cmf`) and source (`*.msgflow`) (Figure C–18).

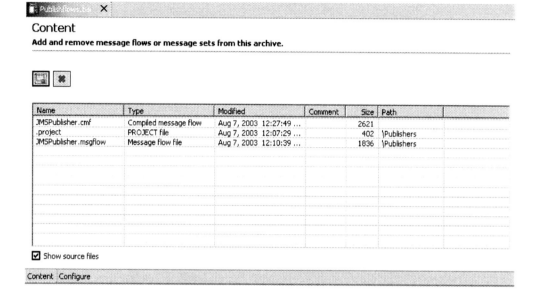

Figure C-18 Populated Broker Archive

6. In the Broker Administration Navigator pane, right-click on the broker archive file **Publishflows.bar** and select **Deploy File**.

7. In the resulting dialog select the default execution group for **JMSBRK** and click **OK** (Figure C–19)

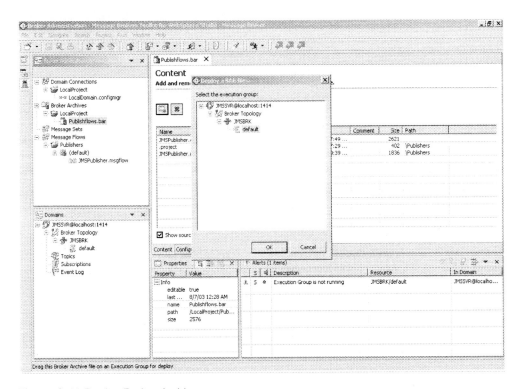

Figure C-19 Deploy Broker Archive

8. You should receive a successful process initiation notification. Double-click the **Event Log** folder in the Domains pane to confirm that the deployment request was successfully processed by the broker (Figure C–20).

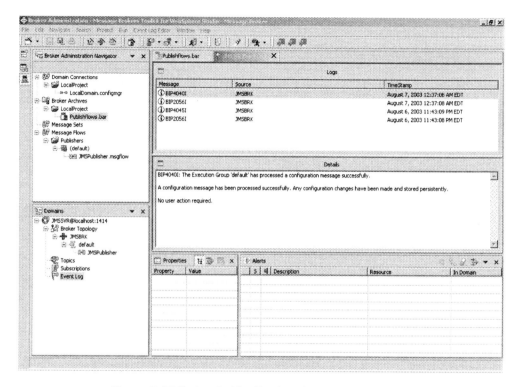

Figure C-20 Broker Archive Deployed

9. You have now completed configuration of the broker. You can close the Message Brokers Toolkit.

With the JMSPublisher message flow deployed, we can now support publishers that send their publications to the MQ queue JMSPUBQ. With our current configuration, we can also support subscribers who will receive their publications using WebSphere MQ. If we wish for publishers or subscribers to use the MQ Real-time Transport, we need to additionally deploy a message flow containing the Real-timeOptimizedFlow node.

Update Application Configuration

In our previous implementation we defined administered objects that bound the JMS clients to the WebSphere JMS Provider. This time we define WebSphere MQ–administered objects that bind the JMS clients to WebSphere MQ and by extension Message Broker. As demonstrated in Chapter 7, we do this using the WebSphere Application Server's administration console. We define `MQTopicConnectionFactory` and `MQTopic` objects to be used by the publisher session bean and subscriber MDBs. We then update associated listener port definitions and resource references to use these new objects.

Create Administered Objects

We create two `MQTopicConnectionFactory` objects for the publisher and subscribers, and we define an `MQTopic` object that binds their interaction. These instructions assume you have implemented scenario 2 in Chapter 7.

1. Launch Application Developer, and start **TestSrv**. Once it is running, launch the **administration console**.
2. In the administration console's menu pane, expand **Resources** and select **WebSphere MQ JMS Provider**. This opens up the provider pane.
3. Click on the **WebSphere MQ Topic Connection Factories** link, and in the resulting page click **New** to open the definitions form.
4. In the definitions form, specify the following:
   - Name: **mq.sample.PubTCF**
   - JNDI Name: **mq.sample.PubTCF**
   - Queue Manager: **JMSSVR**
   - Transport Type: select **BINDINGS**
   - Broker Publication Queue: **JMSPUBQ**
   - Broker Version: select **Advanced**
   - XA Enabled: uncheck the check box
   - Accept all other defaults

   This definition will results in the creation of an `MQTopicConnection-Factory`. Note that any `TopicPublisher` derived from this `TopicConnectionFactory` will publish its messages to the queue `JMSPUBQ` on queue manager `JMSSVR`. This is the queue that our publish message flow **JMSPublisher** retrieves messages from for publication. Note that accepting the default "blank" values in the form results in the defined defaults for the object properties being assigned (see Chapter 6).
5. Click **OK** at the end of the form to save the object definition.
6. Click **New** to open a new definitions form.

7. In the definitions form, specify the following:

- Name**: mq.sample.XASubTCF**
- JNDI Name: **mq.sample.SubTCF**
- Queue Manager: **JMSSVR**
- Transport Type: select **BINDINGS**
- Client ID: **client01**
- XA Enabled: ensure the check box is checked
- Accept all other defaults

Recall from Chapter 7 that we use the XA variant of the `MQTopicConnec-tionFactory` for the subscribers. We also specify a client ID, which is used by the durable subscriber.

8. Click **OK** at the end of the form to save the object definition. You should now have two `TopicConnectionFactory` objects defined (Figure C–21)

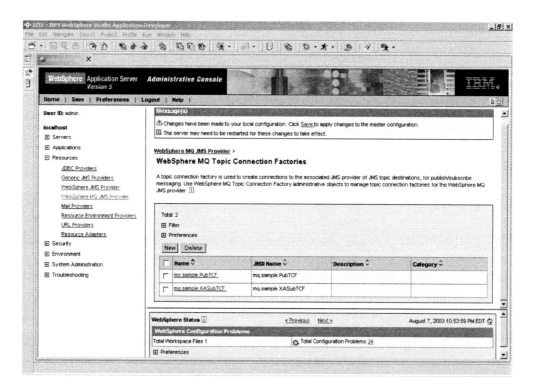

Figure C-21 MQTopicConnectionFactory Objects

9. Return to the WebSphere MQ JMS Provider page and select the WebSphere MQ Topic Destinations link
10. In the resulting page click New to open the definitions form.
11. In the definitions form, specify the following:
    - Name: **mq.sample.Topic**
    - JNDI Name: **mq.sample.Topic**
    - Base Topic Name: **employeeData**
    - Accept all other defaults

    As before we specify a single-level topic name, which defines the topic on which data will be published and subscribed.
12. Click **OK** at the end of the form to save the object definition. You should now have a single Topic defined (Figure C–22).

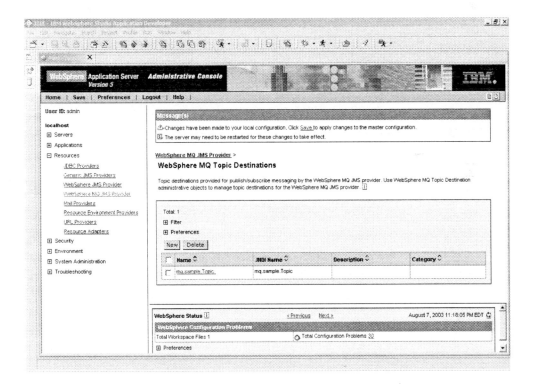

Figure C-22 MQTopic Object

13. In the administration console's menu bar, click **Save** to apply your changes.

Update Listener Port Definitions

1. In the administration console, navigate to the **Message Listener Service** page (via the **server1** application server link).

2. Click on the link for **Listener Ports**.

3. Update the definition for **DurMDBListenerPort** as follows:

   • Connection Factory: **mq.sample.XASubTCF**

   • Destination: **mq.sample.Topic**

4. Similarly update **NonDurMDBListenerPort** with the same values.

5. Your Listener Port page should be similar to that shown in Figure C–23.

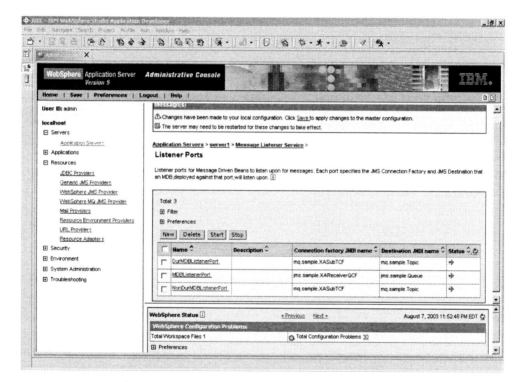

Figure C-23 Listener Port Definitions

6. In the administration console's menu bar, click **Save** to apply your changes.

7. You may log out and close the administration console

Update Resource References and Re-deploy

1. In Application Developer, return to the **J2EE** perspective.
2. Double-click on **EmpRecordPublisherEJB** to open the deployment descriptor, and click the **References** tab.
3. Bind **jms/PubTCF** to **mq.sample.PubTCF**.
4. Similarly, bind **jms/PubTopic** to **mq.sample.Topic**.
5. Save the deployment descriptor.
6. Switch to the **Server** perspective and restart **TestSrv**.

Test the Scenario Implementation

As demonstrated in Chapter 7, we use the Universal Test Client (UTC) to test our implementation.

1. Start **JMSBRK** if it is not already running. In Windows you can go to the Services console and start the service created by the configuration. Alternatively, you can type **mqsistart JMSBRK** in a command prompt. Make sure you check Event Viewer to confirm that the broker started successfully.
2. Launch the UTC and use it to invoke `EmpRecordPublisher`'s `publish` method (see scenario 2 in Chapter 7).
3. You should see the received publications displayed in the server console as before.
4. If you wish, you can use the Message Broker Toolkit to check the current subscriptions registered at the broker.
5. To do this, ensure that the broker configuration manager is running. You can similarly use the Services console or type **mqsistart configmgr** at a command prompt.
6. Launch the Message Broker Toolkit, and in the Domains panel double-click on **Subscriptions**.
7. In the Subscriptions editor, click the **query** button. You should see two registered subscriptions for the topic **employeeData**, one for the durable subscriber MDB and the other for the nondurable subscriber MDB (Figure C–24).

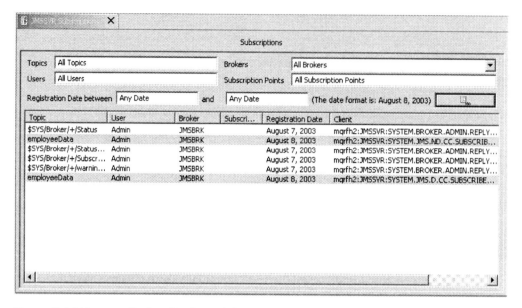

Figure C-24 Message Broker: Registered Subscriptions

Note that the value in the Client column contains the name of the queue manager and the name of the queue where publications that match the subscription should be sent.

We have successfully updated our implementation to use Message Broker as the publish-subscribe broker. Once again we changed the provider used by the JMS clients by simply changing the administered objects retrieved. We implemented a very simple broker configuration using a basic publish message flow to enable its publish-subscribe function over WebSphere MQ. If we wish to use the MQ Real-time Transport, we simply change the value of the `Trans-port` property of the `MQTopicConnectionFactory`. This assumes that we have also deployed the required message flow. Do remember, however, that the MQ Real-time Transport cannot be used with durable subscribers.

Resources

Detailed in this appendix are publications and reference sites that will prove useful should you wish to explore in further detail some of the topics and technologies that we have discussed during the course of this book. The list reflects resources that I have personally used, and I include what I hope are useful comments about the resource where appropriate.

Java-Related Books

Bruce Eckel, *Thinking in Java*, 2nd ed., Upper Saddle River, NJ: Prentice Hall, 2000. One of my personal favorites; if you need to understand the basics of Java programming, this is a good choice.

David Flanagan, *Java in a Nutshell*, 3rd ed., Sebastopol, CA: O'Reilly & Associates, 1999. A useful reference.

David Flanagan, Jim Farley, William Crawford, and Kris Magnusson, *Java Enterprise in a Nutshell*, Sebastopol, CA: O'Reilly & Associates, 1999. Another useful reference, this edition is a bit dated in terms of EJB specification, but the JNDI discussion is very helpful.

Steve Graham, Simeon Simeonov, Toufic Boubez, Glen Daniels, Doug Davis, Yuichi Nakamura, and Ryo Neyama, *Building Web Services with Java*, Sams Publishing, 2002. Has one of the best XML primers I have ever read.

Brett McLaughlin, *Java and XML*, Sebastopol, CA: O'Reilly & Associates, 2000. Provides detailed discussions on XML and its manipulation using Java.

Richard Monson-Haefel, *Enterprise Java Beans*, 3rd ed., Sebastopol, CA: O'Reilly & Associates, 2001. Covers EJB 2.0 and is a good read for EJB developers.

IBM Product Manuals

http://www-3.ibm.com/software/integration/mqfamily/library/manualsa/, *WebSphere MQ and WebSphere Business Integration Message Broker user manuals*. The site acts as a gateway to the various user manuals covering installation, configuration, programming, and system administration. Of particular relevance to this book is the manual *WebSphere MQ Using Java*, which is the user guide for the WebSphere MQ JMS implementation.

http://www-3.ibm.com/software/webservers/appserv/infocenter.html, *WebSphere Application Server Info-Center*. Provides downloadable online documentation source with search capabilities for WebSphere Application Server 5.0

IBM Redbooks

http://www.redbooks.ibm.com/, *IBM Redbooks*, are published by IBM's International Technical Support Organization (ITSO) and are typically compiled by a number of specialists who are very conversant with the technology. They generally provide deep hands-on skills and are a useful resource. The following are particularly relevant to the technologies discussed in this book.

Jill Lennon et al., *WebSphere Application Server and WebSphere MQ Family Integration*, SG24-6878-00, draft, http://www.redbooks.ibm.com/redpieces/pdfs/sg246878.pdf.

Birgit Roehm et al., *IBM WebSphere V5.0 Performance, Scalability, and High Availability: WebSphere Handbook Series*, SG24-6198-00, 2003, http://www.redbooks.ibm.com/redbooks/pdfs/sg246198.pdf.

Carla Sadtler et al., *IBM WebSphere Application Server V5.0 System Management and Configuration: WebSphere Handbook Series*, SG24-6195-00, 2003, http://www.redbooks.ibm.com/redbooks/pdfs/sg246195.pdf.

Ueli Wahli, Wouter Denayer, Lars Schunk, Deborah Shaddon, and Martin Weiss, *EJB 2.0 Development with WebSphere Studio Application Developer*, SG24-6819-00, 2003, http://www.redbooks.ibm.com/redbooks/pdfs/sg246819.pdf.

IBM Supportpacs

http://www-3.ibm.com/software/integration/support/supportpacs/, *WebSphere MQ Supportpacs*, provides access to useful utilities and reports for WebSphere MQ and WebSphere Business Integration Broker. Includes performance reports and configuration guides for high-availability clusters. Examples include:

MP7C: *Message-Driven-Bean Performance using WebSphere MQ v5.3 and WAS V5*, http://www-3.ibm.com/software/integration/support/supportpacs/individual/mp7c.html.

MP7D: *JMS Performance with WebSphere MQ V5.3 on Windows 2000*, http://www-3.ibm.com/software/integration/support/supportpacs/individual/mp7d.html.

IC71: *Configuring WebSphere MQ Integrator for Windows NT/2000 with Microsoft Cluster Server*, http://www-3.ibm.com/software/integration/support/supportpacs/individual/ic71.html.

Reference Websites

http://www.eclipse.org/, Open Source Tooling Framework.

http://java.sun.com/, Java home page.

http://java.sun.com/j2ee/, Java 2 Enterprise Edition (J2EE) Platform.

http://java.sun.com/products/jms/docs.html, JMS Specification.

http://java.sun.com/xml/jaxp/, Java API for XML Processing (JAXP).

http://www-3.ibm.com/software/integration/mqfamily/, WebSphere MQ Family homepage.

http://www-106.ibm.com/developerworks/, Developer's portal. Lots of useful articles and tutorials on various technologies, spanning Java, Linux, Web services, XML, grid computing, and more.

http://www-106.ibm.com/developerworks/toolbox/, IBM Developer's Toolbox subscription.

http://www7b.software.ibm.com/wsdd/, WebSphere Developers Domain. Developer's portal providing access to technical information on the WebSphere software platform.

http://www7b.software.ibm.com/wsdd/downloads/, links to various WebSphere Software downloads.

http://www.cygwin.com/, The Cygwin Toolset, a Linux-like environment for Windows.

http://www.digsigtrust.com/prod_serv/index.html, DigitalSignatureTrust. Certification authority that provides a demo certificate facility.

http://www.jdom.org/, JDOM.

http://www.openssl.org/, The OpenSSL Project.

http://www.saxproject.org/, Simple API for XML (SAX).

http://www.w3.org/XML/, Extended Markup Language (XML).

http://www.w3.org/DOM/, Document Object Model (DO M).

http://xml.apache.org/xerces2-j/index.html, Xerces2 Java Parser.

Technical Articles

Roland Barcia, "Creating and Testing Message Driven Beans using WebSphere Studio Application Developer 5.0," *WebSphere Technical Journal*, November 2002, http://www7b.boulder.ibm.com/wsdd/techjournal/0211_barcia/barcia.html.

Vernon Green, "Simplify Applications by Using WebSphere Extended Messaging," *WebSphere Technical Journal*, March 2003, http://www7b.software.ibm.com/wsdd/techjournal/0303_green/green.html.

John B Jones, "JMS to IMS via WMQ," *MQ Update*, March 2003, pp. 29–43.

Doina Klinger, "Creating Extended Messaging Applications for WebSphere Application Server Enterprise, Version 5," *WebSphere Technical Journal*, April 2003, http://www7b.boulder.ibm.com/wsdd/techjournal/0304_klinger/klinger.html.

Sun Java Tutorial, "Specifying Environment Properties,"http://java.sun.com/products/jndi/tutorial/beyond/env/source.html.

Greg Wadley, "WebSphere V5 Extended Messaging Support," *WebSphere Technical Journal*, February 2003, http://www7b.boulder.ibm.com/wsdd/library/techarticles/0302_wadley/wadley.html.

Kareem Yusuf, "Configuring SSL Connections between JMS Clients and the WebSphere MQ JMS Provider," *WebSphere Technical Journal*, November 2002, http://www7b.boulder.ibm.com/wsdd/techjournal/0211_yusuf/yusuf.html.

INDEX

A

Access methods, for `BytesMessage` interface, 51

`AcknowledgeMode`, 170

Administered objects, 18, 116–140
  creating, 141–146, 309–311
  defined, 115–116
  JMS, creating, 231–233
  WebSphere `QueueConnectionFactory`, 117–118
  WebSphere `TopicConnectionFactory`, 118–120

Administration queues, creating, 297–298

Apache Xerces2 Java Parser, 35

Applets, 58

Application callable receiver bean, 112

Application programming interface (API), 12–13

Application Server Facilities (ASF), 25–26, 59

Application-specific properties, JMS messages, 25

Architecture, enterprise messaging, 5–13

Arithmetic expressions, 255

Arithmetic operators in precedence order, 255–256

Asynchronous messaging, 4

B

Bindings, 167–168

Body, JMS message, 26

Boolean comparison, 255

BROKERCCDSUBQ property, `MQTopic`, 139

BROKERCCSUBQ property, `MQTopicConnectionFactory`, 132

BROKERCONQ property, `MQTopicConnectionFactory`, 129

BROKERDURSUBQ property, `MQTopic`, 138

BROKERPUBQ property, `MQTopicConnectionFactory`, 129

BROKERQMGR property, `MQTopicConnectionFactory`, 129

Brokers, and queue managers, 247–248

BROKERSUBQ property, `MQTopicConnectionFactory`, 129

BROKERVER property:
  `MQTopic`, 138
  `MQTopicConnectionFactory`, 129

`ByteArrayInputStream`, 37

`ByteArrayOutputStream`, 37

`BytesMessage`, 52

`BytesMessage` interface, 25, 37–38, 41, 48–53, 99
  access methods for, 51

C

CCSID property:
  `MQQueue`, 136, 94–95

MQQueueConnectionFactory, 126
MQTopic, 139
MQTopicConnectionFactory, 133
Certification authority (CA), 217
CHANNEL property:
    MQQueueConnectionFactory, 124
    MQTopicConnectionFactory, 128
CLEANUP property,
        MQTopicConnectionFactory, 131
CLEANUPINT property,
        MQTopicConnectionFactory, 131
clearBody() method, 50
clearProperties() method, 44
CLIENTID property,
        MQTopicConnectionFactory, 129
Clones, 250–251
CLONESUPP property, 249
CLONESUPP property,
        MQTopicConnectionFactory, 132
close method, 66, 70
Clustering topologies, 244–251
    high-availability clusters, 245–248
    message broker collectives and clones, 250–
        251
    workload management clusters, 248–249
Collectives, 250–251
com.ibm.mq.jar packages, 95
com.ibm.mqjms.jar, 95, 105
Comparison operators, 255
Component-managed authentication alias,
        WebSphere Application Server, 135
Conditional expressions, 255
Connection, 20–21, 21, 25
    new methods, 84
Connection interface, 84
Connection pools property, WebSphere
        Application Server, 135
ConnectionConsumer, 27
ConnectionFactory, 19–21, 24–25, 77, 84
    new methods, 84
Consumer of messages, 18
Container-managed authentication alias,
        WebSphere Application Server, 135
Context, 63
Control queue (CTRLQ), 107

Create a 2.0 Enterprise Bean dialog, 251
Create a Data Source dialog, 273
Create a JDBC Provider dialog, 271–272
Create new EJB/RDB Mapping dialog, 266
Create New Message Flow dialog, 300
Create New Message Flow Project dialog, 299
createDurableSubscriber method, 77–78
createQueue method, QueueSession, 65
createQueueConnection method, 64
createSubscriber method, 75–76
createTopic method, TopicSession, 74
createTopicConnection, 73
createTopicSubscriber method, 81
Customer relationship management (CRM), 3
Cygwin toolkit, 148

D

Define CMP Attribute dialog, 253
DES (Data Encryption Standard), 219
DESCRIPTION property:
    MQQueue, 136
    MQQueueConnectionFactory, 123
    MQTopic, 138
    MQTopicConnectionFactory, 127
Destination, 20–21, 88
Developer's toolbox subscription, maintaining,
        148–149
Digital certificates, 217
Digital signatures, 216–217
DIRECTAUTH property,
        MQTopicConnectionFactory, 133
Distributed transactions, 27
DOM (Document Object Model), 35–36
DTDs (Document Type Definitions), 34–35
Durable subscribers, 77–78

E

Eavesdropping, 215–216
Eclipse, 90
Electronic Data Interchange (EDI) format, 38
Elements, 30
Embedded JMS server queues, 164
Employee Record entity bean, creating, 260–265

`EmpRecordMDBBean.java`, 170
`EmpRecordSenderBean.java`, 154, 156
`EmpRecordSender.java`, 155–156, 164–165
ENCODING property:
    `MQQueue`, 136
    `MQTopic`, 139
Encryption algorithm, 215–216
Enterprise Application Project dialog, 152
Enterprise Bean Details dialog, 252, 254
Enterprise deployment, 241–252
    clustering topologies, 244–251
    JMS provider location, 241–244
    JNDI namespace provider, 251–252
Enterprise Java Beans (EJB), 15, 58, 92
    message-driven bean:
        administered object, defining, 172–173
        creating, 169–177
        implementing, 169–172
        Listener Port, defining, 173–175
        `QueueConnectionFactory`,
            creating, 173
        receiver enterprise application
            deployment, 175–177
    sender session bean:
        administered objects, creating, 161–163
        administered objects, defining, 157–161
        creating, 150–168
        defining class variables, 154
        `ejbCreate` method, modifying, 154–
            155
        `ejbRemove` method, modifying, 155
        enterprise application, adding to the
            server, 168
        importing package, 154
        JMS client implementation, 153–156
        JMS server configuration update, 164
        resource references, defining, 165–168
        sender enterprise application
            deployment, 164–168
        submit method implementation, 156
Enterprise Java Beans (EJB), exchanging messages
    using, 149–183
Enterprise messaging:
    architecture, 5–13
    connectivity options, 12–13
    defined, 3–4
    interaction patterns, 7–12

message distribution paradigms, 6–7
Enterprise resource planning (ERP), 3
Enterprise resources, 58
Entity beans:
    configuring, 269–278
    Create a 2.0 Enterprise Bean dialog, 251
    Create a Data Source dialog, 273
    Create a JDBC Provider dialog, 271–272
    Create new EJB/RDB Mapping dialog, 266
    creating, 260–278
    data sources, 270
    DB2 resources, configuring, 267–269
    Define CMP Attribute dialog, 253
    deployment code, generating, 277–278
    deployment descriptor, updating, 277–278
    Employee Record entity bean, creating, 260–
        265
    Enterprise Bean Details dialog, 252, 254
    Modify Data Source dialog, 274
    Modify Resources Properties dialog, 275
    table script and mapping, generating, 265–267
    XA JDBC data source, defining, 269–277
ESQL, 103
`ExceptionListener` interface, 80
Exceptions, 256–258
EXPIRY property:
    `MQQueue`, 136
    `MQTopic`, 139
Expressions, 255
Extended Messaging Service, 112
Extensible Markup Language, *See* XML
        (Extensible Markup Language)

F
FAILIFQUIESCE property:
    `MQQueue`, 136
    `MQQueueConnectionFactory`, 125
    `MQTopic`, 140
    `MQTopicConnectionFactory`, 133
Failover, 245
Fields, 30

G
Generic JMP Provider, 111–112
`getBodyLength()` method, 53

getErrorCode() method, 79

getLinkedException() method, 79

getLocalizedMessage(), 79

getMessage() method, 79

getPropertyNames() method, 45

getText method, 26, 53

Global transactions, 27

H

HACMP, 245

Header, JMS messages, 25, 42–44

  JMSCorrelationID, 43

  JMSDeliveryMode, 42

  JMSDestination, 42

  JMSExpiration, 42

  JMSMessageID, 43

  JMSPriority, 43

  JMSRedelivered, 44, 83

  JMSReplyTo, 43

  JMSTimeStamp, 43

  JMSType, 44

High-availability clusters, 245–248

HOSTNAME property:

  MQQueueConnectionFactory, 123

  MQTopicConnectionFactory, 128

I

IBM JMS providers, 89–113

IBM JMS-administered objects, 114–146

  administered objects:

    creating, 141–146

    defined, 115–116

  JMSAdmin, 143–146

  WebSphere Application Server administration

    console, 141–143

  WebSphere JMS Provider (Embedded JMS

    Server), 116–122

  WebSphere MQ JMS Provider, 122–140

IBM WebSphere, 13

IBM WebSphere Software Platform, 89–92

  business integration, 91–92

  business portals, 90–91

  foundation and tools, 90

  WebSphere Application Server, 105–112

  WebSphere Business Integration Message

    Broker, 101–108

WebSphere MQ, 92–100

  WebSphere MQ Everyplace (WMQe), 100–101

Identifiers, 254

IllegalStateException, 80, 85, 257

Impersonation, 216–217

Implementation scenarios, 147–239

  development environment, 148–149

  exchanging messages using EJBs (scenario 1),

    149–183

    See also Enterprise Java beans (EJBs)

  JMS communications, securing (scenario 4),

    213–239

    See also Java Message Service (JMS),

      communications, securing

  non-JMS client communication (scenario 3),

    202–213

    scenario implementation, testing, 211–

      213

    See also Java Message Service (JMS),

      communications, securing

  publish-subscribe interface, scenario

    implementation, testing, 184–202

    See also Publish-subscribe interface

Incoming messages, concurrent processing of, 27

InitialContext, 61–63, 73

Interaction patterns, 7–12

  message consumer, 9

  message producer patter, 8–9

  message producer pattern, 59

  request-reply pattern, 10–12

InvalidClientIDException, 257

InvalidSelectorException, 256, 257

ISO 8879, 31

J

J2EE Hierarchy Panel, 151

Java 2 Enterprise Edition (J2EE) platform, 12, 15–

  16

Java homepage, 101

Java Message Service (JMS), 3, 13, 15–28, *See also*

  Implementation scenarios

  administered objects, 18

  Application Server Facilities (ASF), 25–27

    concurrent processing of incoming

      messages, 27

    distributed (global) transactions, 27

communications, securing (scenario 4), 213–239, 215–219
   eavesdropping, 215–216
   impersonation, 216–217
   scenario implementation, testing, 238–239
   SSL handshake, 217–219
   tampering, 216
   WebSphere MQ SSL configuration, 219–238
environment, 17
exchanging messages using EJBs (scenario 1), scenario implementation, testing, 177–183
implementation scenarios, 147–239
implementations, 17
interface, using, 50–56
JMS 1.1 new features, 23–25
JMS client, 18, 21
JMS provider, 18
key concepts, 15–19
message body, 26, 48–50
message definition, 29–41
message header, 25, 42–44
   JMSCorrelationID, 43
   JMSDeliveryMode, 42
   JMSDestination, 42
   JMSExpiration, 42
   JMSMessageID, 43
   JMSPriority, 43
   JMSRedelivered, 44, 83
   JMSReplyTo, 43
   JMSTimeStamp, 43
   JMSType, 44
message properties, 25–26, 44–47
   application-specific properties, 45
   JMSXAppID, 46
   JMSXDeliveryCount, 46, 83
   JMSXGroupID, 46
   JMSXGroupSeq, 46
   JMSXUserID, 46
   provider-specific properties, 47
   standard properties, 46
message selectors, 47–48
message structure, 41–50
MessageListener interface, receiving messages using, 68–70

messages, 25–26
   browsing, 72
   structure, 41–50
messaging domains, 19–23
programming model, 19–20
provider location, 244–251
QueueRequestor, using, 70–71
specifications, 253–258
   JMS standard exceptions, 256–258
   message selector syntax, 253–256
vendor-specific deployment, 17
Java Naming and Directory Interface (JNDI), 18
   JNDI namespace, 18–19
Java Server Pages (JSP), 90
Java Transaction API (JTA), 58–59
Java Transaction Service (JTS) specification, 27
Java Virtual Machines (JVMs), 58
java.io.InputStream, 37
javax.jms.Queue, 167
JAXP (Java API for XML Parsing), 36
JDOM API, 36–38
JMS API, 57–86
   JMS client, 57–61
   JMS exceptions, handling, 79–81
   local transactions, handling, 81–83
   point-to-point interface, 61–72
   unified interface, 84–85
JMS client, 18, 21, 57–61
JMS provider, 18
JMS server, 110
<jms> folder, 99
jmsadmin, 96, 111
JMSAdmin, 142, 143–146
   verbs/administered objects, 145
JMSCorrelationID, 43, 67, 97
JMSDeliveryMode, 42
JMSDestination, 42
JMSException, 80
JMSExpiration, 42
JMSMessageID, 43, 67, 97
JMSPriority, 43
JMSRedelivered, 44, 83
JMSReplyTo, 43
JMSSecurityException, 257
jms/SenderQCF, 165

JMSTimeStamp, 43
JMSType, 44
JMSXAppID, 46
JMSXDeliveryCount, 46, 83
JMSXGroupID, 46
JMSXGroupSeq, 46
JMSXUserID, 46
JNDI namespace, 18–19
JNDI namespace provider, 251–252

K

Kerberos authentication, 18

L

Listener Port definitions, updating, 312
Literals, 253–254
Local transactions, handling, 81–83
LOCALADDRESS property:
    MQQueueConnectionFactory, 124
    MQTopicConnectionFactory, 128

M

Man-in-the-middle attacks, 216
MapMessage interface, 25, 41, 48–50, 55, 108
    access methods for, 55
<mcd> folder, 99
MC/Service Guard, 245
MD5, 219
Message authentication code, 216–217
Message broker collectives and clones, 250–251
Message Brokers Toolkit for WebSphere Studio,
        103–104, 290–314
    administered objects, creating, 309–311
    administration queues, creating, 297–298
    application configuration update, 309–313
    broker configuration, 290–308
        default, 290–297
    broker details, specifying, 295
    broker domain details, specifying, 294
    creating the broker, 290–297
    deployment configuration, 296
    deployment status dialog, 297
    Getting Started Wizard, launching, 291
    hosting MQ queue manager, hosting, 297

Listener Port definitions update, 312
publish message flow:
        broker archive, 304–308
        broker archive editor, 305
        Create New Message Flow dialog, 300
        Create New Message Flow Project
            dialog, 299
        creating, 299–303
        defining, 298–308
        deploying, 303–308
        message flow editor, 301
        MQInput node properties, 303
        processing nodes, connecting, 302
    publish queue, creating, 298
    scenario implementation, testing, 313–314
    Specify Broker Domain Details dialog, 294
    user account settings, specifying, 293
    Welcome page, 292
Message consumer, 9
Message definition:
    record-oriented physical format, 40–41
    tagged/delimited physical format, 38–40
    XML Extensible Markup Language), 30–38
Message digest, 216–217
Message distribution paradigms, 6–7
Message producer pattern, 8–9, 59
Message Queue Interface (MQI), 96
Message selector syntax, 253–256
    arithmetic operators in precedence order, 255–
        256
    comparison operators, 255
    expressions, 255
    identifiers, 254
    literals, 253–254
    standard bracketing, 255
    whitespace, 254
MessageConsumer, 20–21
MessageConsumers, 21
Message-driven beans (MDB), 26, 150
    administered object, defining, 172–173
    creating, 169–177
    implementing, 169–172
    Listener Port, defining, 173–175
    QueueConnectionFactory, creating,
        173
    receiver enterprise application deployment,
        175–177

`MessageEOFException`, 257
`MessageFormatException`, 257
`MessageListener` interface, 59–60, 68
`MessageNotReadableException`, 257
`MessageNotWriteableException`, 44, 80, 257
`MessageProducer`, 20–21, 84, 86
  new methods, 84
Messaging domains, interfaces, 20
Messaging provider, 5, 12
Microsoft Clusters, 245
Middleware, 89
Modify Data Source dialog, 274
Modify Resouces Properties dialog, 275
MQ API (MQI), 94–95
  mapping JMS API to, 96–98
MQ Messages, 94
  mapping JMS messages to, 98–100
MQ Queue, 94–95
MQ Queue Manager, 92–94
MQCLOSE, 96–98
MQCONN, 96–97
MQDISC, 96, 98
MQGET, 96–97
`MQInput` node, 107
`MQInput` node properties, 303
mqjbndxx, 95
MQOPEN, 96–97
MQPUT, 96–97
`MQQueue`, 209
`MQQueueConnectionFactory`, 98, 123–127
  advanced properties, 125–126
  basic properties, 123–124
  transport dependencies, 124
MQSeries classes, 96
`MQTopicConnectionFactory`, 105, 127–134, 249
  advanced properties, 131–134
  basic properties, 127–129
  transport dependencies, 130
`MQXAQueueConnectionFactory`, 134
MSGBATCHSZ property:
  `MQQueueConnectionFactory`, 125
  `MQTopicConnectionFactory`, 132
MSGSELECTION property,
  `MQTopicConnectionFactory`, 132

MSGSELECTION property,
  `MQTopicConnectionFactory`, 141
MULTICAST property:
  `MQTopic`, 138
  `MQTopicConnectionFactory`, 128

N
NAME property:
  `MQQueue`, 136
  `MQQueueConnectionFactory`, 123
  `MQTopic`, 138
  `MQTopicConnectionFactory`, 127
`NamingException`, 63
Nondurable subscribers, 74–77
Non-JMS clients, communicating with, 202–213
  WebSphere MQ JMS Provider, using, 206–211
  WebSphere MQ resources, defining, 209–210

O
`ObjectMessage` interface, 41, 48–50, 56
  access methods for, 56
`onException` method,
  `ExceptionListener` interface, 80–81
OpenSSL tookit, 148
`orderValue`, 45

P
PeopleSoft, 91
PERSISTENCE property:
  `MQQueue`, 136
  `MQTopic`, 139
Point-to-point messaging, 6, 21–22, 61–72
  connecting to a provider, 62–65
  `InitialContext` class, creating, 61–63
  `QueueConnection`, creating, 63–64
  `QueueConnectionFactory`, retrieving, 63
  `QueueSession`, creating, 64–65
  receiving messages, 66–70
  sending messages, 65–66
Polling, 9
POLLINGINT property:
  `MQQueueConnectionFactory`, 125
  `MQTopicConnectionFactory`, 132

PORT property:
    MQQueueConnectionFactory, 123
    MQTopicConnectionFactory, 128
PRIORITY property:
    MQQueue, 136
    MQTopic, 139
Producer of messages, 18
Properties, JMS messages, 25–26, 44–47
    application-specific properties, 45
    JMSXAppID, 46
    JMSXDeliveryCount, 46, 83
    JMSXGroupID, 46
    JMSXGroupSeq, 46
    JMSXUserID, 46
    provider-specific properties, 47
    standard properties, 46
Provider-specific properties, JMS messages, 26
PROXYHOSTNAME property,
    MQTopicConnectionFactory, 128
PROXYPORT property,
    MQTopicConnectionFactory, 129
PSC<psc> folder, 99–100
PUBACKINT property,
    MQTopicConnectionFactory, 131
Publication node, 106
Publication queue (PUBQ), 107
Publish message flow:
    broker archive, 304–308
    broker archive editor, 305
    Create New Message Flow dialog, 300
    Create New Message Flow Project dialog, 299
    creating, 299–303
    defining, 298–308
    deploying, 303–308
    message flow editor, 301
    MQInput node properties, 303
    processing nodes, connecting, 302
Publish-subscribe interface, 6–7
    additional facilities, 78–79
    application flow, 22
    connecting to a provider, 73
    development environment, 289
    implementing, 184–202, 289–314
    Message Broker, 290–314
    publisher enterprise application:
        adding to the server, 192
        deploying, 191
        resource references, defining, 191

publisher session bean:
    creating, 186–192
    ejbCreate and ejbRemove
        methods, modifying, 186–190
publishing messages, 74–75
subscriber message-driven beans:
    administered objects, defining, 196–197
    application deployment, 197–198
    creating, 192–198
    implementing, 192–195
    Listener Ports, defining, 196–197
    TopicConnectionFactory,
        creating, 196
subscribers:
    creating, 74–78
    durable subscribers, 77–78
    nondurable subscribers, 74–77

Q

QMANAGER property, 249
    MQQueue, 136
    MQQueueConnectionFactory, 123
    MQTopicConnectionFactory, 127
Queue, 20, 120–121, 163
Queue, defined, 5
Queue managers, 93–94
    and brokers, 247–248
Queue, properties, 120
QueueBrowser, 20, 72
QueueConnection, 20, 64, 66–68, 98
QueueConnectionFactory, 20, 24, 63, 73,
    117–118, 162
    properties, 117
QueueReceiver, 20, 66–72, 76
QueueRequestor, 70–71, 78–79
QueueSender, 20, 65–66, 70–71
QueueSession, 20, 22, 23, 64–66, 67, 71–73,
    97–98

R

RC2, 219
Real-timeOptimizedFlow node, 106–107
receiveNoWait, 76
RECEXIT property:
    MQQueueConnectionFactory, 126
    MQTopicConnectionFactory, 133

RECEXITINIT property:
  MQQueueConnectionFactory, 126
  MQTopicConnectionFactory, 133
Record-oriented physical format, 40–41
Request-reply pattern, 10–12
RESCANINT property:
  MQQueueConnectionFactory, 125
  MQTopicConnectionFactory, 133
reset() method, 53
ResourceAllocationException, 258
rmm.jar, 95
Rogue agents, 216–217

S
SAP, 3, 91
SAX (Simple API for XML), 35
SECEXIT property:
  MQQueueConnectionFactory, 126
  MQTopicConnectionFactory, 134
SECEXITINT property:
  MQQueueConnectionFactory, 126
  MQTopicConnectionFactory, 134
Secure Socket Layer (SSL), 93
Selectors, 255
Sender session bean, creating, 150–168
SENDEXIT property:
  MQQueueConnectionFactory, 126
  MQTopicConnectionFactory, 134
SENDEXITINT property:
  MQQueueConnectionFactory, 126
  MQTopicConnectionFactory, 134
ServerSession, 27
ServerSessionPool, 27
Servlets, 58, 90
Session beans, 150
  configuring, 280–282
  creating, 278–282
  implementing, 278–280
Session interface, 20–21, 50–56, 84
  new methods, 84
Session pools property, WebSphere Application
    Server, 135
Session.AUTO_ACKNOWLEDGE, 64
Session.CLIENT_ACKNOWLEDGE, 65
Session.commit(), 82–83

Session.DUPS_OK_ACKNOWLEDGE, 64–65
Session.rollback(), 82–83
setObjectProperty() method, 45
setText method, 26, 53
SHA (Secure Hash Algorithm), 219
Shared queues, 248
SIEBEL, 3
SOAP, 32
Soft cluster configuration, 247
SPARESUBS property,
    MQTopicConnectionFactory, 132
Specify Broker Domain Details dialog, 294
SSL client, 217–218
SSL handshake, 217–219
SSL server, 217–218
SSLCIPHERSUITE property:
  MQQueueConnectionFactory, 125
  MQTopicConnectionFactory, 133
SSLCRL property:
  MQQueueConnectionFactory, 126
  MQTopicConnectionFactory, 133
SSLPEERNAME property:
  MQQueueConnectionFactory, 126
  MQTopicConnectionFactory, 133
Standard bracketing, 255
Standard Generalized Markup Language (SGML),
    31
Standard properties, JMS messages, 25–26
STATEREFRESHINT property,
    MQTopicConnectionFactory, 131
StreamMessage, 112
StreamMessage interface, 25, 41, 48–50, 108
String comparison, 255
Subscribers:
  creating, 74–78
  durable subscribers, 77–78
  nondurable subscribers, 74–77
SUBSTORE property,
    MQTopicConnectionFactory, 131
SWIFT, 39–40
Symmetric algorithms, 216
Synchronous messaging, 4
SYNCPOINTALLGETS property:
  MQQueueConnectionFactory, 126
  MQTopicConnectionFactory, 133

T

Tagged/delimited physical format, 38–40
    processing, 39–40
    tagged delimited, 39
    variable-length delimited, 38
Tampering, 216
TARGCLIENT property:
    MQQueue, 136
    MQTopic, 140
TEMPMODEL property,
        MQQueueConnectionFactory, 125
TemporaryQueue, 67, 68, 75
TemporaryTopic, 75, 79
TEMPQPREFIX property,
        MQQueueConnectionFactory, 125
TextMessage interface, 41, 48–50, 53–54, 99
    access methods for, 53
Time to live (TTL), 11
Topic, 20, 120–121
    properties, 120–121
TOPIC property, MQTopic, 138
TopicConnection, 20, 24, 73, 74, 76–78
TopicConnectionFactory, 20, 24, 73, 78,
    84, 118–120
    properties, 118–119
TopicPublisher, 20, 74, 76
TopicRequestor, 78–79
TopicSession, 20, 22, 23, 73, 74
TopicSubscriber, 20, 77–78
Transaction manager, 81–82
TransactionInProgressException, 258
TransactionRolledBackException, 258
TRANSPORT property:
    MQQueueConnectionFactory, 123
    MQTopicConnectionFactory, 127
TripleDES, 219

U

Unicode character encoding, 253
Universal Test Client (UTC) homepage, 177–178
USECONNPOOLING property:
    MQQueueConnectionFactory, 125
    MQTopicConnectionFactory, 132
<usr> folder, 99

V

Variable-length delimited, 38
Veritas Clusters, 245
VERSION property:
    MQQueue, 136
    MQQueueConnectionFactory, 126
    MQTopic, 140
    MQTopicConnectionFactory, 133

W

WebSphere Application Server, 90, 92
    Enterprise package, 105, 112
    Express package, 105
    Extended Messaging Service, 112
    Generic JMP Provider, 111–112
    JMS administration facilities, 111–112
    JMS support, 109–112
    Network Deployment package, 105
    transaction management and MDB support,
        109
    WebSphere JMS Provider (Embedded JMS
        Server), 109–111
    WebSphere MQ JMS Provider, 111
WebSphere Application Server administration
    console, 141–143
WebSphere Business Integration Event/Message
    Broker, 148
WebSphere Business Integration Message Broker,
    91–92, 101–108, 250
    broker runtime, 102–103
    defined, 101
    definition tools, 103–104
    JMS support, 104–108
    Message Brokers Toolkit for WebSphere
        Studio, 103–104
    system components, 102–104
WebSphere Commerce, 90–91
WebSphere Evaluation Download Center, 148
WebSphere JMS Provider (Embedded JMS
    Server), 109–111, 162
    administered objects, 116–122
        WebSphere QueueConnectionFac-
           tory, 117–118
        WebSphere TopicConnectionFac-
           tory, 118–120
    WebSphere Queue, 120–121

WebSphere Topic, 120–121
WebSphere MQ, 91–100, 103
    JMS support, 95–100
    MQ Message, 94
    MQ Queue, 94–95
    MQ Queue Manager, 92–94
    system components, 92–95
WebSphere MQ 5.3, 218
WebSphere MQ Everyplace (WMQe), 91, 100–
        101
    JMS support, 100–101
WebSphere MQ JMS Provider, 111, 122–140
    administered objects, 122–140
    JMSWrapXAQueueConnectionFactor
        y, 135
    JMSWrapXATopicConnectionFactor
        y, 135
    MQQueue, 136–138
    MQQueueConnectionFactory, 123–127
    MQTopic, 138–140
    MQTopicConnectionFactory, 127–134
    MQXAQueueConnectionFactory, 134
    MQXATopicConnectionFactory, 134
    WebSphere Application Server runtime
        properties, 135–136
WebSphere MQ Mobile Transport, 105
WebSphere MQ Multicast Transport, 105–106
WebSphere MQ Real-Time Transport, 105
WebSphere MQ SSL configuration, 219–238
    digital certificates, obtaining, 219–229
    generic JMS provider, creating, 233–236
    JMS client's certificate, generating, 226–227
    JMS-administered objects, creating, 231–233
    JVM properties, setting, 236–237
    MQ queue manager's certificate, generating,
        220–226
    public certificates, exchanging, 228–229
    resources, configuring, 229–238
    sender session bean, modifying resource
        references of, 237–238
    server connection channel, configuring, 229–
        231
WebSphere MQ Telemetry Transport, 105
WebSphere Portal Server, 90–92
Whitespace, 254
Windows Pocket PD platforms, 100
Workload management clusters, 248–249

WSDL, 32

X
XA global transactions:
    entity bean:
        configuring, 269–278
        Create a 2.0 Enterprise Bean dialog, 251
        Create a Data Source dialog, 273
        Create a JDBC Provider dialog, 271–272
        Create new EJB/RDB Mapping dialog,
            266
        creating, 260–278
        data sources, 270
        DB2 resources, configuring, 267–269
        Define CMP Attribute dialog, 253
        deployment code, generating, 277–278
        deployment descriptor, updating, 277–
            278
        Employee Record entity bean, creating,
            260–266
        Enterprise Bean Details dialog, 252, 254
        Modify Data Source dialog, 274
        Modify Resources Properties dialog, 275
        table script and mapping, generating,
            265–267
        XA JDBC data source, defining, 269–
            277
    implementing, 259–287
    MDB, modifying, 282–284
    scenario implementation, testing, 284–287
    session bean:
        configuring, 280–282
        creating, 278–282
        implementing, 278–280
    using, 259–260
XAConnectionFactory, 27
XA-enabled property, WebSphere Application
        Server, 135
XASession, 27
XML (Extensible Markup Language), 30–38
    defined, 31
    documents:
        anatomy of, 32–34
        processing, 35–38
    DOM (Document Object Model), 35–36
    DTDs and XML schemas, 34–35
    element names, 33

JAXP (Java API for XML Parsing), 36
JDOM API, 36–38
SAX (Simple API for XML), 35

start tags, 33
XML Schemas, 34–35, 41